LIVING ECONOMY

LIVING ECONOMY

The Reuters guide to the economy of modern Britain

Jenny Scott

REUTERS

An imprint of **Pearson Education**

London / New York / San Francisco / Toronto / Sydney / Tokyo / Singapore

Hong Kong / Cape Town / Madrid / Paris / Milan / Munich / Amsterdam

PEARSON EDUCATION LIMITED

Head Office:
Edinburgh Gate
Harlow CM20 2JE
Tel: +44 (0)1279 623623
Fax: +44 (0)1279 431059

London Office:
128 Long Acre
London WC2E 9AN
Tel: +44 (0)20 7447 2000
Fax: +44 (0)20 7240 5771
Website: www.business-minds.com

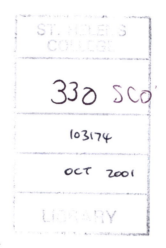
First published in Great Britain in 2001

ISBN 0 273 65017 3

British Library Cataloguing in Publication Data
A CIP catalogue record for this book can be obtained from the British Library.

10 9 8 7 6 5 4 3 2 1

Typeset by Pantek Arts Ltd, Maidstone, Kent
Printed and bound in Great Britain by Biddles Ltd, Guildford and King's Lynn

The Publishers' policy is to use paper manufactured from sustainable forests.

CONTENTS

CHAPTER 5 ▪ WORKING FOR A LIVING

CHAPTER 6 ▪ FINANCIAL MARKETS

CHAPTER 7 ▪ BEST OF BOTH WORLDS

CHAPTER 8 ▪ REDRAWING THE EUROPEAN ECONOMIC MAP

ABOUT THE AUTHOR

Born in 1970, Jenny Scott studied economics at Cambridge University before spending two years working as an analyst at the Bank of England. She joined Reuters in 1994 and, after an early posting in Amsterdam, returned to London to write about international capital markets.

She joined the Reuters UK economics desk in 1998 and spent two and a half years covering everything from monthly inflation and unemployment data to interest rate decisions and the government's annual budgets.

She is currently the BBC's economics reporter.

INTRODUCTION

"Do you have anything on economics?" asked a colleague in his local bookshop. 'Over there,' replied the assistant, 'beyond fiction.'"

Anonymous, quoted in 'Men and Matters', *Financial Times*, November 1981

Economics does not belong in textbooks. It is not a crusty subject that should be learned for the sake of it, the sole preserve of City wannabes looking to make a fortune on the stock market. It is a living subject. It tries to make sense of everyday events, such as why people lose their jobs, why prices in supermarkets rise or why some people earn more than others. That is why it is so important. Economics has a direct impact on your wallet. Looking at it from a more philosophical angle, it attempts to explain how a motive as selfish as wanting to make money is compatible with an environment where people live together in relative harmony.

“For the study of political economy you need no special knowledge, no extensive library, no costly laboratory. You do not even need textbooks nor teachers, if you will but think for yourselves.”

Henry George (1839–97)

This book tells you how economics applies to everyday life. It gives you the background you need to make informed decisions on everything from whether to take out a loan to which political party to vote for. Economics can help you to decide when to invest in the stock market or when to buy a house. It can give you an idea of whether interest rates will change and therefore which mortgage to pick. It can tell you if a recession is around the corner and you are in danger of losing your job, or if inflation is going to whittle away all your savings.

However, this is not a book about personal finances – economics goes way beyond that. It is about jobs and wages and houses and happiness. It brings in politics, psychology and ethics. It can suggest ways of reducing the gap between rich and poor, and equally, it can explain why the opposite often happens.

But it will not give you all the answers. Economics can tell you that your pension is in danger of being worth a good deal less than you thought (Chapter 6) but it won't tell you which pension plan to choose. It can tell you the advantages and disadvantages of joining monetary union, but it offers no guarantees of success either way. There are no formulas to learn or theories to memorise, no foolproof answers. That's one of the reasons it is so fascinating – and so frustrating. It takes you halfway there and then leaves you to come to your own, informed conclusions. But as one of the greatest economists of the 20th century, John Maynard Keynes, said: 'I'd rather be vaguely right than precisely wrong.'

66 The first law of economics says that for every economist there exists an equal and opposite economist. The second law says they are both wrong. 99

The reason for the gaps is that economics is very far from an exact science. The main actors are people, you and me, everyone who works and spends money. There is too much psychology involved to come up with water-tight laws (which is why economists are always saying 'on the one hand ...'). You can't just plug some numbers into a computer and get a print-out telling you what to do with interest rates or taxes. It means governments get things wrong, people lose money on the stock exchange and companies go belly up. But it also means that *anyone* can have a crack at it. With a bit of common sense and some basic theory, you can judge for yourself whether borrowing costs should be raised or whether the country is on the brink of recession. You may not always be right but at least you'll have an opinion.

This book takes care of the theory. It strips out the jargon and makes what can seem a baffling and complicated subject clear and easy to understand. I find examples help, and there are lots of those. There are also case studies that take modern-day issues and look at what economics has to say about them. This subject is constantly evolving and adapting to the world around it. Ideas conceived more than 200 years ago can be tweaked and teased into theories capable of explaining the economic impact of the Internet or turned into suggestions for curing technology-induced unemployment.

This is not a definitive guide to the subject – that would take too long and would probably be a little tedious. Instead, the boring bits have been left out (ISLM curves and cobweb theorems would stretch anyone's patience) and only the topics relevant to everyday life have been included. This book also focuses mainly on macroeconomics, the big picture stuff such as unemployment and inflation and growth. It discusses issues such as why the job for life has disappeared, what makes house prices rise, and whether it matters that Britain's manufacturing industry seems to be in terminal decline.

> **“In economics,**
> # everything depends on everything else –
> ## and in more than one way.”
>
> Anonymous

The inspiration behind this book was the inquisitiveness of my friends and family. Apart from the usual questions about when to buy holiday money and whether to invest in the stock market, they asked about issues such as whether interest rates were likely to rise and why the government didn't cut taxes despite having pots of money to spare. This book is the conversation that might have followed.

Among other things, it talks about:

- **the ideas and insights of the economic masters of the past 250 years**. Economists are notoriously argumentative – it is the only subject where two people can win a Nobel prize for saying completely opposite things. George Bernard Shaw once summed it up perfectly, declaring: 'If all economists were laid end to end they would not reach a conclusion.' However, there would be some pretty heated debates, some of which are examined in Chapter 1, courtesy of arguably the greatest economists in history. The patron saint of the subject, Adam Smith, is discussed, along with the revolutionary Karl Marx, John Maynard Keynes and staunch free-marketeer Milton Friedman. Each thought his theories were conclusive, yet each conclusion was different;

■ **what an economy is and how it grows**. Living standards in Britain have risen fivefold in the past 100 years and have the potential to increase even further. That means more money for Joe Average and a longer, more comfortable life. But it won't be a smooth ride. Growth can fluctuate wildly, setting a cracking pace one year then slowing to a reluctant crawl the next. The second chapter explains why and explores what causes recessions. It gives a couple of pointers on how to spot a downturn before the dole queues lengthen – useful if you are thinking of buying a house or shares, both of which could take a hit if the economy contracts. It also considers the impact of the Internet, and whether it spells more growth and better living standards for everyone;

■ **the role of the government in economics**. Everything British workers earn each year up until the middle of May goes to the government in the form of taxes, so it's little wonder they want value for money. Chapter 3 assesses whether they are getting it. It looks at the economics behind petrol taxes and considers how governments can achieve that vote-winning formula of lots of jobs, strong growth and low inflation, and considers how something as simple as a country's currency could hold the key to all three. It discusses how the Internet could help reluctant taxpayers circumvent the Inland Revenue, and ends by considering why government debt is of the remotest interest to anyone outside parliament and the financial markets;

■ **why interest rates move**. You don't have to be a bond dealer or a banker to benefit from being able to predict changes in the cost of borrowing. If you are taking out a mortgage or making an investment, for example, it could be invaluable. Chapter 4 gives a few tips on how to anticipate interest rate changes by going back to the root of the problem – inflation. It explains what makes prices rise, what effect that can have on your everyday life, and what authorities can do to douse the inflationary flames. It discusses whether the Bank of England is doing a good job of keeping inflation at bay and considers what impact the Internet will have on the prices we pay for everything from food to furniture;

■ **why people lose their jobs and what can be done about it**. Unemployment is a sensitive subject. It affects us personally – our lifestyle and self-esteem – more than anything else the economy can throw at us, be it inflation, trade or taxes. Chapter 5 looks at what economics has to say on the subject. It explains why people lose their jobs and suggests ways the government and businesses can get people back to work. It looks at why more and more people feel insecure in their jobs today, and why millions still live in (relative) poverty. It also assesses the British government's New Deal plan to get the young and long-term jobless back to work, looks at the economics behind the minimum wage, and explains why the UK is still split, economically, on north/south lines;

- **the relationship between economics and financial markets such as bonds and shares**. Share prices move for all sorts of reasons: the level of company profits, expansion plans, the resignation of a chief executive. But underlying all that is the state of the economy. A shock increase in a country's inflation rate can wipe billions off stock markets (as it did in the US in April 2000). Understanding the link between markets and economics is therefore key to your investment decisions. Chapter 6 traces that link for bonds and shares, peeling away the jargon that encompasses both. It explains what bonds are, why their prices move and how they can affect the value of your pension. It explores why share prices change, what stock markets do, and gives a few tips on how to predict a stock market crash. Finally, it takes a simple look at derivatives, those horribly complicated financial instruments that strike fear into the heart of anyone without a maths PhD;

- **why countries trade with each other, and how you may gain or lose from that**. Trillions of dollars of goods and services are traded internationally every year. It means Finns can eat oranges, landlocked Austrians can eat cod and Britons can drive Renaults and Fiats. Chapter 7 looks at what motivates trade and whether it is unambiguously a good thing. It explains exactly what globalisation is and discusses whether it spells penury or progress for the world's population. It also explains what makes a currency move, so the next time you are heading abroad on holiday, you will know the best time to buy your spending money;

- **the basics of European Economic and Monetary Union in plain English**. EMU began on 1 January 1999 when 11 countries on the Continent fixed their currencies against each other. True to form, Britain stayed out. But that could change. The decision on whether to relinquish the pound in favour of the euro will have an impact on everyone's lives, affecting inflation, jobs, interest rates, share prices and taxation. You probably have a gut reaction about the issue, but you may not fully understand the details of the debate. Chapter 8 won't try to change your view but it will lay out the economic arguments for and against euro membership in simple, impartial terms, enabling you to hold your own in any argument on the subject;

- **the world economy and the institutions pulling the economic strings**. It is not just elected politicians who can influence the path of an economy. Central bankers and experts at organisations such as the International Monetary Fund also have a say. The final chapter gives a simple account of how three major central banks operate – the Bank of England, the US equivalent the Federal Reserve, and the European Central Bank – and of the workings of three major institutions that regularly crop up in newspapers – the IMF, the World Bank and the World Trade Organisation.

By all means dip into specific chapters of *Living Economy*. If you have a burning desire to know whether current account deficits matter, go straight to Chapter 7. If you have always wondered what was so special about Keynes, flick to Chapter 1. Each chapter can stand alone, but if you have the patience to read the book sequentially, you will get much more out of it. Each part of economics is a piece to a giant jigsaw puzzle and you won't get a complete picture until the last bit is slotted into place.

Lastly, I should make it clear that this book is not ground-breaking and it is not biased. It won't present a brilliant new theory and it won't try to change your political colours. But it will equip you with the knowledge you need to understand the world around you. The rest is up to you.

CHAPTER I

ECONOMICS – THE BUSINESS OF LIFE

Major economists and what they thought

"Arthur awoke to the sound of argument and went to the bridge.

Ford was waving his arms about. 'You're crazy Zaphod,' he was saying.

'Magrathea is a myth, a fairy story, it's what parents tell their kids about at night if they want them to grow up to be economists, it's …'."

Douglas Adams, *Hitchhiker's Guide to the Galaxy*, Chapter 16

INTRODUCTION

Economics is about finding out how a society knits together, how it evolves and expands. It's about discovering how a selfish motive like making money is compatible with a world where people can live together. Or, as the late economist Alfred Marshall put it, rather more succinctly: 'Economics is the study of mankind in the ordinary business of life.'

This book delves deeper into that 'business of life'. It explores how jobs are created, what determines how much we earn, why prices of things like cars and houses move, and why we buy and sell some goods abroad. But first, it is useful to examine how the subject has evolved. An understanding of the main schools of thought in economics provides a solid foundation for tackling problems such as unemployment and inflation.

“ Economics is at once the most artistic of the sciences
and may hope to become
the most scientific of the arts. ”

R.J. Ball and Peter Doyle, *Inflation*, 1969

Economics is not a proper science. You cannot conduct controlled experiments, observing people as you would laboratory rats. Economics depends upon human action and interaction – and humans aren't always predictable or rational, which makes devising theories difficult. Yet it is not an art either. Although there is no universally accepted formula for getting the most out of an economy, there are a number of popular approaches which use models and statistical evidence to 'prove' their worth. This chapter examines four of those approaches, courtesy of some of the greatest minds in the business: Adam Smith, Karl Marx, John Maynard Keynes and Milton Friedman.

There are many more economists who deserve a mention, but space precludes it (see the panel below for a rundown of some other famous names). Despite the omissions, however, in Smith, Marx, Keynes and Friedman you have a potted history of economic thought that will hold you in good stead for the remainder of the book.

Adam Smith (1723–1790): Smith was the founding father of modern economics. His 1776 tome, *The Wealth of Nations* described the principle of market forces for the first time. Smith believed that if left to its own devices, free from government intervention or restricted competition, changes in price would ensure society got everything it needed. He was the original free-marketeer and he forged what became known as the 'classical' school of economics.

Thomas Robert Malthus (1766–1834): Malthus (pronounced Malthiss) is one of the most controversial and pessimistic figures in the history of economics. Two of his theories stand out. Firstly, he believed that it is impossible to raise people's living standards. He argued that greater wealth encourages higher birth rates (because of a human instinct for sexual pleasure), which eventually leads to starvation and death since food production cannot keep up with the population increase. Secondly, he

▶

opposed any government assistance for the poor, arguing that this only leads to more poor people, for exactly the same reasons as above. These apocalyptic predictions prompted Thomas Carlisle to call economics 'the dismal science', a tag that has stuck for more than 200 years.

David Ricardo (1772–1823): Along with Smith and Marx, Ricardo was one of the three giants in classical economics, which dominated from the late 18th century to the late 19th century. Born in London to prosperous Jewish parents, he later married a Quaker and converted to Christianity. Ricardo is best known for his theory of comparative advantage, which says that free trade is always worthwhile, and results in greater global economic growth. He also did a lot of work on income distribution.

Karl Marx (1818–1883): Marx, philosopher, sociologist and revolutionary, believed that far from imposing a kind of discipline over people, market forces allowed a few people to make more and more money at the expense of exploited workers. He argued that those workers would become increasingly alienated and would end up rebelling against the system and bringing about the downfall of capitalism.

Alfred Marshall (1842–1924): If one person is responsible for putting economics on the academic map, it's Alfred Marshall. Thanks to him, the subject became a discipline in its own right at Cambridge University in 1903, a move soon followed by other academic institutions around the world. Marshall devised a host of important, and simple, theories that still form the mainstay of any student's exploration of the subject, including the laws of supply and demand (*see* box, Economists and Models, in Chapter 2) and the principle of price elasticity (*see* glossary).

John Maynard Keynes (1883–1946): Born into an academic family, Keynes challenged the efficacy of classical economics. He believed markets were far from the be all and end all and suggested the government should intervene when necessary to either stimulate growth or dampen it down. In other words, the government should try to manipulate demand. Keynes is best known for his 1936 book the *General Theory of Employment, Interest and Money*, which changed the face of economics. It instantly struck a chord and for more than 20 years his so-called demand management policies held sway.

Milton Friedman (1912–): A Nobel prize winner and modern-day champion of free markets, Friedman is typically associated with the theory that inflation is a direct consequence of changes in the money supply. Margaret Thatcher was an enthusiastic disciple of this so-called monetarism, and for years British interest rate decisions were based on the size of the money supply.

ADAM SMITH (1723–1790)

THE FOUNDING FATHER OF ECONOMICS

'It is not from the benevolence of the butcher, the brewer, or the baker that we expect our dinner, but from the regard to their own interest.'

Adam Smith, *The Wealth of Nations*

Adam Smith was as much a philosopher as an economist. His pioneering description of market forces (which still underpins the subject more than 200 years later) is based on his observations of human nature.

Smith believed that people want to 'better their condition'. He observed that 'every man, as long as he does not violate the laws of justice, is left perfectly free to pursue his own interest his own way ...'. That then raised the question, how can such a selfish society be compatible with an orderly and fair one? How can we stop the desire to make money from getting out of hand and polarising the community into the very wealthy and the very poor? (For as Smith noted: 'No society can surely be flourishing and happy, of which the far greater part of the members are poor and miserable.')

MARKET FORCES RESPONSIBILITY

The answer lies in the market. Smith argued that the **'invisible hand'** of the price mechanism pressured selfish individuals into socially responsible ways, preventing any one person from accumulating excessive profits. How? Imagine exotic coffee is all the rage (not an example that Smith used). Filter is no longer good enough; people want cappuccinos and lattes and beans roasted in Columbia. But there's only one coffee shop in town. It can charge whatever it likes, and before long it will be pulling in enormous profits. That will attract other firms into the industry which are willing to undercut to take some market share. In time there will be a new coffee shop on every street corner. Prices will fall and so will profits. The 'invisible hand' of the market has ensured that no one makes an excessive amount of money, while consumers get the coffee they want at the price they want.

The market, observed Smith, is a hard taskmaster – provided there are two essential conditions in place. Firstly, there should be plenty of competition – in this case, a lot of coffee shops. This is where Smith's theories tend to break down as more restricted forms of competition often prevail in reality. Secondly, there should be no government intervention. Politicians should leave well alone, he said, thus creating a *laissez-faire* society.

Despite his conviction of the power of the market, Smith recognised that it did have its limitations. It would not provide services such as defence, for example. No one person would fund a country's army since that would benefit society as a whole, not just the individual. In that case, the government should step in. As a rule, however, self-interest and a drive to make money created their own discipline. The market was self-regulating.

THE DIVISION OF LABOUR

That was the first of Smith's theories that was to endure for centuries. The second was an extension of it. Once he had explained how the market worked, Smith turned to the question of wealth creation. How did an economy grow? Smith recognised that a desire for more profits would spur greater productivity, and therefore greater growth. This was achieved via the **division of labour**.

To illustrate his point, Smith described the activities of a pin factory. He told how if one man tried to do everything – draw out the wire, straighten it, cut it, grind it and then make the head – he would be capable of making only a few pins a day. But if workers specialised, doing just one or two parts of the operation, their output would soar.

'I have seen a small manufactory of this kind where ten men only were employed and where some of them consequently performed two or three distinct operations,' he wrote in *The Wealth of Nations*. 'These ten persons, therefore, could make among them upwards of forty-eight thousand pins a day... But if they had all wrought separately and independently ... they could certainly not each of them make twenty, perhaps not one pin in a day.'

Thus productivity is improved not only by specialisation but also by better machinery – principles still used in factories today from car plants to breweries.

GREED ISN'T GOOD

Adam Smith laid the foundations for modern economics. He exposed the power of the markets and described how a tendency to self-betterment was kept in check by the price mechanism. He was careful not to advocate greed, however. In an earlier book, *The Theory of Moral Sentiments*, Smith described how 'power and riches ... keep off the summer shower, not the winter storm … leave [their possessor] always as much, and sometimes more exposed than before, to anxiety, to fear and to sorrow; to diseases, to danger, and to death'. He had a lot of sympathy for the poor and believed that the happiness of others was necessary to man. Above all, the economic freedom he so zealously endorsed was to be exercised with consideration and attention to the justice of others.

PORTRAIT OF A SCOTTISH PHILOSOPHER

Adam Smith was born into a relatively well-to-do family in the small town of Kirkcaldy, a few miles north of Edinburgh, in 1723. His father, a customs officer, died a few weeks before his birth, leaving Smith in the sole care of his much-loved mother, Margaret Douglas.

© 2000 Getty Images, Inc.

Smith had a sickly childhood, which left him with a tendency to hypochondria in later years. Illness aside, the most striking event in his early years occurred at the age of about four, when he was stolen by gypsies. The alarm was soon raised and the boy returned to his mother (which was just as well, according to an early biographer John Rae, who declared: 'He would have made, I fear, a poor gypsy.').

Smith enjoyed a good education at the local, two-room school in Kirkcaldy, graduating from the grammar system in 1737. He went straight to Glasgow University at the age of 14 – normal practice in his time – where he developed a keen interest in Newtonian physics and mathematics. By all accounts it was a stimulating three years. His principal inspiration was the 'never to be forgotten' Francis Hutheson, a controversial philosopher who taught Smith to respect liberty, reason and free speech. These tenets were to underlie the young academic's moral code in later years and form the basis of his system of economics.

Smith graduated from Glasgow in 1740, having won a highly prized scholarship to Oxford. However, his six years there were to prove an intellectual anti-climax. The absence of formal teaching spurred him to do extensive, but by all accounts sporadic, reading on his own initiative (in a letter to his mother in 1743, Smith wrote: 'I am just recovered from a violent fit of laziness.').

He left Oxford in 1746, a number of years before his scholarship expired, and went back to his native Scotland where he became a freelance lecturer in Edinburgh before being elected professor at the University of Glasgow in 1751.

He later described his 13 years in that post as 'by far the most useful and, therefore, by far the happiest and most honourable' of his career. He soon developed a tendency towards the archetypal absent-minded professor, a characteristic that was to stay with him throughout his life. Despite his academic success, he is described as being an unpretentious man, with a harsh voice and a conversational style similar to lecturing that belied an extremely kind nature.

Smith left Glasgow in 1764, having been offered the job of tutor to the Third Duke of Buccleuch. This post took him to Toulouse, Geneva and Paris, where he met a number of eminent European academics, including his 'hero' Voltaire.

On his return, he went to London where he spent three years putting the final touches to his seminal work, *Inquiry into the Nature and Causes of the Wealth of Nations*. The book was published in 1776 in five parts to great critical acclaim, and is arguably still the most influential book on economics ever written.

In 1778, Smith was appointed to a comfortable post as commissioner of customs in Scotland and he went back to Edinburgh to live with his mother. He died there on 17 July 1790 at the age of 67.

The Adam Smith Institute has a website at www.adamsmith.org.uk

KARL MARX (1818–1883)

A RADICAL ECONOMIST

'The mass of misery, oppression, slavery, degradation and exploitation grows; but with this there also grows the revolt of the working class ...'

Karl Marx

Karl Marx has been labelled many things: anthropologist, philosopher, sociologist and revolutionary, to name a few. He was also one of the most radical economists ever to have lived.

His theories were unlike any before them. Although he and Smith shared a common starting point – both saw profit as the prime motivator in society – they were like chalk and cheese in every other respect.

Smith believed competition would keep that profit motive under control and prevent any individual from amassing too much money. Marx, however, predicted it would make a few people rich at the expense of everyone else, sparking tensions that would eventually destroy capitalism.

That was the nub of Marx's teaching. He believed capitalism, where firms hire workers in order to make a profit, was inherently unstable and would eventually self-destruct. Why? Because it exploited people, who would feel increasingly alienated by their rich employers and would end up banding together and forcing change.

Much of Marx's work centred on explaining how those dangers of exploitation and alienation arose.

EXPLOITATION OF WORKERS

Take the first problem, exploitation. Marx believed that the value of a good depended on how much it cost to make. This entailed three expenses: constant capital (the machines needed), variable capital (the workers needed) and surplus value (in other words, profit). Workers don't own capital, therefore they have no choice but to work for someone else. They start each day by making enough things to pay for their wages, then for the wear and tear on the machinery they use, so by the end of the day they are working simply to enrich their employers. In other words, they don't receive the full value of everything they produce. They are being exploited.

Since the essence of capitalism is to make money, those workers will be increasingly exploited as time goes on. Faced with growing competition, employers may make staff work longer or harder or they may cut their wages and hire cheaper workers like women and children. Either way, profits will increase and so will worker dissatisfaction.

ALIENATING WORKERS

This soon leads to the next problem, alienation. Not only do workers resent enriching their employers while surviving on subsistence wages themselves, they also take less and less pride in their work. The division of labour advocated by Smith destroys creativity and prevents workers from getting the satisfaction of actually making something. In addition, the drive to make profits encourages factory owners to cut corners, so workers end up making shoddy, cheap goods that no one can be proud of.

Eventually, predicted Marx, the feelings of resentment and alienation from being exploited will become overwhelming and a struggle will ensue between workers and capitalists. Competition between companies ensures continuous pressure to make more profits and pay workers less. Revolution follows and the system implodes.

So far, Marx's predictions have proved unfounded. Some believe that may be because he underestimated the flexibility of capitalism. He recognised, for example, that governments could mitigate worker exploitation by providing public libraries, making income tax progressive and running transport networks, but added that that would not prevent the system's downfall. He also believed that capitalists would 'buy out' governments, preventing them from enforcing minimum wages, maximum hours and worker rights.

Others say Marx overlooked the positive aspects of capitalism. True, he recognised that it would encourage new technology and better living standards and spur a move away from the 'idiocy of rural life' towards towns, but he believed those advantages paled into insignificance against the disadvantages.

Whatever the reason for the resilience of capitalism, Marx still has a huge following among economists. Some believe his predictions may yet prove prescient as the trend towards multinational corporations and ever bigger profits intensifies, alienating more and more people. His call for the workers of the world to unite may yet be heeded.

A REBEL WITH A CAUSE

By all accounts, Karl Marx was a cantankerous individual who didn't suffer fools gladly. An insomniac who was susceptible to ill-health, he is commonly depicted as vicious towards his enemies and domineering to his friends.

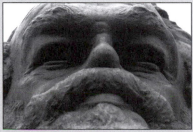
© Reuters 1998.

He was also incredibly loyal and one of the most original thinkers that ever lived. His theories on capitalism and the exploitation of workers inspired many 19th-century employees to unite and rebel against oppression, and they continue to provoke action today. He made people question the status quo.

Marx was born in Trier in Germany in 1818, the son of Jewish parents who converted to Christianity for social reasons. He studied law at Bonn University on his father's advice but later changed schools and subjects, taking up history and philosophy at Berlin and receiving his doctorate in the latter at the age of 23.

Already fiercely critical of the social system, Marx began to write inflammatory articles for a radical newspaper, the *Rheinische Zeitung*. However, his journalistic career was cut short in 1843 when the paper, of which he was by then editor-in-chief, was suppressed by the authorities. Labelled a dangerous revolutionary, Marx was forced to flee Germany. By this time he had married his childhood sweetheart, Jenny von Westphalen, the daughter of a baron, and the couple set up home in Paris.

His experiences during the following two years influenced him greatly. Shortly after he arrived in Paris, which was fast becoming a gathering place for radicals from all over Europe, Marx met Friedrich Engels, who was to become his lifelong friend. The son of a wealthy German cotton manufacturer, Engels had had first-hand experience of the atrocious working-class conditions of the day when managing one of his father's factories, and he introduced Marx to the miseries of working life.

After a couple of years in the French capital, Marx moved to Brussels, where he penned what was to become the world's best-selling political pamphlet, the *Communist Party manifesto*. This enduring piece of prose had been commissioned by the Communist League in December 1847, after a 10-day brainstorming session in a room above the Red Lion pub in Soho. Its opening and closing sentences have since been immortalised: 'The history of all hitherto existing society is the history of class struggles … The proletarians have nothing to lose but their chains. They have a world to win. Workers of the world, unite!'

Shortly after the publication of the manifesto – which caused barely a ripple at the time – Marx moved to London, where he was to remain for the next 33 years, until his death. There, he and his family lived in abject poverty, almost entirely dependent on handouts from Engels. Marx did try to find a job once, as a clerk in a railway office, but was turned down because of his illegible handwriting. Instead, he spent his time soaking up information in the reading room at the British Museum, punctuated by the occasional rowdy pub-crawl along Tottenham Court Road.

According to biographers, Marx mellowed in later life and took to reading *The Times* over breakfast before retiring to his study or taking long walks on Hampstead Heath with his grandchildren. The first volume of his great masterpiece, *Das Kapital*, was published in 1867, the only one of four volumes to be released during his lifetime. (Engels worked tirelessly after his friend's death, editing volumes II and III for publication. Volume IV was released unedited after Engels died.)

Towards the end of his life, Marx became increasingly frail. He never recovered from the death of his wife, on 2 December 1881, and when his eldest daughter also died, just over a year later, it proved too much. Two months later, on 14 March 1883, Marx passed away in an armchair in his study. He was buried at Highgate cemetery. On hearing of the loss of his friend, Engels wrote: 'Mankind is shorter by a head, and that the greatest head of our time.'

> **"**In economics the basic questions do not change –
> # it is the answers that change from
> ### time to time.**"**

Anonymous

JOHN MAYNARD KEYNES (1883–1946)

AN ECONOMIC REVOLUTIONARY

'I would rather be vaguely right than precisely wrong.'

John Maynard Keynes

Marx's teachings were undoubtedly powerful and revolutionary. However, perhaps understandably, they failed to impress contemporary policymakers, who were keen to maintain the status quo. Hence Smith's doctrine of free markets endured, with few exceptions, for the best part of 150 years.

Then, in the late 1920s, the Great Depression hit Britain and the US like a whirlwind and confidence in the power of the 'invisible hand' waned. While classical economics could reasonably *explain* the mass unemployment that ensued – restrictions on competition rendered market forces impotent – it did not seem to have the practical solutions to the problem.

Both the public and the government were eager for an alternative answer. Then, in 1936, John Maynard Keynes (pronounced canes, not keens), a Cambridge fellow and British Treasury official, published his seminal work, the *General Theory of Employment, Interest and Money*, which challenged classical economic theory. It was lapped up.

KEYNES QUESTIONS THE CLASSICAL ECONOMISTS

Keynes turned contemporary economic thinking on its head. He claimed that market forces could not be relied upon to produce the goods people wanted and the jobs they needed. Instead, it was up to the government to intervene in the economy and provide the extra money necessary to generate full employment.

This is Keynes' legacy. It has become known as **demand management** and it works like this. Imagine there is unemployment. The market *may* be able to create jobs eventually, but it could take years and years (and as Keynes famously declared, 'in the long run we are all dead').

In the meantime, the government should increase its spending on programmes like public buildings, roads, hospitals, etc. This generates the multiplier effect (discussed in Chapter 2). Construction workers spend part of their wages on things like clothes or food, pumping money into local shops and supermarkets. They in turn increase their output and hire more workers, who spend their wages on holidays or cars, etc. And so on until the total income in the economy has increased significantly, generating jobs along the way. Government spending has pushed the country towards full employment.

Moreover, said Keynes, if that initial government spending is funded by borrowing, it will have an even greater impact because it is soaking up previously idle money. If it is funded by tax increases, it will still stimulate employment, but not by as much because people would have spent that money anyway. When newspapers talk about deficit spending, that is what they mean – government spending financed by borrowing.

In this way, Keynes' demand management was inherently **counter-cyclical**, in that it went in the opposite direction to the business cycle. When growth slows, the government should spend more so as to ward off recession, even if it means getting into debt. Conversely, in good times, the government should spend less, and use buoyant tax receipts to pay off what it has borrowed.

> 66 Whenever I ask England's six leading economists
> # a question, I get seven answers –
> ## two from Mr Keynes. 99

Winston Churchill, 1874–1965

A NEW THEORY OF UNEMPLOYMENT

Keynes made many contributions to economics, of which demand management was arguably his most significant. However, his thoughts on wages and unemployment also deserve a mention. Classical economists believed unemployment arose because real wages were too high. In other words, workers were asking for too much money, relative to the rate of inflation and output in the economy. To reduce the number out of work, therefore, it was just a case of lowering salary demands.

Keynes disagreed. For a start, he said, it is very hard to reduce wages. No doubt you can appreciate that from a personal view. If your boss tried to cut your salary by 10 per cent, you would probably either seek union support or try to find another job.

Besides, continued Keynes, even if wages could be cut, that might not do much good. He argued that any fall in earnings would be ineffective in stimulating job growth, and would have at best a marginal, temporary impact.

Classical	VS	Keynes
General principle: The market knows best, so leave it alone. This *laissez faire* attitude will ensure the right goods are produced and sold at the right price, creating the optimum number of jobs. Government should play a very limited role.		**General principle:** The market is not the be all and end all. If left to its own devices, it won't deliver the best outcome. Therefore it's up to the government to step in and steer the economy towards full employment and strong growth.
Unemloyment: Unemployment arises because wages are too high, making it unprofitable for firms to hire more workers. This occurs because of impediments to the free market, like trade union power and generous unemployment benefits.		**Unemloyment:** It's very hard to push wages down (in reality, it's impossible to force British workers to take a wage cut, it has to be voluntary). Therefore an economy can easily come to rest at less than full employment. It is up to the government to intervene and generate jobs by spending more money or reducing taxes.
Inflation: Prices rise because there is too much money in the economy. The speed at which money changes hands and the number of times it changes hands both tend to be stable. Therefore, if the supply of money increases, all that happens is that prices go up. This theory was extended by monetarists.		**Inflation:** Prices are forced up by *real* factors, not money. If there is more demand in an economy than supply, there will be **demand-pull inflation**. If the cost of hiring workers rises, or the price of raw materials goes up, the price of the final product will also increase. There will be a **cost-push inflation** (see Chapter 4).
Recommended policies: Control the money supply to control inflation. Use supply-side policies to reduce unemployment and encourage growth. In other words, break down the barriers to a free market. Improve the amount and the quality of workers through education, lower benefits (which encourage people to look for work) and weaker trade unions (which lower wage demands). Alternatively, encourage more investment by offering tax breaks and reducing unnecessary regulations. Former British Prime Minister Margaret Thatcher relied heavily on supply-side policies, while the Labour government elected in 1997 favours a more hybrid approach.		**Recommended policies:** Government should **reflate** the economy if there is a shortfall in demand and there is a recession, or **deflate** the economy if there is excess demand and inflation. Reflation could include lowering taxes or increasing government expenditure (fiscal policy), or reducing interest rates or allowing the money supply to increase (monetary policy). Deflation entails the opposite – increasing taxes, reducing government spending, increasing interest rates or reducing the money supply, all of which will stifle demand and therefore inflation.

FIG. 1.1 The great debate: Keynes versus the Classical economists

Thus Keynes totally contradicted classical economics. It took just 10 years for most western economists to be won over by his ideas, an incredibly short time for an intellectual revolution. British politics was essentially governed by demand management by 1950 and in the United States, Roosevelt was an enthusiastic follower. By 1947 Keynes had even made it into elementary economic textbooks.

The debate between Keynesian and classical economics continues (*see* Fig. 1.1). The efficacy of the former was questioned in the 1970s thanks to rampant inflation and high unemployment and since then, governments have tended to take a hybrid approach to economic management. They still tend to provide grants and increase spending in lean times, yet leave the bulk of provision to the market.

> **"Evidently I knew more about economics**
>
> **than my examiners."**
>
> J.M. Keynes, commenting on the results of his civil service exam

PORTRAIT OF A GENTLEMAN ECONOMIST

John Maynard Keynes was a phenomenally successful economist, both in the academic and real world. By the time his ground-breaking *General Theory* was published in 1936, he was worth about £10 million in today's money, thanks to a talent for speculation on the currency markets.

© 2000 Getty Images, Inc.

He was born in Cambridge in 1883 (the year Marx died) into a solidly middle-class, academic family. His father, John Neville Keynes, was a lecturer in logic and political economy at Cambridge University, and his mother, Florence Ada Keynes, graduated from the university's Newnham College and later became the city's first woman mayor.

After what appears to have been a happy childhood, Keynes won a modest scholarship to Eton before attending King's College, Cambridge to read classics and mathematics. There, he forged friendships that were to last a lifetime. In particular, he fell in with a group called the Apostles, a small, secret society of dons and undergraduates who met periodically to discuss ethical and political questions. Many of his contemporaries there went on to form the core of the artistic crowd known as the Bloomsbury Group (a name invented by a journalist to describe the group of Bohemian painters and writers living in and around Bloomsbury in central London).

Keynes graduated from Cambridge in 1905 at the age of 22 and joined the Civil Service. After coming second in the entrance exams out of the 10 who were accepted that year, he took up a post in the India office, where he worked for more than two years.

During his spell there, he reworked his dissertation on probability that was to earn him a fellowship at King's in 1909, and he subsequently returned to his hometown. Once war broke out, however, he was back in London, working for the Civil Service again. Despite his pacifist objections, he found himself representing Britain at the Peace Conference at Versailles in 1919. However, he became increasingly disheartened by the harsh terms being imposed on Germany by the allies and resigned his post to return to Britain.

There, he immersed himself in journalism and currency speculation. In 1925 he married a Russian ballerina, Lydia Lopokova, in a match which surprised his friends. Keynes had never shown much interest in women before, and his Bloomsbury contemporaries initially resented his wife's presence, and her broken, strange English. It was a very happy marriage, however, and in time Lydia is said to have won over even the most aloof of her husband's friends.

The couple bought a farmhouse near Firle, in Sussex, and when Keynes wasn't in his London flat or his Cambridge rooms, he would spend long vacations in the country. He founded the Arts Theatre in his hometown in 1936, the same year as his *General Theory* was published, but a year later suffered a severe heart attack, which marked the end of his contributions to economic theory.

However, he continued to take an active interest in British politics and economics. When war broke out again, he re-entered the Treasury as an unpaid adviser to the Chancellor (or, as he put it, a demi-semi-official). He took up a seat in the House of Lords shortly thereafter, and died in his Sussex farmhouse on 21 April 1946 at the age of 62. He was survived by both his parents.

❝Economists, indeed, never seem in danger **of unemployment, because, while new** problems are constantly arising, **old ones are never settled.❞**

Warren B. Catlin, *The Progress of Economics*

MILTON FRIEDMAN (1912–)

MONEY AND FREEDOM

'Inflation is always and everywhere a monetary phenomenon.'

Milton Friedman

For a number of years after Keynes revolutionised economic theory, governments were given carte blanche to intervene in the running of a country. They spent more in times of trouble, and less in times of wealth, and even dictated the size of people's pay rises in the belief that it would help to control inflation.

However, once again, a nasty upset to economic growth called the prevailing doctrine into question. This time, it was stagflation that allowed the doubts to creep in. A fourfold rise in oil prices in the early 1970s triggered the double whammy of high in*flation* coupled with low growth, or a *stag*nant economy. That should not be allowed in a Keynesian world. Rising prices should be associated with high growth and hence falling unemployment, and vice versa. Just as the Great Depression had shaken the foundations of classical theory and popularised Keynes, so stagflation did the opposite. Maybe the market did know best after all.

Once again, there was an economist waiting in the wings, ready to show governments where they had gone wrong. His name was Milton Friedman.

Friedman's approach to the economy is based on two principles: money matters and freedom matters. Money matters because it is changes in the money supply that affect economic activity and fuel inflation, and freedom matters because economies work better when governments are not trying to control everything from prices to exchange rates and jobs.

FRIEDMAN VS KEYNES

Hence Friedman led the crusade against Keynesian economics, turning the spotlight on inflation rather than the unemployment that had so preoccupied Keynes. His attack was three-pronged.

Two of his arguments are tackled in subsequent chapters. The first – that it is changes in money supply that lead to changes in inflation, rather than moves in demand – will feature in Chapter 4. The second – that every economy has a certain, natural level of unemployment, and that it is futile to try to reduce that level by stimulating demand – will be addressed in Chapter 5.

For now, we will concentrate on his argument that Keynesian demand management is ineffective in guiding growth.

Friedman believes that the amount of money people spend depends on how much they expect to earn over a very long period of time, not just how much they are earning right now. He calls this the *permanent income hypothesis* and it allows him to show that government intervention to boost jobs and growth is pointless.

Why? Imagine the economy is in trouble. There are lots of people out of work and growth is slowing, hence the government spends more money on things like roads and hospitals. In a Keynesian world, the recipients of that extra money, the road builders etc., would go out and spend their wages, triggering a multiplier effect that boosts jobs and growth in the country as a whole. According to Friedman, however, just because they have a bit more money in their pockets now doesn't mean every road builder will go on a huge spending spree. If they expect to be unemployed again when their contract expires, they will save the extra money instead. Hence government spending does nothing to boost growth. Keynesian demand management is pointless.

PERSUADING THE POLITICIANS

Friedman's trust in money and freedom was taken up by a number of governments in the early 1980s, particularly those in Britain and the US. Former Prime Minister Margaret Thatcher introduced money supply targets in the early 1980s in a bid to control inflation, and former US President Ronald Reagan was an ardent free-marketeer.

However, as is always the case in economics, Friedman's theories are far from foolproof. Many economists still swear by Keynes and believe the only way to make sure everyone has a job is by spending government money when needed. Others still favour the theories of Adam Smith – remarkable, considering their age. As economist Kenneth Boulding put it: 'It's always depressing to go back to Adam Smith, especially on economic development, as one realises how little we have learned in nearly 200 years.'

PORTRAIT OF A FREEDOM FIGHTER

Milton Friedman was born in Brooklyn, New York, in 1912 to a family of poor Jewish immigrants from the Austro-Hungarian empire. He and his three sisters spent most of their childhood in Rahway, New Jersey, where their parents bought a dry-goods store. The family lived above the shop, which was soon expanded to incorporate an ice-cream parlour, although neither enterprise was particularly profitable and money was scarce.

© 2000 Getty Images, Inc.

Friedman attended the local high school where he developed a love of maths and an ambition to be an insurance actuary. His interest in economics only really took off when he won a scholarship to attend the local college, Rutgers. There, he showed an early flair for making money by selling second-hand books and college ties to first-year students, thus helping to fund his studies.

After majoring in both economics and maths, Friedman went to the University of Chicago to do his post-graduate studies. There, in an economics course on price and distribution theory, he met his future wife, Rose. They got to know each other in the romantic setting of the statistics laboratory and married some six years later.

A varied career in both academia and the media followed. Apart from brief stints at Columbia and Minnesota Universities, Friedman spent the bulk of his time at the University of Chicago, fathering a son and a daughter along the way. He wrote a regular economics column in *Newsweek* magazine between 1966 and 1984 and has penned a number of best-selling books. His TV series, *Free to Choose*, plus his role as economic adviser to both Richard Nixon and Ronald Reagan when they were presidential candidates, have made Milton Friedman a household name.

His work on monetary theory and inflation helped to earn him a Nobel prize in 1976. He retired from Chicago University the following year and moved to San Francisco, where he has lived with his wife ever since.

▶

Throughout his years as teacher and journalist, Friedman has remained one of the world's most ardent and effective advocates of free markets. That faith in freedom stretches way beyond textbook economics. He supports educational choice, privatising television channels and legalising drugs. He wants an all-volunteer army and the deregulation of private life to the fullest extent possible. Friedman is a champion of human rights, not just from an economic but also from a social perspective. Many economists regard his only rival over the past 100 years to be John Maynard Keynes.

IF YOU REMEMBER FOUR THINGS FROM THIS CHAPTER …

- Classical and neo-classical economists believe in the supremacy of market forces. They claim the market is self-regulating, and will ensure that all goods are produced at the right price, leaving no room for government intervention. (How many classical economists does it take to change a light bulb? None – if the light bulb had needed changing, the market would have done it already.)

- Keynesian economists believe the opposite. They think governments should intervene in an economy, increasing spending in times of trouble and reducing it in times of wealth. Such counter-cyclical demand management will smooth business cycles and ensure maximum employment. (So, how many Keynesian economists does it take to change a light bulb? All of them, because that will generate employment and more consumption, so the economy will grow.)

- Karl Marx questioned the stability of the whole capitalist system, where firms hire workers in order to make a profit. He believed it was inherently unstable and would eventually self-destruct because it exploited people. These people would feel increasingly alienated by their rich employers and would end up uniting and forcing change.

- Milton Friedman believes in money and freedom. He claims inflation is caused solely by changes in the money supply, and says government intervention in an economy is counterproductive.

CHAPTER 2

ECONOMIC HEALTH, WEALTH AND HAPPINESS

A simple guide to growth and recessions

A gentleman ...

is one who has money enough

to do what every fool would like to do

if he could afford it:

... consume without producing.

George Bernard Shaw

INTRODUCTION

Many of us want to 'better our conditions', as the grandfather of economics, Adam Smith, put it. Maybe you'd like a bigger house, a faster car or a better job. It is this drive for self-betterment that helps an economy to grow. It is what makes people start businesses or invest in the stock market. It spurs scientific research and encourages us to learn. It is the reason we are not still living in houses with outside toilets and no electricity.

Economic growth is central to everyone's quality of life. It lifts people out of poverty and allows us all to live longer and in greater comfort. On a personal level it can affect whether you have a job, what kind of house you live in and whether you can afford a new car or a couple of holidays a year. But it is the next generation that really stands to benefit. If Britain carries on expanding at the pace it has been, everyone will earn twice as much as they do today in 30 years' time. Instead of earning just over £20,000 a year, as the average full-time worker does now,[1] your children will have more than £40,000 to live on – and that is in real money, excluding inflation.

Growth not only helps to determine how comfortable you are, it could also influence your investment decisions. If you are planning to buy shares, for example, the state of the economy could be key. If growth is forging ahead and inflation is low, companies can expect to make healthy profits in future, which spells good news for the stock market. The value of US shares almost doubled between April 1997 and January 2000,[2] a surge that owed a lot to the US economy's unprecedented nine-year expansion. Knowing if and when that economic expansion is going to falter could be useful if you own a pension plan or an endowment with exposure to the US market.

Similarly, if you are thinking of buying a house, the last thing you want to worry about as you juggle surveys, solicitors and recalcitrant vendors further up the chain is whether a recession is going to plunge you into negative equity as soon as you complete.

This chapter will help you with all those investment decisions. It is not a guide to personal finance, it will not tell you which life assurance plan to buy or whether to risk your life savings on a dot.com. But it will give you the background knowledge you need to forge intelligent, informed views about the future.

To that end, it tackles the following issues:

- **It looks at how an economy grows.** Each country has workers, natural resources (maybe coal or precious metals) and money, all bound together by technology. Using those in the right combination will make everyone better off.

- **It considers why we get recessions.** Three times in the past 30 years the British economy nosedived into mass unemployment as one downturn after another sapped the country of both money and confidence. The Labour government elected in 1997 vowed to expel the pernicious boom–bust cycle, but it is too early to say yet whether it has been successful. In the meantime, this chapter explains why we get recessions and gives some tips on how to spot a downturn before it is too late.

- **It puts growth in context.** If you have ever come across a story about economic growth in the paper, you would be forgiven for passing right over it. To the uninitiated it is practically meaningless. So the economy has grown by 2 per cent – is that good, bad or indifferent? You read that services are growing but manufacturing is stagnant, that domestic demand is strong but exports are weak. It is hard to make sense of it all, hence the tendency to gloss over it and pass swiftly on to the sports pages. This chapter makes things less opaque. It explains how an economy is measured, how to find out which parts are doing well and which are falling behind. It looks at what constitutes a decent rate of growth, and what falls into the 'could do better' category. In short, it will allow you to assess whether a country is on the road to prosperity or penury.

■ **It discusses potential problems for Britain and other developed countries.** New technology means Britain and much of the industrial world could be on the threshold of a prolonged period of expansion. But that doesn't mean all our problems are over. Growth can generate losers as well as winners – the environment could suffer, while the gap between rich and poor may widen. Reading the economic tea leaves, however, should be attempted with caution. As one economist once put it: forecasting is like trying to drive a car blindfolded and following directions given by a person who is looking out of the back window.

■ **It examines the impact of the Internet.** Any self-respecting economic fortune teller must mention the World Wide Web. It is a recurring theme throughout the book and kicks off here with a look at the net's impact on economic growth. We are all assured that cyberspace will revolutionise our lives, but it is not immediately obvious what it means for the economy as a whole. This chapter explores the dot.com revolution and explains how it could translate into solid, old-fashioned growth.

■ **It considers how life in Britain compares with that in the rest of the world.** For years the UK has been the laggard among its contemporaries. But it seems the tide is turning at last. The chapter finishes with a look at why it is hard to compare living standards in different countries, and at how Britain is finally shedding that excess flab and shaping up.

HOW DOES YOUR COUNTRY GROW?

If you are reading this book at home, chances are you are within easy reach of a washing machine, telephone, fridge and probably car. If you are on the way to work, you may spend your day in a comfortable, centrally heated office with access to a computer and the Internet. The last century has seen incredible change (*see* Fig. 2.1), and it's all thanks to economic growth.

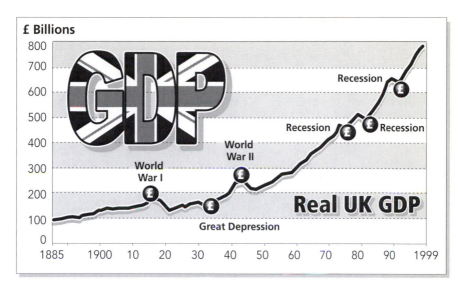

FIG. 2.1 Real UK GDP

Source: Reuters/EcoWin

To understand how an economy evolves, how everyone can enjoy a better standard of living, it helps to consider a simple economic model called the **circular flow of income**.

> **«**You can make even a parrot into
> a learned political economist –
> all he must learn are the two words
> 'supply' and 'demand'.**»**
>
> Anonymous

ECONOMISTS AND MODELS

Economic models are just what their name implies – blueprints of how things should be in an ideal, model world. Just as a road atlas is a streamlined version of an A-Z, so a model is a way of simplifying an economy and squashing it down into a manageable form. It sketches out a basic scenario to which all the complications of real life can be added.

Economists divide models into two categories: **positive** and **normative**. Positive models give objective, scientific explanations of events that can be proved

▶

or refuted using hard evidence and statistics. One example is the **model of price determination**. This is probably the most important concept – and the most intuitive – that you will come across in economics. It says that prices are determined by supply and demand. If supply of a product outweighs demand, prices will fall until enough people are persuaded to buy the excess. If there is more demand than supply, prices will rise. That principle applies to just about everything: the price of labour, or wages, the price of money, in other words interest rates, and the price of land, such as the rent you may pay for your flat. Evidence that it works can be found everywhere – even in the school playground. A craze for Pokémon cards among British children in early 2000 meant particularly prized single editions of the mini monster characters were changing hands for up to £30 behind the bike sheds – far more than the shop price of £2.49 for a random pack of six.

The second type of model, the normative model, is based on what *ought* to be. It is usually a subjective statement that comes from opinions or, as economists put it, value judgements. For example, many people believe firms should pay for the pollution they generate. There are valid arguments to support that position – the price of a car, for example, should reflect the full cost of making it, including any bill for cleaning up environmental damage inflicted in production – but no doubt the champions of heavy industry would disagree. It is difficult to prove the idea with hard facts.

Both positive and normative models are often criticised for being based on outlandish *assumptions*. A classic example is the ubiquitous **model of perfect competition**. This describes a highly competitive marketplace where there are plenty of firms all producing the same thing, there is nothing to stop new companies from setting up rival businesses, and shoppers have perfect knowledge. All highly unlikely in the real world, but that doesn't stop the model from forming the basis of many other theories.

This reliance on unrealistic assumptions is often portrayed as the subject's Achilles heel, the reason that even those in the business maintain a healthy dose of cynicism and self-mockery. Renowned economist Paul Samuelson sums it up perfectly: 'A physicist, a chemist and an economist are stranded on an island with nothing to eat. A can of soup washes ashore. The physicist says: 'Let's smash the can open with a rock.' The chemist says: 'Let's build a fire and heat the can first.' And the economist says: 'Let's assume we have a can opener.'

THE CIRCULAR FLOW OF INCOME

This model divides the economy into four parts – consumers, companies, the government and the overseas sector. The relationship between the first two is key.

Consumers and companies are like Morecambe and Wise, Gilbert and Sullivan. Having one without the other just wouldn't work. Firms produce goods or offer services using workers to whom they pay a salary. The workers then use this salary to buy the goods and the services the firms make. In that way, money gets sent around the economy, with each group relying on the other for survival. There is a circular flow of income. Every time you buy a newspaper or a new pair of shoes or maybe a sandwich for lunch, you are perpetuating that flow.

That's all very well, but it doesn't explain growth. No one is becoming better off. To achieve that, firms need an injection of money in the form of investment. They can then use that money to buy new machines, train workers or pump money into research and development. In 'economic speak', they *improve the quality and quantity of the* **factors of production**, the things that go into making something. This is absolutely key to growth (*see* Fig. 2.2).

One last stroke completes the circle. Firms need money from somewhere to make those investments. They can either go to their bank for a loan, raise money on the stock market or issue a bond. Either way, it is consumers who ultimately provide the cash. Growth relies on households saving part of their income, which they deposit in banks or use to buy shares or bonds, which in turn get recycled as investment by firms. (There is nothing new in the virtue of thrift. Confucius advised back in 550 BC that 'when prosperity comes, do not use all of it'.)

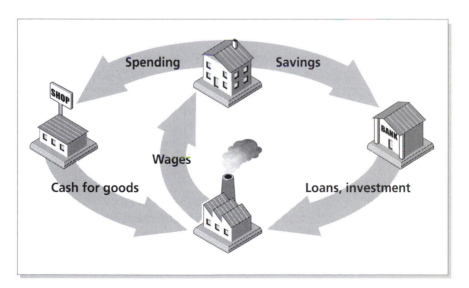

FIG. 2.2 The circular flow of income

The consumer is king in this model. It is his or her demand for, say, cars or clothes that persuades firms to open factories, hire workers and make things. The promise of strong sales and healthy profits attracts investment, which fuels growth. Crudely put, the desire to make money powers growth.

Economic growth comes from improving the quality and quantity of the factors of production, of which there are four: natural resources, employees, capital or money, and ideas and technology. The latter allows existing goods to be made more efficiently, and creates opportunities for making new goods.

MAKING THE MOST OF THE FACTORS OF PRODUCTION

As a rule, four factors go into making everything we buy, from toothpaste to televisions. They are:

- natural resources
- workers
- money
- technology.

Each can be improved, either in quantity or quality, to increase growth.

Natural resources

The discovery of North Sea oil in Britain in the late 1970s gave a welcome boost to growth and still contributes a modest 2 per cent to the economy. Most economists argue that resources play a minor part in the development of advanced countries but can be a significant help to poorer nations.

Workers

The quantity of workers could be increased by population changes, growing participation of women in the paid workforce, or immigration (a skills shortage in Britain at the end of the 1990s persuaded the government to speed up the visa process for selected overseas applicants, for example). Their quality will be improved by education and training. If you plucked a bell-bottomed, platform-shoed worker from the 1970s and put him in front of a computer workstation today, for example, he would probably struggle to make any use of it whatsoever. It is only through training that technological advances can be capitalised upon.

Much of the growth in Britain in the early part of the 20th century came from improved quality of labour. Better education and new technology paved the way for mass production and a burgeoning middle class populated by accountants and doctors and lawyers who demanded higher-quality goods and services, such as cars and radios.

Money and capital

This covers things such as machinery, buildings and factories. Without improvements in this factor of production we would all still be eking a living off the land. Progress in Britain in the 19th century was forged partly through the exploitation of natural resources and partly through capital. The industrial revolution was in full swing by the 1800s and inventions like George Stephenson's 'Rocket' in 1829, a locomotive capable of racing along at 30 miles per hour, helped to make industry more efficient as goods could be transported quickly and cheaply. Which also encompasses the final factor – technology.

Technology

Technology provides the last piece of the jigsaw puzzle. It helps to push out what economists call the **production possibility frontier**. This is an imaginary line that represents the maximum a country can produce given all its land, workers and money. An improvement in technology plus better educated workers, more factories and machines and more raw materials will allow more goods to be produced for less money.

In other words, **productivity** – the amount produced per worker – will increase and that production possibility frontier will move out. This lies at the very core of progress.

Britain has a notoriously low rate of productivity growth. Experts estimate that British workers produce about 20 per cent less than their French and German counterparts and 30 per cent less than Americans. Many believe that gap exists because of chronic under-investment in Britain over the years, a problem that is being tackled with tax incentives and, more importantly, by fostering strong, stable economic growth.

BALANCING SAVING AND INVESTMENT

A country's growth prospects clearly hinge on the amount of investment it makes (and of course the use to which that investment is put. It's no good spending millions on telephone cables just as the world is turning to mobiles). But what is to say that money will be forthcoming? You can't force people to put their wages into a deposit account, so what is to stop investment funds from drying up?

The market, say economists. Many believe that interest rates – in other words the price of money – help to match saving and investment. That keeps the circular flow evenly balanced so that injections into the system (investment) equal withdrawals (saving). The logic is appealing.

Firms spend more on computers. There is an increase in investment → The demand for money rises → Interest rates rise in response (demand for money outweighs supply so the price of money increases) → People are attracted by higher rates on their deposit accounts and increase their savings → Balance has been restored. The interest rate has ensured that investment = saving again.

GOVERNMENT AND GROWTH

So far, money is only circulating between companies and consumers. Now add in the public sector. Whether you like it or not governments raise money through taxes to finance spending on services, such as health and education. Thinking along the same lines as before, taxes are a withdrawal from the system and spending an injection. Again, at some point withdrawals must equal injections to stop the model from either drying up or being flooded with cash. This gives theoretical credence to the global trend at the beginning of the new millennium towards balanced budgets.

THE OVERSEAS SECTOR AND GROWTH

The same goes for foreign trade. Britons buy some of their goods and services from overseas, which represents money leaving the domestic system, flowing out of the country. In other words, imports are a withdrawal. But they also sell goods and services to overseas customers, injecting money back into the system. Again, using the same logic, the three withdrawals – imports, taxation and saving – must equal the three injections – exports, government spending and investment.

Injections:	=	Withdrawals:
▪ Exports		▪ Imports
▪ Government spending		▪ Taxation
▪ Investment		▪ Saving

That sounds like a mighty big coincidence. But remember, this is only a model. In reality, countries run trade surpluses and deficits and governments spend more than they receive in taxes. Both these issues are considered in later chapters.

PUTTING GDP GROWTH IN CONTEXT

A country's growth rate is measured in terms of its **gross domestic product**. Known as **GDP**, this is the total amount of goods and services an economy produces, including government spending and the net contribution from exports and imports.

The focus of GDP data is on how much the economy has grown compared with the previous quarter (quarter-on-quarter growth rate) or with the same quarter in the previous year (year-on-year growth). That is the rate you are most likely to read about in newspapers. When economists talk about annualised growth they simply take the quarter-on-quarter rate and multiply it by four to get an idea of what annual growth would be if the economy carried on expanding at the current rate. This way of looking at the data is more common in the US than in the UK or Europe.

What is considered a decent rate of growth? In Britain, anything around 2½ per cent a year is about normal, although it can fluctuate markedly around that level. Since 1948, it has been as high as 5.5 per cent (in 1964) or as low as –2.2 per cent (in 1980 – in other words, the economy shrank). *See* Fig. 2.3. The United States tends to manage a higher rate of growth, more like 3½ to 4 per cent a year.

GDP figures are a useful way of seeing which parts of an economy are most vibrant. In Britain's case, industry used to be the dominant force, but nowadays it is the trading floor, not the factory floor, that powers the country. The service sector makes up around 70 per cent of the total economy, leaving industry with 28 per cent and farming with just 2 per cent.

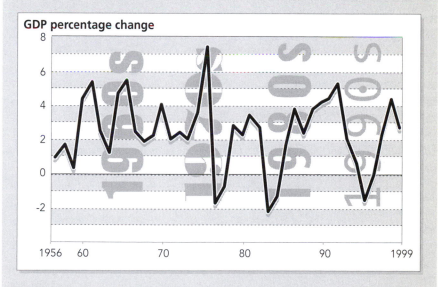

GDP percentage change

FIG. 2.3 Economic growth in Britain between 1956 and 1999   Source: Reuters/EcoWin

HOW DOES BRITAIN MEASURE UP?

Try to work out how much you are worth. If you have ever had to fathom your way through a tax return, you probably know how difficult that is. Now try to do the same thing for everyone else in your family, then everyone in your street, then everyone in your town. You get the picture. Adding up the size of the entire British economy is a huge task, and one that falls to statisticians at the government-run National Statistics office.

Data are compiled in three ways: in terms of output produced, income generated and money spent. All three are measured separately and in theory should add up to the same amount. In practice that is impossible, due partly to the sheer size of the country and partly because of a 'black economy' that cannot be officially recorded. Any differences that arise between the three measures are averaged away.

The *income* measure of GDP tots up all wages, rents, interest and profits in the economy. In other words, it adds up the payments to the factors of production: the land, labour and capital. The statistics office initially estimates the total wage bill using its employment and earnings figures, but longer term it uses more accurate numbers from the Inland Revenue. Similarly for profits, in the short term it interviews the top 1,600 companies in Britain to gauge their earnings and then extrapolates them for all firms. Two or three years down the line it has access to more accurate profit data from the taxman.

The income method does not include *transfer payments* when money changes hands but nothing is produced in return. For example, the unemployed receive a jobseekers' allowance from the government but do not produce anything in return, hence benefits are excluded from GDP data. Similarly, a person selling a second-hand car gets money for it but no new car has been created so that is also left out.

The *output* measure of GDP records everything that is made in Britain, from widgets to warships. There is a danger here of double counting which is remedied by only adding up the value of the *final* output of goods and services. For example, suppose you spend 45 pence buying a pint of milk. If the GDP data counted that final output *and* the intermediate output – the cost to the supermarket of buying the milk from the dairy – the pint will have been added up twice. Service-sector firms such as hairdressers or restaurants are assessed by turnover.

Lastly, the *expenditure* method uses survey data to record how many goods and services are sold across the country, plus figures on government spending and trade.

GDP figures are released every quarter but tend to be of limited interest to financial markets such as shares and bonds because they are backward looking and initially fairly inaccurate. It can take up to four years before a complete set of data is available.

For example, when figures for the first quarter of 1996 initially came out, it was estimated that real GDP (adjusted for inflation) was 0.4 per cent higher than in the previous quarter. Subsequent revisions meant three years later that figure had been revised up to 1.0 per cent. Spare a thought for the policymakers who are trying to decide interest rates, taxes or government spending with such misleading data. It is little wonder things can go horribly wrong.

National Statistics has a website at www.statistics.gov.uk

TURNING THE WHEELS OF THE BUSINESS CYCLE

> **"Recession is when your neighbour loses his job; depression is when you lose yours."**
>
> Harry S. Truman

Countries grow at different rates from one year to the next. In the good times an advanced economy can expand by up to 5 or 6 per cent, in the bad times growth may fade to nothing, or even turn negative. This ebb and flow, which tends to repeat itself in waves, has been going on for centuries and is known as the **business** or **trade cycle**.

Even the Bible talks of the natural rhythm of years of plenty followed by years of want. Back then it was the richness of crop harvests that powered the cycle. These days, most economists attribute it to changes in spending.

WHY ECONOMIES MOVE IN CYCLES, AND WHY THAT MATTERS

Knowing what causes business cycles, and being able to predict a downturn before the unemployment queues lengthen, is tricky, but useful if you can crack it. Share markets tend to sag in recessions and house prices often fall as both spending and jobs dry up. The economy's growth prospects are therefore vital to any investment decisions you make.

Sadly, there is no easy checklist of factors that cause recessions. But economics is not totally impotent. The section below explains their most likely cause, while the box entitled 'How to spot a recession' gives a few tips on forecasting a downturn ahead of time.

Consider the four groups mentioned earlier: consumers, companies, the government and the overseas sector. To understand how the spending patterns of each group fuel the business cycle and make the difference between prosperity and penury, it helps to consider two simple principles, both devised by John Maynard Keynes – the **accelerator theory** and the **multiplier effect**.

THE ACCELERATOR THEORY

Some economists believe investment – in other words, spending by companies – is determined by interest rates and past profits. The lower the cost of borrowing and the more cash available from previous years, the higher the investment. Some believe, however, that it is dictated by total demand and income in the economy. This latter principle is known as the accelerator theory. This says that if people go out and spend more (so that overall demand and income in the economy rise), firms will buy more machines to make the extra goods needed to meet that demand. For example, if the government lowered taxes, you may decide to spend the extra money you are left with on, say, a new car. If enough people did that, firms such as Ford would have to expand production by building new assembly lines. In other words, an increase in total spending in the economy has prompted a rise in investment.

THE MULTIPLIER EFFECT

Which leads to the second principle, the multiplier effect. Imagine Ford has built a car plant in Britain, at a cost of £100 million, to satisfy the increase in demand. A good chunk of that money will be spent hiring construction workers to build the factory. They will spend their wages on anything from clothes to a holiday, so now demand for, say, jeans has risen, too. Denim manufacturers will hire more workers to make more jeans, increasing their income, which will also be spent. And so on. The £100 million invested by Ford has triggered a chain reaction and increased overall GDP by much more than the original amount. There has been a multiplier effect.

The extent of that multiplier effect depends on people's **propensity to consume** – their tendency to spend. If the original construction workers hired by Ford saved all the money they earned, there would be no multiplier. The money would stop with them. If they spent most of it, however, that chain reaction would be set in motion, until it eventually petered out (some of the money spent down the line would go on foreign goods, some would be lost in tax, some saved).

FUSING THE TWO...

Now bring both theories together. Imagine the economy is roaring away at 5 per cent growth and it feels like the good times will roll for ever. However, sooner or later there will not be enough workers available to make all the goods people want. The economy will be bumping up against its production possibility frontier. This puts a brake on things. As growth slows and people scale back their spending, investment by firms falls (because of the accelerator theory), which has a knock-on downward effect on the whole economy (because of the multiplier effect). Growth spirals lower. At some point, however, firms will be forced to invest, if only to replace defunct machinery and depleted stockpiles. Similarly, eventually consumers will use their savings or borrow money to buy things, as they are loath to suffer any further decline in their living standards. With both consumer and business spending on the increase, the economy will start to turn higher again.

...AND ADDING IN THE GOVERNMENT AND OVERSEAS SECTORS

This is easy. The government can manipulate consumption and investment by changing taxes or it can directly affect the output of the economy by its own billions of pounds in spending (though nowadays the government is very proud of its balanced fiscal policy). Demand for exports and imports will change as growth fluctuates abroad or as the exchange rate changes. Both of these factors will help shape domestic growth (and both are considered in more detail in later chapters).

The accelerator/multiplier theory of business cycles is based on principles developed by Keynes. It has two defining characteristics. Firstly, fluctuations in growth rely on changes in *real* variables such as investment and labour (as opposed to simply changes in money), and secondly, those fluctuations are driven by *endogenous* factors. In other words, GDP changes thanks to forces from *within* the model – the investment and spending – rather than any outside influence. In this Keynesian model, it is the private sector that generates business cycles.

Monetarists disagree. They believe changes in growth are driven by changes in the amount of money there is in an economy, for which they blame governments. It is the misguided actions of authorities, they say, that put us all through the pain and uncertainty of recession.

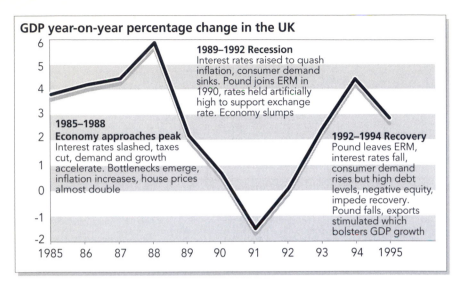

GDP year-on-year percentage change in the UK

1989–1992 Recession
Interest rates raised to quash inflation, consumer demand sinks. Pound joins ERM in 1990, rates held artificially high to support exchange rate. Economy slumps

1985–1988
Economy approaches peak
Interest rates slashed, taxes cut, demand and growth accelerate. Bottlenecks emerge, inflation increases, house prices almost double

1992–1994 Recovery
Pound leaves ERM, interest rates fall, consumer demand rises but high debt levels, negative equity, impede recovery. Pound falls, exports stimulated which bolsters GDP growth

FIG. 2.4 Anatomy of a business cycle

Source: Reuters/EcoWin

HOW TO SPOT A RECESSION

'Economists set themselves too easy, too useless a task if in tempestuous seasons they can only tell us that when the storm is long past the ocean is flat again.'

J.M. Keynes, 1923

There have been three major recessions in post-war Britain: in 1974/5, 1980/81 and 1990/91. Together, they wiped £27 billion off the economy, and put more than three million people out of work. In retrospect, it is clear the country was on a collision course with disaster on each occasion, but at the time governments thought they were invincible.

Here is a quick guide on how to spot a recession.

Interest rates too high

You probably know from personal experience how crippling high interest rates can be. They spell bigger mortgage payments and hefty credit card bills, encouraging you to tighten your belt and cancel all spending sprees. Demand in the economy falls and firms start to cut back on production by laying off workers. Higher borrowing costs also discourage investment by companies, triggering that negative multiplier effect. A downward spiral develops and recession beckons.

Unfortunately, there is no handy benchmark signalling when rates are too high. What might seem ludicrously tight to you may be too lax for a central banker intent on keeping inflation under control. As a general rule of thumb, if rates rise far and fast, there could be trouble ahead. When borrowing costs almost doubled to 14 per cent in one year up to May 1989, recession was quick to follow.

Badly timed tax change

Profligate public spending (maybe ahead of an election) could sink the government into unsustainable debt and force an ill-timed tax increase. Consumers will have less money to spend and will start cutting back on luxuries. Warning signs include a massive build-up of government debt (and an unpopular government faced with the prospect of losing an election).

Sustained decline in exports

A prolonged fall in the demand for exports could also cause domestic GDP to fall – the 1929/32 UK depression was almost entirely due to a fall in exports. Warning signs include an overseas recession (when Asian economies collapsed in the late 1990s there was widespread fear of a knock-on global downturn as demand from the region plummeted) and a sharp rise in the currency. This makes exports more expensive (see Chapter 4) and therefore lowers demand for them. Exports make up about 30 per cent of the British economy, so a sharp fall in their demand could be damaging.

A random shock

An unexpected event outside the country, such as a war, a natural disaster or an overseas stock market crash, could knock growth off course and precipitate a downturn. For example, in the early 1970s an agreement by oil-producing nations to restrict supply sent oil prices through the roof. Inflation in Britain soared, the country got into huge debt and recession followed.

IS THE RECESSION DEAD?

Between the end of the Second World War and the 1970s Britain had no recessions. It had business cycles, in the sense that growth was as high as 5 per cent in some years and as low as 1 per cent or less in others, but the economy never actually contracted. Growth never turned negative (technically, economists define a recession as two consecutive quarters of negative growth, though some say it is an annual decline in GDP). In an ideal world that would be the norm – certainly the latest trend among governments is to banish the boom–bust cycle of the past. Maybe we will look back in 30 years' time at the 1970s–1990s as an aberration in an otherwise recession-free post-war era.

Maybe. Interest rates in Britain are now controlled by experts at the Bank of England rather than politicians, so there is less chance of them rising too high too fast. It's a similar story elsewhere: in the US, the Federal Reserve controls the cost of borrowing and in much of Europe it's the European Central Bank. In addition, in Britain the Labour government elected in 1997 imposed strict rules on public borrowing, mitigating the chances of heavy debts and crippling tax rises. Again, there are similar rules limiting the accumulation of public debt in much of Europe. So the danger from the first two potential trouble spots mentioned in the box above has receded.

However, even the canniest of politicians can do little about natural disasters. Thus the threat of an outside shock remains, as does the danger of an overseas recession hitting exports. Almost a fifth of British goods and services sold abroad go to the US, so a sudden fall in demand across the Atlantic would put a damaging hole in the UK's accounts.

Economist Arthur Okun put his finger on it in 1970 when he said the danger of recession had not disappeared. 'Recessions are now generally considered to be fundamentally preventable, like airplane crashes and unlike hurricanes,' he said in his book *The Political Economy of Prosperity*. 'But we have not banished air crashes from the land, and it is not clear that we have the wisdom or the ability to eliminate recessions.'

DOTTY ABOUT GROWTH

The dot.com revolution has arrived. There was a time at the end of the 1990s when you couldn't switch on the TV, open a newspaper or turn on the radio without hearing about another Internet entrepreneur striking it rich in the knowledge economy. (Francis Bacon was way ahead of his time when he declared in 1597: 'For also knowledge itself is power.') Thousands of Britons are getting online every day, seduced by the promise of cheap books, cut-price airfares and more information than you could absorb in a lifetime.

But what does the Internet mean for good old-fashioned growth? It may be a useful way of booking a holiday or buying a CD, but can it really raise living standards and generate economic expansion?

The answer could lie in an economic theory developed almost 100 years ago. In 1911, Austrian economist Joseph Schumpeter identified three periods of growth that occur simultaneously in an economy: a short-run cycle lasting three to four years, a medium-term one that runs for between eight and 11 years, and a longwave cycle that goes on for 45 to 60 years.

Schumpeter suggested that these long cycles were triggered by innovation (in other words, by an *exogenous* force, something that comes from outside the model). During periods of slow growth, firms are less likely to invest in research and development because there is little money to spare. Potential breakthroughs pile up because entrepreneurs cannot secure the funds to finance their inventions. Once growth does improve – maybe thanks to an investment boom – all those inventions come on stream at once, releasing a flood of money for copycat developments that drip-feed growth for years.

Schumpeter identified the Industrial Revolution in 1750 as the beginning of one expansion, the railroad and construction boom in the mid 19th century as the start of another, and the spread of electricity, cars and chemicals at the start of the 20th century as a third. That begs the question, could the Internet be the catalyst for the next long wave of growth?

It certainly has the potential to cut costs and boost efficiency, particularly in the so-called business to business (B2B) market. For example, many multinationals now use the web as a single connection point to suppliers, instead of conducting business with hundreds of individual companies, effectively making information cheaper. US car giants Ford, General Motors and DaimlerChrysler hope to save up to 20 per cent by establishing such an online exchange for the motor industry (it can be likened to paying one big bill, instead of 10 different ones in 10 different ways to 10 different people).

GlobalNetExchange does the same thing for supermarkets, linking firms like Sainsbury in Britain with Carrefour in France and Sears in the US. Competing head to head in such a transparent market may force suppliers to trim prices to maintain market share, driving overall costs lower. The B2B market is booming. Forrester Research, which specialises in looking at the Internet, estimates it will be worth $1.3 trillion in Europe alone by 2004.

The web also allows firms to cut the cost of selling. Firstly, when customers buy online, administration and processing costs are lower, and secondly, Internet companies have less need for expensive branch networks. Web pioneer Amazon.com offers 1.5 million books to its 13 million customers without owning a single shop.

All these cost savings have the potential to deliver those prized productivity gains. Put another way, the Internet could help to squeeze more and more out of the factors of production, shifting the production possibility frontier further out. Exactly how far out remains in contention, however. Economists at top investment bank Goldman Sachs estimate that British GDP could be just over 5 per cent higher in the long term thanks to the savings from B2B and its knock-on effects – that amounts to more than £40 billion, a figure worthy of any dot.com entrepreneur.

66Forecasting is very difficult,
especially if it is about the future.**99**

Anonymous

THE DOWNSIDE TO GLOBAL GROWTH

The global economy, including Britain, could be on the threshold of a sustained period of economic growth. Some predict the world economy will double in size between 1997 and 2020, allowing living standards to rise by almost 70 per cent – a cheering thought for the next time you can't afford the computer you want or the car you crave.

But that growth could come at a price. Possible costs of economic expansion you may want to keep an eye on include:

- **growing income inequality:** some believe that expansion favours the strong and neglects the weak, thus widening the gulf between rich and poor. But evidence is inconclusive. There are also those who argue that growth benefits everyone equally – and they have the statistics to prove it. While you are waiting for the economists to make up their minds, you may as well assume the worst and prepare to fight for your piece of the growth action. That means getting wired to the web and staying ahead of the dot.com revolution. Equality of access to the Internet will be essential to prevent society from polarising into two camps: the web savvy and the web illiterate;

- **environmental damage:** expansion brings pollution in its wake, a *negative externality*. In other words, by poisoning rivers etc. a firm imposes a cost on society that is not reflected in its profits. Many economists believe a pollution tax would limit this kind of environmental damage (a normative statement). It would internalise the externality;

- **depletion of non-renewable resources:** the faster an economy grows, the more oil, coal and gas, etc. it uses, depleting the stock of resources available for the next generation. However, growth also brings technological advances and the money for exploration. For example, in the ten years after the 1973/74 Opec (Organisation of Petroleum Exporting Countries) crisis, when oil prices rose fourfold, carmakers halved average fuel consumption per mile by designing more efficient engines. Brazil even developed cars which ran on fuel made from sugar. In addition, exploration means there are almost double the amount of known global oil reserves now than there were in 1977;

- **an ageing population:** growth and technological advance tend to prolong life. For example, life expectancy in Britain averages 77 now, compared with 48 in 1900 and 37 in 1805. That means there will be a growing number of pensioners for every worker in future. The National Statistics office estimates that by 2011 there will be almost 12 million pensioners in Britain, an increase of 11 per cent since

1998. By contrast, the number of people of working age will have gone up by just 6 per cent, to 38.5 million. Not only does that mean fewer workers generating growth for more people, it also means more money will have to be found for services such as healthcare.

LIVING IT UP

Material progress in Britain has been startling in recent years. According to the National Statistics office, about 90 per cent of the UK population had washing machines in 1998, 89 per cent had central heating (up from about 60 per cent in 1981) and 70 per cent owned a car (against 62 per cent in 1981).

That is a pretty comfortable lifestyle by anyone's standards, but it still falls a touch short of many other developed countries.

According to GDP figures – adjusted for differences in prices between countries – each Briton could lay claim to $21,675 in 1998, more than the $21,150 per Frenchman, but less than the $22,998 per German and $32,328 per American.[3] In fact, Britain was way down in 17th place out of 29 OECD (Organisation for Economic Co-operation and Development) countries in terms of GDP per capita (a measure of wealth per head of the population), below the likes of Norway, Austria, Iceland and the Netherlands.

Up until the 1980s, Britain put in a poor economic performance compared with her main competitors, Germany, France and the US. Problems centred around a failure to match productivity growth. British workers produced less than their Continental and US counterparts, with the result that the economy could not grow as fast. Ironically, one of the UK's biggest handicaps was its Second World War victory, which deprived industry of the opportunity to start again from scratch with the latest technology. Partly as a result of that, the country spent years saddled with the demeaning title 'sick man of Europe'.

Figure 2.5 shows GDP per head in 14 countries, based on 1999 figures.

LIMITATIONS TO GDP

But all is not lost. Before Britons pack their bags and head for a life of luxury in Florida, they should bear in mind the following:

- **British growth is picking up.** Between 1982 and 1991, the UK notched up real annual growth of 2.7 per cent on average, the same as that in Germany. However, between 1992 and 2001, it is expected

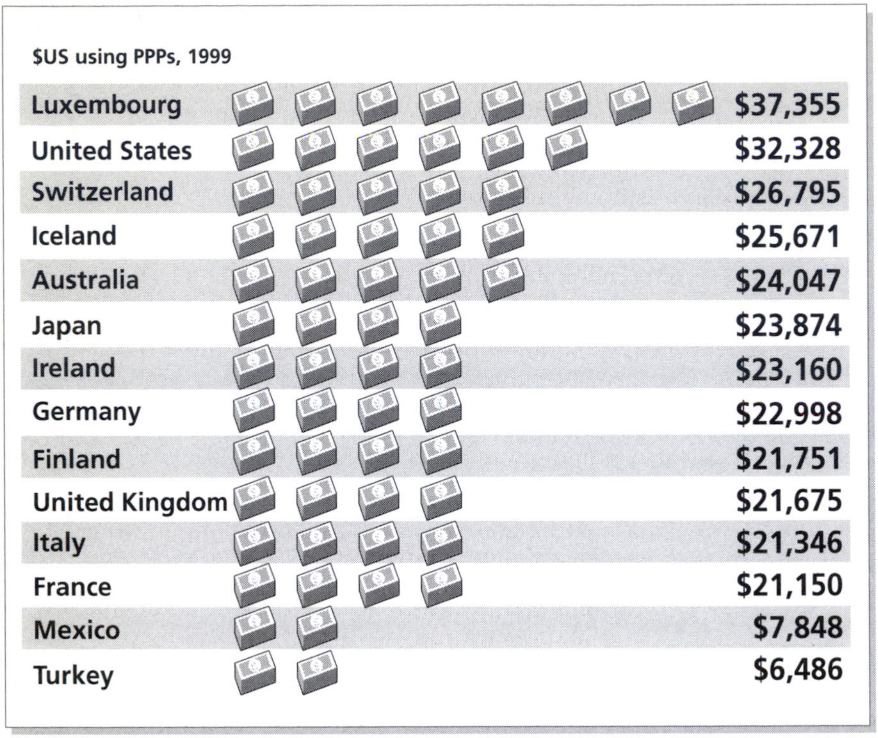

$US using PPPs, 1999

Country	GDP per head
Luxembourg	$37,355
United States	$32,328
Switzerland	$26,795
Iceland	$25,671
Australia	$24,047
Japan	$23,874
Ireland	$23,160
Germany	$22,998
Finland	$21,751
United Kingdom	$21,675
Italy	$21,346
France	$21,150
Mexico	$7,848
Turkey	$6,486

FIG. 2.5 GDP per head in selected countries   Source: OECD Economic Outlook, December 1999

to average 2.5 per cent, significantly higher than the 1.7 per cent in Germany and the 2.0 per cent in France.[4]

■ **GDP changes can be misleading.** The general rule that higher GDP is good and lower GDP is bad has a number of exceptions. Changes in gross domestic product do not take into account changes in quality. For example, air travel is much better today than 50 years ago but it is also much cheaper, relatively speaking (Britons flew seven billion kilometres on domestic flights in 1998 against 200,000 in 1952). This lower price would register as lower GDP, wrongly implying that living standards had fallen.

■ **Not all production is of equal worth.** GDP is an all-encompassing measure of the economy. It covers luxuries such as sports cars and yachts, but also includes things like the cost of running jails. It does not distinguish between the two, so it is hard to know whether a rise in GDP is entirely good or bad. For example, making more tanks will add to GDP but some would say that is less worthwhile than building more schools or printing more (economics) textbooks.

■ **GDP fails to show the distribution of income.** GDP measures the wealth of a country as a whole, but it does not show how evenly distributed that wealth is. For example, Saudi Arabia has similar GDP to Finland but a far more uneven distribution of income.

■ **GDP is a blunt tool for measuring living standards.** The total amount of income generated in an economy is just one way of judging a population's wellbeing. Other factors such as tax and benefit laws are also important, as are more esoteric measures like pollution, infant mortality, crime rates and even the amount of space per person. As political scion Robert F. Kennedy put it: '(The gross national product) does not allow for the health of our families, the quality of their education, or the joy of their play. It is indifferent to the decency of our factories and the safety of streets alike. It does not include the beauty of our poetry or the strength of our marriages, the intelligence of our public debate or the integrity of our public officials.'

■ **Cross-country GDP comparison is flawed.** The prevalence of these non-quantifiable factors make cross-country GDP comparisons difficult. For example, Finland and Italy had almost identical GDP/capita values in 1998, but Finns have to spend a greater proportion of their income on heating than Italians. It is a trivial example but one that illustrates the dangers of ranking countries' quality of life according to GDP figures alone.

IF YOU REMEMBER SIX THINGS FROM THIS CHAPTER ...

■ Economies grow through the exploitation of the factors of production: natural resources, labour, capital and technology. Minerals are mined, labour is educated, money is used to build factories, and technology allows goods to be produced more efficiently.

■ In the 21st century the exploitation of knowledge and information technology and the emergence of the digital economy could power the world through a prolonged period of growth.

■ The risk of recession remains, however. Interest rates may be too high, the government grip on the economy too tight, or an external shock such as a natural disaster or stock market crash could trigger a downturn.

■ Gross domestic product is the total amount of goods and services produced in an economy. It is measured in terms of output, income or expenditure and can take up to four years to compile accurately.

▪ Britain's service sector accounts for around 70 per cent of output. Industry contributes about 28 per cent and farming the remainder. The British economy amounted to around £790 billion in 1999.

▪ Britain has traditionally lagged behind its major counterparts in GDP growth but has put in a better performance in recent years compared with France and Germany. Whether that lead can be maintained is open to question.

ENDNOTES

1 Based on average, full-time weekly earnings of £400.10, according to the New Earnings Survey.

2 Based on the Dow Jones Industrial Average.

3 OECD National Accounts, March 2000.

4 IMF World Economic Outlook, Spring 2000.

CHAPTER 3

POLITICAL CORRECTNESS

The government, the Chancellor, his job and your money

"The government solution to a problem

is usually as bad

as the problem.**"**

Milton Friedman

"My experience

in government is that when things

are non-controversial,

beautifully co-ordinated

and all the rest,

it must be

that there is not much going on.**"**

John F. Kennedy (1917–63)

INTRODUCTION

Every year, Britain's Chancellor of the Exchequer stands at the dispatch box in the House of Commons and delivers his annual Budget. With the tipple of his choice at his side (former Conservative Chancellor Kenneth Clarke opted for whisky, Labour's Gordon Brown prefers Scottish mineral water), the man of the moment spends around an hour laying out his spending and taxation plans for the coming 12 months.

It is the one occasion when he has the electorate's undivided attention. British taxpayers give the government around £375 billion a year to run the country, equivalent to roughly £7,400 per adult.[1] Exactly what happens to that money will have an impact on the lives of everyone in the country. It could affect the standard of education in British schools, the service received from local doctors, the length of time it takes to get the train into work. It may affect how much money people have to spend after tax, how much it costs to fill up the car or the price of a pint in the local pub.

But it is not just about spending as much money as possible within an acceptable rate of taxation. The Budget also has ramifications for the economy as a whole. Voters may welcome more money for the NHS, particularly if taxes aren't going up to pay for it. But if that extra spending takes place when economic growth is already quite strong and inflationary pressures are bubbling below the surface, it could elicit a sharp interest rate rise from the Bank of England. What the Chancellor has given in more spending, the Bank could simply take away in higher mortgages and more expensive credit card bills. In this way, monetary policy (changing borrowing costs) is used to discipline fiscal policy (government spending).

The Budget is therefore one big balancing act. Naturally, the individual measures are key and can make an enormous difference to people's lives, but it should also be judged in a wider context. The prize for skillful execution is another term in office, the punishment for incompetence is expulsion to the opposition benches (not to mention a hard time for the general public).

To help you judge for yourself whether the government is doing a decent job of running the country, this chapter discusses the following ideas:

- **It considers why we have to pay taxes.** Taxes not only help pay for a country's hospitals, schools and armies, they also redistribute income, making society a fairer place.

- **It assesses whether British taxpayers are getting value for money**. Most people don't like paying taxes, so when they do, they want to be sure their hard-earned cash is being spent wisely. This chapter goes on to consider that question by looking at how the British tax burden has changed over the years, and how it compares with that in other countries.

- **It traces the history of taxation in Britain.** Everything from watches to dogs to windows has been taxed at some point in Britain. This chapter charts the surprisingly colourful history of those and other levies, from the 2nd century Roman tax on British cattle through to self-assessment of income tax, introduced in 1996/97.

- **It considers the future of taxation, particularly where the Internet is concerned.** Cybershopping poses considerable problems for the taxman, as does the opportunity afforded by the net to evade taxation. This chapter looks at whether the web will lower your tax bill, and at what the Inland Revenue may have up its sleeve to stop that from happening.

- **It looks at how governments use taxes and spending to control the economy.** Taxes are raised to finance spending, but they can also help to manipulate the economy, creating jobs or stifling inflation. The chapter considers how this so-called fiscal policy works, and suggests its limitations.

- **It explores how else the government tweaks the economy.** Taxes are not the only tool governments use to achieve that vote-winning formula of strong growth, plenty of jobs and low inflation. Exchange rates and so-called supply-side policies are also useful.

- **It discusses why government debt matters to you and me.** Just as you or I cannot keep adding to our credit cards without paying them off, so the government cannot keep borrowing ad infinitum. The chapter ends with a look at how much Britain owes and why a country's debt levels matter to you and me. While I wouldn't lose any sleep over government debt, it is one of those issues that is worth keeping an eye on, to make sure it doesn't get out of control.

A TAXING ISSUE

WHY DO WE HAVE TO PAY TAXES?

❝There is no such thing as a good tax.❞

Winston Churchill (1874–1965)

Imagine a world without governments. Who would make sure roads were built and armies were trained? Who would install streetlights and traffic lights? Who would build, staff and fund hospitals, then provide free healthcare to everyone who wanted it?

As the philosopher Plato observed almost 2,500 years ago: 'A state comes into existence because no individual is self-sufficing, we all have many needs.' Even the most hardened free-marketeer recognises that and will tolerate limited taxation and spending as a result. The following are reasons (some more universally accepted than others) why we need to pay taxes.

- **To pay for nationwide services such as defence.** Nearly all goods are *private goods*. Once they are consumed, no one else can use them.

For example, if you buy a car, no one can drive it unless you give them the keys (assuming it's not stolen). A few goods, however, are *public goods*, which, as their name suggests, are available to everyone, regardless of who pays for them. Defence is a classic example. The British army affords protection to everyone living in the UK, irrespective of whether they want that protection or not. It is **non-excludable**. It is also **non-rival** in that an increase in the population will not reduce the defence protection available to anyone else. These two characteristics give rise to a **free rider problem**. Given that public goods are available to everyone, regardless of who pays for them, some people will inevitably attempt to free load. If enough people do that, the good won't be provided at all, hence the government must step in.

- **To pay for healthcare and education.** Hospitals and schools eat up more than a quarter of British government spending, yet unlike defence, both can be, and are, provided by the private sector. The trouble is, free markets will not provide enough of either to go around. Most people cannot afford Eton or Bupa, yet both education and healthcare are considered basic rights in a modern society. Private provision of these so-called **merit goods**, things that are good for you, must therefore be supplemented by state provision. Fervent free-marketeers disagree, arguing that free schools impose the government's choice of education on everyone, preventing people from making their own decisions.

- **To pay unemployment and other benefits.** Social security, which covers benefits such as unemployment and housing, gobbles up almost a third of British government spending, far and away the largest single proportion. The foundation of the welfare state by the Labour government in 1945 established the principle of provision from cradle to grave, creating an enduring tax bill in the process. Again, a true free-marketeer would oppose a comprehensive benefits system, arguing that it deters the unemployed from taking a job and therefore prevents wages from being bargained lower.

- **To discourage pollution.** Just as governments spend money on hospitals and schools to nurture a healthy, learned population, so they can tax pollution, cigarettes and other harmful products so as to discourage their use. In other words, they can penalise **demerit goods**. For example, when extra taxes meant leaded petrol became slightly more expensive than unleaded in Britain, most drivers bought cars which ran on the latter, thereby cutting down on pollution. In fact, it worked so well that leaded petrol disappeared from service station forecourts at the end of 1999.

- **To manage the economy as a whole.** Taxation can influence the level of demand and inflation, hence it is a useful way of tweaking growth and prices in the economy. More on that later.

- **To redistribute income.** The market may be efficient if left to its own devices, but that does not mean it will be fair. Smith's 'invisible hand' is blind to poverty. Money talks, hence since 'we can't have our cake of market efficiency and share it equally', as the economist Arthur Okun put it, there is arguably a role for taxation to redistribute income.

> 66 It is not the possessions
> # but the desires of mankind
> which require to be equalised. 99
>
> Aristotle (384–322 BC)

WEALTH REDISTRIBUTION UNDER NEW LABOUR

The New Labour government that swept to power in May 1997 had to tread extremely carefully when it came to wealth redistribution. Instead of being treated as a badge of honour, diverting income from rich to poor via high income taxes had come to be associated with fiscal laxity thanks to the disastrous tax and spend policies of their predecessors in the 1970s.

Yet around 80 per cent of Britons (70 per cent of Conservatives) believe that the income gap between rich and poor in the UK is too large and almost three-quarters say it is the government's responsibility to do something about it.[2]

With higher income taxes off the agenda, other, more subtle means of redistribution had to be found. Measures such as the working families tax credit (which ensures working parents get a certain, minimum income), the minimum wage and help for pensioners were introduced to divert money to the worse off. These were partly paid for by the abolition of the married couple's allowance, an increase in stamp duty on expensive properties and the scrapping of mortgage interest tax relief (Miras). Equality of opportunity, not equality of income, became the battle cry of the new Labour party.

Research suggests the strategy worked. According to the Institute for Fiscal Studies (IFS), a highly regarded independent think-tank, following Labour's first four budgets, the poorest 10 per cent of people in the country were just over 9 per cent better off – equivalent to an extra £9 a week. The next 10 per cent were 8 per cent better off, and the next 10 per cent were 5 per cent wealthier. At the other end of the scale, the richest 20 per cent of the population had lost out slightly. Gordon Brown's reputation as the quietly redistributing chancellor appears to be well earned.

Until, that is, you look at a wider measure of inequality. The National Statistics office has estimated that the gap between the wealthy and the poor in Britain was, in 1998/99, at its widest since 1990, the last year of Margaret Thatcher's premiership. Its index of income distribution, based on a complicated mathematical formula called a Gini Coefficient, rose to 35 in 1998/99 from 34 the previous year (a value of zero being total equality). However, there is an important caveat attached – this coefficient was calculated before measures such as the minimum wage and the working families tax credit were introduced.

The IFS has a website at www.ifs.org.uk

> 66 Nobody who has wealth to distribute
> # ever omits himself. 99

Leon Trotsky (1879–1940)

LIMITS TO TAXATION

Very few people like paying taxes, hence their use as a means of redistribution is limited. Surveys regularly show that voters would be happy to pay higher taxes if it meant a better health service or more schools, but get them into a polling booth and it is often a different matter. Penalise top income earners too heavily and governments run the risk of being voted on to the opposition benches.

But that is not the only incentive for keeping the tax burden under control. By increasing income tax rates, particularly those at the top of the scale, governments run the risk of:

- **reducing the incentive to work.** The top rate of income tax under the Labour government between 1974 and 1979 was 83 per cent. A surcharge of 15 per cent was applied to unearned income (such as interest on investments) above a certain threshold. In other words, for every one pound earned by a top-rate taxpayer with investment income, the government took 98 pence of it, leaving the worker with just 2 pence to show for his labour (high earners supposedly needed to make £10,000 to buy a suit). By cutting those tax rates, people will be encouraged to work harder, say some economists, therefore spurring economic growth. This will add to revenues further down the road;

- **triggering a brain drain.** With such punitive tax rates, high earners are likely to flee overseas, taking their money and their skills with them. On the day of the 1992 election, when it looked like Neil Kinnock's Labour Party might win, the *Sun* newspaper famously asked its readers: 'If Kinnock wins today, will the last person to leave Britain please turn out all the lights.';

- **Encouraging tax avoidance.** The higher the tax rate, the harder the wealthy will try to bypass it. They may do this via legal means of tax avoidance, or illegal ones of tax evasion. The gap between the two is narrow, but it is important. As former Chancellor Denis Healey once put it, 'The difference between tax avoidance and tax evasion is the thickness of a prison wall.'

TYPES OF TAXATION

'It was as true', said Mr Barkis, 'as taxes is. And nothing's truer than them.'

David Copperfield, Chapter 21
Charles Dickens (1812–70)

Taxes are classified in the following ways:

- **direct:** this is a tax levied directly on an individual or an organisation, such as income tax (which is raised on earnings) or corporation tax (which is raised on company profits).

- **indirect:** this is a tax on a good or service, such as value added tax (VAT), fuel duty, or the tax paid on cigarettes and alcohol. In other words, it is levied on spending.

Within those two classes, taxes are further broken down depending on their impact:

- **progressive:** this is a tax where the proportion paid rises as the income of the taxpayer rises. Britain's income tax system is progressive because high earners pay higher tax rates than low earners. This is considered the fairest type of tax;

- **regressive:** this is where the proportion of income paid in tax falls as the income of the taxpayer rises. The notorious poll tax introduced in England in 1990 by Margaret Thatcher was regressive since someone earning, say, £10,000 paid the same amount as someone earning £100,000. The unfairness of the tax sparked violent riots in central London, forcing the Conservatives to back down and introduce council tax instead;

> ■ **proportional:** a proportional tax is one where everyone pays the same percentage of tax, no matter what the income of the taxpayer. VAT is an example of a broadly proportional tax. Apart from a few exceptions, it is levied at a flat rate of 17.5 per cent on all goods and services (some items such as books and food are zero rated, while domestic fuel carries a levy of just 5 per cent).

THE STRAIN ON THE TAXPAYER'S PURSE

HOW MUCH DO BRITONS PAY IN TAX?

The question of how much money to raise in taxation is not a straightforward one. On the one hand, services like the NHS arguably need more funds, but that could be bad news for the beer-drinking, cigarette-smoking, car-driving taxpayer who has to foot the bill. Equally, extra money for schools is almost guaranteed to win votes, but if that means penalising top-rate taxpayers, it may be politically (and economically) counterproductive. Alternatively, the government could bypass taxpayers altogether and borrow the money to pay for projects like road building and improved public transport. But that would risk the ire of the financial markets, and although they cannot cast votes directly, they can show their disapproval in many other ways, such as driving interest rates higher or the pound lower.

In short, the Chancellor must pick his way through a fiscal minefield, raising enough money to nurture the economy and impress the markets without alienating a typically tax-shy electorate.

> ❝The point to remember is
> # that what the government gives
> it must first take away. ❞
>
> John S. Coleman (1897–1958)

Figure 3.1 shows the end result of this delicate balancing act. Britons have paid between 33 and 39 per cent of their total income in taxes in the past 20 or so years. Immediately after Margaret Thatcher came to power in 1979, the tax take rose, but then it started to drop off as the Conservative privatisation programme got under way and income taxes

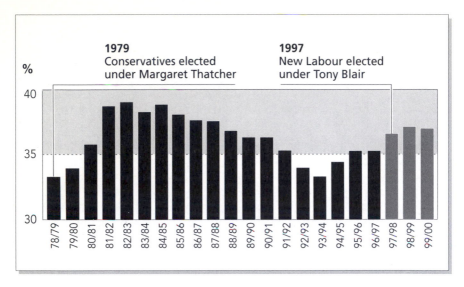

FIG. 3.1 UK tax as a percentage of GDP

Source: Red Book 2000

were cut. It increased slightly in the early years of the New Labour government, elected in 1997, but has since levelled off.

> ❝That which angers men most
> # is to be taxed above their neighbours.❞

Sir William Petty (1623–87)

BRITISH VERSUS OVERSEAS TAXATION

Comparing tax takes across similar countries helps to put those figures into context. Figure 3.2 gives OECD calculations of total tax receipts as a share of GDP in 1996. It shows the tax burden shouldered by Britons is about average – larger than that borne by Americans, but smaller than that borne by Swedes.

That could imply that UK taxpayers get a raw deal – after all, the US is the richest nation on the planet, yet Americans hand over much less money to the government than the Brits do. But have a look at the comparative spending data in Fig. 3.3, and the reasons for the anomaly become clear.

Government spending in the United States amounts to only around 30 per cent of GDP, so it is no wonder Americans pay less in taxes. They live in a

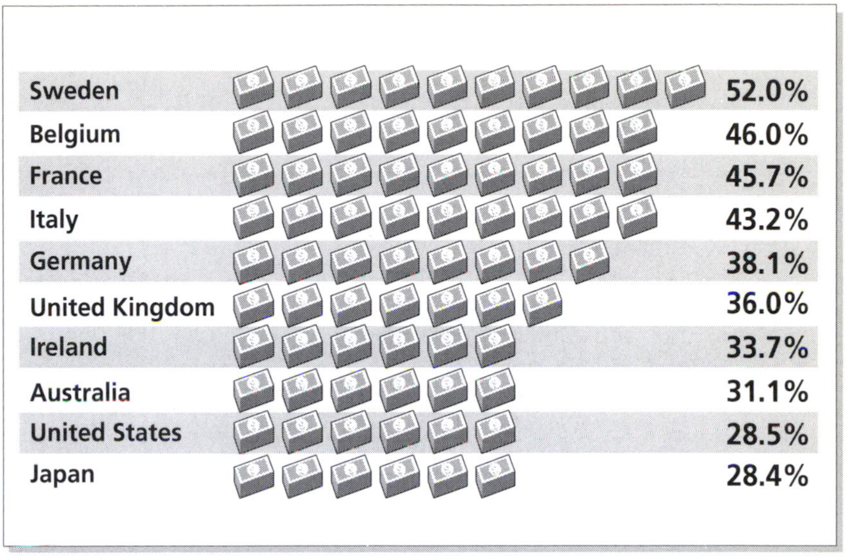

Sweden		52.0%
Belgium		46.0%
France		45.7%
Italy		43.2%
Germany		38.1%
United Kingdom		36.0%
Ireland		33.7%
Australia		31.1%
United States		28.5%
Japan		28.4%

FIG. 3.2 Tax take as a share of GDP, 1996   Source: OECD

broadly **free market economy**. The state provides public goods such as defence, it maintains a sound currency and it enforces a legal framework. But most other goods and services are provided by the market – something Adam Smith would have applauded. The obvious example is healthcare. Only the very poor and the old receive government help with their medical bills under Medicaid and Medicare. The rest have to pay their own way, relieving the taxpayer of a huge burden.

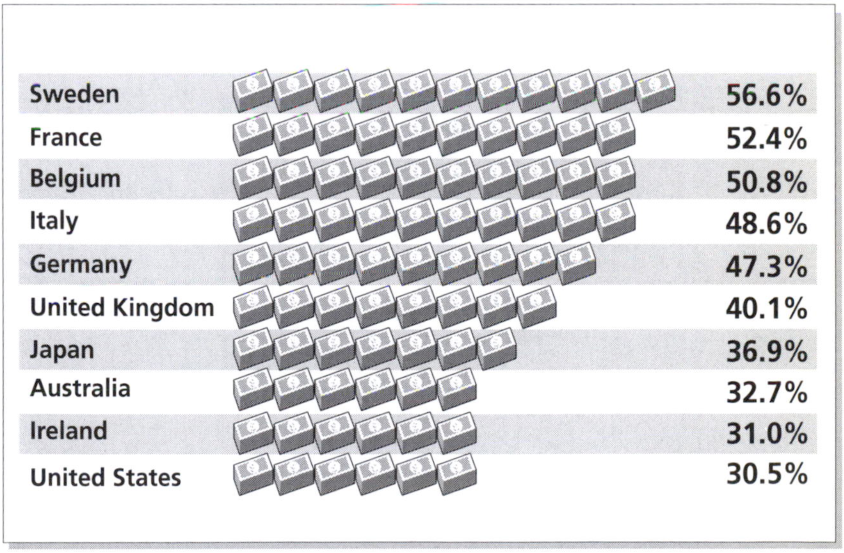

Sweden		56.6%
France		52.4%
Belgium		50.8%
Italy		48.6%
Germany		47.3%
United Kingdom		40.1%
Japan		36.9%
Australia		32.7%
Ireland		31.0%
United States		30.5%

FIG. 3.3 Government spending as a share of GDP, 1998

Source: OECD Economic Outlook, December 1999

Sweden has a completely different ethos. Government spending there accounts for almost 57 per cent of GDP thanks to the country's generous cradle-to-grave welfare system. State benefits include healthcare, childcare and elderly care, usually extended regardless of wealth and in generous amounts compared with the rest of the world. There is also compensation for short-term income loss and ample unemployment benefits. The result is an onerous tax burden which leaves Swedes with less than half of their income to spend as they choose.

Britain lies somewhere in between. Most argue it is a **mixed economy**, a half-way house between Smith's ideal, free-market world and the **command economy** popularised by Marx. In the latter, the government decides who gets what through a rigorous planning mechanism, a system associated with the former communist countries of Eastern Europe. Thatcher's privatisation and deregulation crusade in the 1980s pushed the UK towards the US free-market model, but the move petered out before the country became a fully-fledged member of the *laissez-faire* club.

Nevertheless, as Fig. 3.2 shows, Britons pay less than many of their European counterparts in tax. But the distribution of that tax varies markedly. For example, petrol tax in Britian is much higher than on the continent – an argument that has been used in the past to call for a cut in fuel duty.

WHERE DOES ALL THE MONEY COME FROM AND WHERE DOES IT GO?

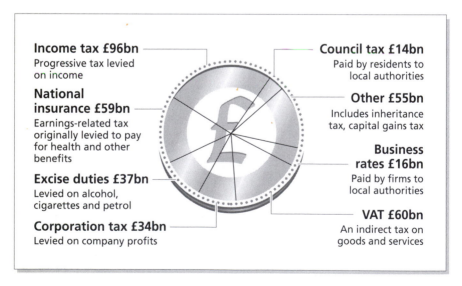

Income tax £96bn
Progressive tax levied on income

National insurance £59bn
Earnings-related tax originally levied to pay for health and other benefits

Excise duties £37bn
Levied on alcohol, cigarettes and petrol

Corporation tax £34bn
Levied on company profits

Council tax £14bn
Paid by residents to local authorities

Other £55bn
Includes inheritance tax, capital gains tax

Business rates £16bn
Paid by firms to local authorities

VAT £60bn
An indirect tax on goods and services

FIG. 3.4 Where the UK government gets its money   Source: Red Book 2000

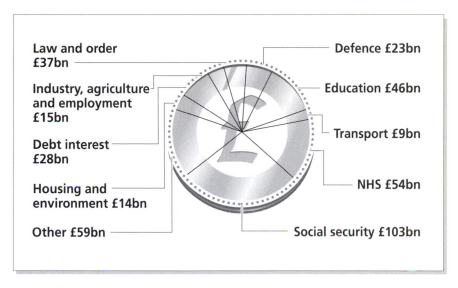

Law and order £37bn

Industry, agriculture and employment £15bn

Debt interest £28bn

Housing and environment £14bn

Other £59bn

Defence £23bn

Education £46bn

Transport £9bn

NHS £54bn

Social security £103bn

FIG. 3.5 Where taxpayers' money is spent   Source: Red Book 2000

The average worker in Britain spends almost 40 per cent of her working week slaving away just to pay her tax bill – in other words, all of Monday and most of Tuesday is spent working effectively for the government. Figure 3.4 shows exactly where all that hard-earned cash comes from and Fig. 3.5 shows where it goes. Together, social security and the National Health Service eat up more than 40 per cent of public spending, while interest on debt alone takes up around 7.5 per cent. That is even more than the share swallowed by defence, which has assumed a shrinking slice of government money in recent years.

FROM DANEGELD TO SELF-ASSESSMENT: A HISTORY OF UK TAXATION

'And it came to pass in those days, that there went out a decree from Caesar Augustus, that all the world should be taxed.'

Bible, Luke Ch 2 v 1

People have never liked paying taxes. Lady Godiva rode naked through the streets of Coventry in the 11th century to persuade her husband to reduce them. Part of the reason King Charles I lost his head was because they were excessive. And American patriots, armed with axes and pistols, dumped 340 chests of tea into Boston Harbour in 1773 in protest against them.

Yet, as Benjamin Franklin famously quipped in 1789, they are as inevitable as death. The first recorded tax in Britain was the scriptura, levied on cattle by Julius

Caesar in the 2nd century. Some 800 years later, long after the fall of the Roman Empire, the more comprehensive Danegeld was introduced. Levied by Ethelred the Unready at a rate of four shillings per hide of land (around 120 acres), this tax was used to buy peace from the marauding Vikings. It was later transformed into a general tax and was collected until 1162.

In the meantime, following the Norman Conquest in 1066, land was confiscated and ownership became confused, which made tax collection difficult. Faced with empty coffers and the threat of invasion from Flanders and Denmark, William the Conqueror needed money. So he commissioned a survey of his kingdom to ascertain who owned what. The result was the Domesday Book, the largest tax return in history, and so called because, like the day of judgement, there could be no appeal against it.

Another legacy of the Normans was the Court of the Exchequer, the main financial department of the English government in the 12th century. Named after the chequered tablecloth which served as a counting board for the royal revenue, it helped to formalise the fragmented and haphazard system of tax collection (and also later gave its name to the minister in charge of the country's finances, the Chancellor of the Exchequer).

Taxes became more sophisticated in the years that followed, and in the late 14th century, three highly unpopular poll taxes were introduced in the space of four years. Levied at a flat rate per head of the population (initially at one groat, or 4 pence, on everyone over the age of 14), the taxes precipitated widespread evasion and culminated in the peasants' revolt in June 1381 (an uprising Thatcher would have done well to note before imposing the 1990 poll tax).

That evasion meant the expected yield from the tax did not materialise, forcing authorities to seek revenue from all manner of sources. Female servants, watches and dogs were all used as indicators of ability to pay (in the case of the latter, assessors would patrol the streets at night, kicking on doors and counting the number of animals that barked inside). The most celebrated was the 1696 window tax (the legacy of which can still be seen today in the form of bricked-up windows).

By the close of the 17th century, control of the economy and taxation had passed from the crown to politicians. But it wasn't until 1799 that the seeds of the modern tax system were sown, with the foundation of a direct tax on income. Such a measure had long been resisted, as it required gentlemen to tell someone what their income was, an act 'repugnant to the customs and manners of the nation', as Prime Minister William Pitt argued in 1798.

However, the escalating war against Napoleon was proving expensive and 'certain duties on income' were *temporarily* applied. The initial levy was 10 per cent on income above £60, with reductions on income up to £200. Technically speaking, income tax is still 'temporary' – it expires each year on April 5 when parliament must reapply it by an annual Finance Act.

For the next 100 years or so, successive politicians promised to abolish income tax, only to balk at the prospect at the last minute. In the end, it was briefly suspended in 1816, a year after the Battle of Waterloo, only to be reintroduced in 1843 in the face of a growing national debt.

In 1875 it fell to less than 1 per cent, with most of the population exempt. The First World War put an end to such low levels for good, however. The standard rate rose to 30 per cent at the outbreak of fighting, realising £257 million. When the Second World War erupted 25 years later, the government was quick to react, setting hefty standard and surtax rates for incomes over £50,000. As Chancellor John Simon said at the time: 'Finance is the fourth arm of defence'.

The widening of the tax net during the war prompted the foundation of the more efficient Pay As You Earn (PAYE) scheme in 1944, shortly before the NHS and the welfare state changed the social and economic make-up of Britain for good. In the decades that followed, the top rate of income tax hit 83 per cent before falling again to less than half that.

Corporation tax and capital gains tax were introduced in 1965 and VAT replaced purchase tax in 1973. The most recent innovation to the tax system was the introduction of self-assessment in 1996/97, which affected 9 million people.

66An economy breathes
through its tax loopholes.99

Barry Bracewell-Milnes, *Daily Telegraph*, July 1979

COULD THE INTERNET LOWER YOUR TAX BILL?

The Internet has prompted some frantic head-scratching at Customs and Excise. Its ability to transcend national borders, conduct business virtually instead of physically, and cloak users in anonymity undermines the core principles of the taxation system.

However, the tenacious tax collector has been devising ingenious ways of making the public pay its dues ever since Biblical times, so the chances are he won't allow a bit of technology to thwart him. But it will not be easy to come up with a foolproof system of taxing e-commerce and in the meantime, there are gaping loopholes.

Take a simple example. Imagine you want to buy a CD. You have four choices. You could get one at your local record shop, order one via a UK Internet company, order one from a US web firm, or download it directly from the Internet on to your PC. In the first two cases, you will automatically pay VAT at 17.5 per cent. However in the third case, because the CD is coming from outside the European Union, you will only be liable to VAT if it costs more than £18. That is the tax threshold for any goods that come into Britain via the postal import system (excluding the EU). So if you order one or two CDs at a time, providing the cost of postage and packaging is not too high, you will probably save money.

Of course, the government could lower that threshold or eliminate it so that all goods bought over the Internet are subject to tax. However, there would soon come a point when enforcement costs would outweigh the revenue collected – postmen would be forever knocking on doors asking for VAT.

In the case of digitally downloading the music directly from the Internet, the problems for the taxman are even greater. If you did it from a UK site, you would be charged VAT as normal. However (at the time of writing), there is absolutely no legislation that would require you to pay tax on digital content from a site outside the EU. Your music would be completely tax-free (and the same applies to videos, software, or anything else that can be digitally downloaded).

How can the government close that loophole? Firstly, it is probably not worth even trying to at the moment. Only a fraction of goods are bought over the web, and most cannot be digitally downloaded. Customs and Excise lose far more revenue from cigarette smuggling than they do from consumers buying products over the Internet (lost revenue from cross-Channel tobacco smuggling tops £2.5 billion a year). And anyway, to go cybershopping you need to buy a computer, pay for Internet access and pay your phone bills, all of which are subject to VAT.

However, if forecasters are right and we will be spending almost £7.5 billion shopping on the Internet and interactive TV by 2004,[3] the hole in tax revenues could start to hurt. With that in mind, the OECD has proposed a solution. Taxation of digitally downloaded material should arise in the country of consumption rather than origin. It sounds simple enough, but it raises huge compliance and collection problems. Firstly, a firm like Amazon.com would have to register for taxation in each country in which it had customers – there are more than 140 different VAT and sales tax systems worldwide. Apart from the added costs that would entail, there is the question of who would make it comply with each system. Britain does not have jurisdiction over US tax matters, for example, so who would make sure Amazon charged its UK customers?

Secondly, tracking purchasers could mean forcing banks and credit card companies to keep tabs on who buys what – expensive, bureaucratic, and extremely inconvenient.

While there is no clear solution to the problem of taxing cybershopping, it could pale into insignificance compared with the headache of tracking multinationals around the web. The Internet gives companies considerable flexibility in delivering their products and services, which in turn may allow them much more leeway in managing their liability to tax. They may, for example, seek to base themselves in low-tax countries and sell their products from there to customers anywhere on the planet. Competition between countries trying to attract lucrative e-businesses would increase as a result, simultaneously pushing corporate tax levels lower and the number of tax avoidance rules higher.

Alternatively, the slipperiness of the web could mark a return to more solid sources of taxation. Just as declining revenues in the 14th century (thanks largely to the unpopular poll tax) forced the crown to search for other indicators of ability to pay, so the Internet could signal a move towards taxing things such as land or pollution. Not only would the latter plug the shortfall, it would also protect the environment, reduce the risk of smothering nascent high-tech firms in red tape, and keep the tax burden off the all-important voter. A tantalising prospect for any government.

HOW DOES THE GOVERNMENT CONTROL THE ECONOMY?

"Englishmen never will be slaves: they are free to do whatever the government and public opinion allow them to do."

George Bernard Shaw (1856–1950)

The Budget is not the only chance the government has to impress voters. Having delegated interest rate policy to the Bank of England, it has three other means of manipulating the British economy: **fiscal policy, exchange rate policy** and **supply-side policies**.

FISCAL POLICY

Fiscal policy is that part of government policy concerned with raising revenue through taxation and deciding on the level and pattern of spending. Fiscal literally means of public revenue.

Taxes are levied to finance hospitals and schools, pay for defence forces and to redistribute income. They are also a useful way of controlling the economy. By changing both direct and indirect tax rates, and by varying the amount it spends, the government can influence how much money people have, and therefore how much you and I are able to spend. In other words, it can use fiscal policy to manage demand.

For example, Chancellor Gordon Brown abolished the married couples' tax allowance with effect from April 2000. Taken in isolation, that meant a typical husband and wife lost almost £200 a year. Adding that up across the whole population, some £1.6 billion was sucked out of the economy in 2000/01.

On the other hand, at about the same time, he pumped an extra £2 billion into the NHS and promised to increase spending on health by more than 6 per cent a year above inflation. That had a counterbalancing expansionary effect. More money for nurses, for example, means they can afford to spend more, which, via the multiplier effect (*see* Chapter 2), will increase jobs and growth in the whole country.

Co-ordinating monetary and fiscal policy

The Chancellor must carefully weigh up the expected impact of each of his budget measures in order to gauge the net effect on the economy. If he does not spend enough money, if he squeezes the economy too hard, he could trigger an economic slowdown, putting thousands out of work. However, if he spends too much – in other words, reflates the economy too vigorously – he may spark inflation.

This link between fiscal and monetary policy is key. There may be strong social arguments for pouring millions of pounds into services like health and education, but such largesse could be counterproductive if it draws a sharp rate rise from the Bank of England's Monetary Policy Committee (MPC). What the Chancellor gives voters with one hand, the Bank will take away with the other. Co-ordination between the two is vital.

This was shown to clear effect in April 2000 when the Treasury raised an unexpectedly large £22.5 billion by auctioning mobile phone licences. Calls to spend the money were deafening. Everyone from pensioners to nurses to teachers wanted a slice, but the government stood firm and pledged not to increase public spending or reduce taxes.

At first glance this looked stingy. Public finances were in good shape and the money was a bonus, so why not spend it on the country's run-down hospitals and schools? Because to do so would have risked a sharp rise in inflation and therefore interest rates. The Bank of England was already increasing borrowing costs. Throwing another £20 billion into the economic ring – equivalent to 2.5 per cent of the size of the whole country – would have made matters worse. For one thing, higher rates would have meant an even stronger pound, which would have made life tougher for exporters. More manufacturers would probably have gone bankrupt and jobs would have been lost. There was only one sensible thing the government could do – put the money in its back pocket and prevent it from stoking inflation.

The breakdown of fine-tuning

In the 1950s and 1960s, governments began to believe that changes in taxation and spending could be used to **fine-tune** growth and inflation. Flushed with the success of stable prices, low unemployment and relatively robust growth in the two post-war decades, they took Keynes' theory on demand management to the extreme, assuming a constant, predictable relationship between fiscal policy and the economy.

However, just as it looked like economics had made a major breakthrough, which could elevate it to the status of a true science, things began to deteriorate. In the 1970s, fine-tuning propagated the infamous boom–bust cycles that proved so destructive to long-term growth, largely because policymakers had failed to give the dangers of inflation the respect they deserved. Time lags between different policies also proved problematic. A tax rise was felt on spending and growth fairly quickly, but an offsetting increase in, say, transport spending could take years to work its way through the economy, as roads were built and train tracks improved. There was also the perennial problem of inaccurate data. The Chancellor must assume various growth and inflation rates before he can estimate the impact of his policies, making the whole exercise riddled with pitfalls.

Fine-tuning has therefore largely been discredited. Chancellors now prefer to nurture balanced budgets, where spending equals revenues, or even foster surpluses in case of a rainy day, rather than spend their way out of trouble. However, that fashion may change. As long as fiscal policy is in the hands of politicians, the country's finances will only be as healthy as the Chancellor is wise.

An independent fiscal policy to match independent monetary policy?

In order to mitigate against profligate future chancellors, some economists support the idea of an independent authority to control fiscal policy, rather like the independent central banks that control monetary policy. While the idea of unelected officials deciding tax rates may be alarming, they argue that is far outweighed by the advantages of such a system – namely that politicians would not be able to 'bribe' voters with irresponsible tax cuts ahead of elections. The country's financial health would be in the hands of unbiased experts who could add continuity and stability to the economy, free from the dictates of the ballot box.

In practice, however, such an authority seems improbable. For one thing, politicians are unlikely to relinquish the power to decide spending and taxation, and anyway, voters are unlikely to go for a system that deprives them of democratic control over such issues. A far better idea, say some, would be to create an independent fiscal agency to oversee tax and spend decisions, thereby acting as a public safety net against irresponsibility.

The closest Britain has to that at present is the Code for Fiscal Stability. This lays out the broad aims of fiscal policy and requires that the government sets out its borrowing plans each year for full public scrutiny, thereby introducing an element of discipline into the process.

EXCHANGE RATE POLICY

Extreme Keynesian demand management has proved unpopular. Fiscal policy is still used to regulate the economy, but given the modern predilection for sound finances and balanced budgets, governments must find additional ways to tinker with growth, jobs and inflation.

Another variable they may target is the exchange rate. The box, 'Is a strong currency a good thing?', shows how movements in the external value of money can affect everyone in the country, not just holiday-makers, making the currency a potentially potent weapon in the government's armoury.

IS A STRONG CURRENCY A GOOD THING?

Strong currencies have a certain cachet. They lend countries an air of popularity and success. They are a seal of international approval – politicians must be doing something right with the economy if everyone wants a piece of the action. But as usual, things aren't that simple. It is not always obvious if we should celebrate or commiserate a robust currency. Here is a quick guide to the highs and lows of a mighty exchange rate.

STRONG MEANS GOOD

■ The most obvious advantage of a strong currency to you and me is *cheaper overseas holidays*. More dollars to every pound means more rides at Disneyland for British tourists and cheaper Mickey Mouse souvenirs for friends back home.

■ A strong currency also means *lower inflation* (Chapter 4 has a more detailed explanation). Just as a rise in the pound makes croissants cheaper when you go to France, it also makes them cheaper when they are imported into Britain. The same goes for all other imports so that the overall effect is to keep a lid on prices and inflation. That means interest rates will not have to rise as high as they would otherwise, which means cheaper mortgages and overdrafts for everyone.

STRONG ALSO MEANS PROBLEMS

■ But it's not all good news. The higher the pound went in 1999, the louder the cry for help from Britain's manufacturers. Its 30 per cent rise between 1996 and 2000 put an enormous strain on UK industry. Many rely on overseas sales for survival, and a strong pound means foreign customers have to pay more for British products, making them uncompetitive. In order to retain market share, UK firms were forced to slash prices and profit margins, sending many out of business and many workers out of a job.

As far as exporters are concerned, therefore, the weaker the currency the better. That makes their products cheap to overseas customers, allowing them to clean up. Flagging growth in Europe was given a welcome fillip by the 20 per cent depreciation of the single currency in its first 14 months, for example.

WEAK MEANS PROBLEMS, TOO

■ However … Just like a strong currency means lower inflation, a weak one means higher inflation. More expensive imports feed through the price chain and show up as higher prices in shops. In the case of Europe, the steady depreciation of the euro helped nudge inflation in Germany to its highest level for two years in March 2000.

As ever, it is a case of everything in moderation. However, in today's world of (mainly) floating exchange rates, that may not always be possible. Currency values are set by fickle markets intent on making money, not guiding dollars, pounds or euros to their job-creating, inflation-busting optimum levels. One consolation is that exchange rates typically end up following economic fundamentals … eventually. In the meantime, however, there could be a lot of pain all round.

However, controlling the exchange rate for policy purposes is not easy. While spending and taxation might be hard to exploit with any accuracy, it is child's play compared with trying to manipulate the currency.

The pound has been allowed to fluctuate freely against other currencies since June 1972. Its value is determined by a number of factors such as interest rates both at home and abroad, rumours, and trade flows (all of which are discussed in more detail in Chapter 7).

The government has no control over most of these factors, so it must rely on *intervention* if it wants to try to alter the value of the currency. In other words, it must buy or sell pounds using some of the $23 billion worth of foreign currencies it owns (as of February 2000) in case of emergencies. That sounds like a lot of money, but compared with the $1.5 trillion of currencies traded daily in the markets, it is a drop in the ocean. Hence intervention is often futile, as was highlighted to humiliating effect when currency speculators forced the pound out of Europe's Exchange Rate Mechanism in September 1992 (*see* Chapter 7).

A more effective method of manipulating the pound may be to 'jawbone' it lower. Powerful politicians can call for a weaker currency, in the hope that traders will latch on to the comments and turn them into self-fulfilling prophesies. This can be a dangerous game, however. Despite all the disadvantages of a strong pound, it may be preferable to one that is becoming increasingly worthless by the day, making imports more expensive and putting Britons at a disadvantage when they spend money abroad.

SUPPLY-SIDE POLICIES

Both taxes and exchange rates are relatively blunt tools when it comes to manipulating the economy. Therefore, in recent years, governments have relied increasingly on **supply-side policies**.

As their name suggests, these work on manipulating the *supply* of factors like labour and money, rather than altering *demand* for them as fiscal policy does. For example, tax breaks on Individual Savings Accounts (ISAs) encourage people to save more, thereby increasing the supply of funds for investment. Likewise, some argue that taxes should be lowered to encourage greater work effort, or benefits cut to persuade the unemployed back into the jobs market. Both increase the supply of labour available to firms, and hence have the potential to push out the production possibility frontier.

Margaret Thatcher was a fervent believer in supply-side policies and spent 10 years dismantling barriers to so-called labour flexibility. She cut unemployment benefits, slashed income tax rates, emasculated trade unions and made it easier to hire and fire, all with the aim of releasing more people on to the jobs market. Not only would that increase the country's capacity to grow, it would also allow it to do so with lower inflation since the surplus of workers would keep a lid on wage demands.

> Supply-side policies attempt to increase the supply of money and workers in an economy so as to promote stronger growth and low inflation. They became popular in the late 1970s and formed a central plank of the Conservative government's economic strategy in the following decade.

Supply-side policies in action

Many government initiatives over the years have fallen under the umbrella of supply-side policies. The following are examples, split into two familiar categories: the Keynesian approach, followed by a neo-classical formula.

> ❝All governments like to interfere;
> ## it elevates their position to make out
> that they can cure the evils of mankind.❞

Walter Bagehot, former editor of *The Economist* (1826–1877)

The legacy of Keynes

You will recall from Chapter 1 that Keynes' central criticism of the classical school was that markets fail. A lack of competition and stubborn wages will generate mass unemployment and low growth, hence the government must interfere in order to correct any problems. Among other things, therefore, Keynesians recommend:

- **government-sponsored education and training**. More skilled workers mean higher productivity and greater growth. Therefore, in addition to free education up to the age of 18, governments have poured money into a number of schemes over the years, such as the Youth Training Scheme in 1983 and the Employment Training

Scheme in 1988. The New Deal programme to help the unemployed back to work is the latest initiative. It offers both on-the-job training and subsidised education (more on that in Chapter 5);

- **industrial grants and tax incentives.** This is a thorny issue. Governments have used various cash carrots over the years to attract firms to high unemployment areas, with differing degrees of success. Some economists argue that subsidising industry is a waste of money and simply postpones an inevitable collapse, others see it as a useful way of revitalising regions and allowing British firms to compete with cheap imports;

- **tax breaks for research and development.** Innovation is the seed of success (particularly if you agree with Schumpeter). Therefore if governments can encourage investment in research and development via tax breaks, they may improve the country's capital stock, boosting productivity and growth.

The neo-classical philosophy

Strictly speaking, those free-marketeers who swear by supply-side policies are called, imaginatively, supply-side economists, but they are often lumped together with the neo-classicals. They believe that free markets hold the key to efficiency, and therefore that it is the government's role to eliminate any barriers to those markets. They therefore recommend the following:

- **Curb the power of trade unions.** By taking collective action, unions artificially raise wages, goes the argument, pricing workers out of a job. Unemployment can therefore be reduced by stripping unions of their power. Thatcher led an all-out assault on unions in the 1980s, passing legislation that made it harder for members to strike and made collective pay bargaining much more difficult. Without fear of reprisal from workers, firms found it easier to hire and fire people and could also negotiate lower pay awards.

- **Cut benefits.** Research shows that almost half of the British public believe that the present welfare system discourages work. One problem is that unemployment benefits put an artificial floor under wages and deter people from looking for a job. By cutting benefits, the government can alleviate the poverty trap, a demoralising situation where finding work leads to a fall in income after taxes have been paid and benefits docked. Labour's working families tax credit is a variant on this. It is a means-tested benefit paid to those in work on low incomes who have children to support. It is intended to make work pay, a central theme of the Labour government.

- **Cut marginal tax rates.** As explained earlier, high income taxes reduce the incentive to work and therefore reduce the supply of labour. The top tax rate in Britain (at the time of writing) is 40 per cent, less than half the 83 per cent in the mid 1970s. By the same token, reducing corporation tax will leave firms with higher profits, which may encourage greater investment and growth.

- **Reduce the penalties from changing jobs.** Portable pensions and better information about job vacancies increase mobility, encouraging people to go where the work is. At the beginning of 2000, the government announced it was spending £18 million on an online employment service which would allow the unemployed to use the Internet in libraries and job centres to look for work.

- **Make it easier for firms to hire and fire.** Easing redundancy obligations and eroding worker rights make the labour force more flexible to employers. Thatcher introduced reams of legislation in the 1980s to that end, with the result that British workers are among the most adaptable in the European Union (which is good news for employers, but not so pleasant for the disposable worker, a point revisited in Chapter 5).

- **Privatisation.** Supply-siders argue that the government is in no position to decide how money is best invested, therefore it should put such weighty decisions in the hands of the market by privatising as many industries as possible. This strategy will be forever synonymous with Margaret Thatcher. Between 1979 and 1995, the Conservatives raised around £60 billion by privatising companies such as British Telecom, British Gas and British Petroleum. The number of shareholders in Britain had tripled to 9 million in 1987 (almost half of whom only owned stock in privatised companies) from 3 million in 1979. The Labour Party did nothing to reverse Tory privatisations when it came to power in 1997. Instead, it implicitly agreed with the strategy by abolishing its ancient 'Clause Four' commitment to mass nationalisation and common ownership.

- **Deregulation.** Ridding the public sector of its many rules and regulations will encourage competition and boost efficiency, say supply-siders. With those aims in mind, the Conservative Party allowed schools to opt out of local authority control, let hospitals put their cleaning contracts out to tender and opened up bus routes to private firms. In other words, where it couldn't privatise, it introduced competition into publicly provided services. It also abolished many regulations in the financial markets, including exchange controls, which had restricted the amount of sterling people could move into and out of Britain.

A MATTER OF LIFE AND DEBT

GOVERNMENT BORROWING AND WHAT IT MEANS FOR YOU

'Annual income twenty pounds, annual expenditure nineteen nineteen six, result
happiness. Annual income twenty pounds, annual expenditure twenty pounds
ought and six, result misery.'

Mr Micawber, in *David Copperfield*,

Charles Dickens, 1850

When there is not enough tax revenue to pay for all the hospitals,
schools, roads and armed forces that the UK needs, the government has
to borrow money, either from the British public or from people overseas. It does so by issuing bonds, which are discussed in Chapter 6.

Most of the government's economic decisions are plain to see. Tax
changes soon show up in pay cheques and spending plans will affect
the state of public transport or the length of hospital waiting lists. But
it is a lot harder to gauge the impact of accumulating debt.

There is a natural assumption that it is bad (as Polonius, the Lord
Chamberlain, advised in Shakespeare's *Hamlet*, 'Neither a borrower or a
lender be'). But it is not immediately obvious why. What difference does it
make to you or me if the government borrows £10 billion or £100 billion?

Public debt affects us in three ways:

- **It increases the financial burden on future generations.** If we
  indulge ourselves today, our children will pay for it tomorrow,
  which to some may be dissuasive.

- **It transfers money from taxpayers to bond holders via interest payments.** Some may argue there is nothing wrong with that – it is just a
  redistribution of income. But when you consider that Britain expected
  to spend around £28 billion in 2000/2001 on interest, it does not look
  so harmless. That is double the amount set aside for housing and the
  environment and three times the amount to go on transport – arguably
  much needier causes. (Italy has been running a primary budget surplus
  for years, which strips out interest payments, but because past fiscal
  laxity means debt is so high, its overall budget is still in the red.)

- **It puts pressure on a country's currency, which could destabilise the
  whole economy.** Just as you would be reluctant to lend money to
  someone who already has an overdraft, a loan and a host of credit card
  bills, so investors will become increasingly wary of buying into countries with enormous debts. The currency may fall as a result, triggering
  inflation, higher interest rates and ultimately a bigger mortgage bill.

Given that all money borrowed accumulates interest and must ultimately be repaid, surely it follows that each country should aim to wipe out its debt altogether? That is what the United States intends to do. In 1999, the US government owed the world $5.7 trillion. By 2013 it intends to be debt free.

> **"Public money is like holy water; everyone helps himself to it."**

Italian proverb

THE DOWNSIDE OF DEBT REPAYMENT

However appealing the idea of no debt may be, in reality things are a little different, for three reasons. Firstly, as already discussed, a country's spending and therefore debt levels will depend on the level of services the government provides. More generous health and welfare provision demands either higher taxes or more debt. (Of course, it is important that any public sector money is spent wisely – it is pointless borrowing to finance inefficiency.)

Secondly, it depends why the government needs to borrow. If it is just to cover 'everyday' expenses such as unemployment benefits (known as *current spending*), then clearly the position is unsustainable. If, however, it is to cover investment in, say, new technology, which may increase economic growth in the future, it is a different matter. Just as a student loan that allows a budding doctor (or maybe economist) to go to university could be considered money worth borrowing, so public debt for the purposes of investment is arguably worthwhile.

Thirdly, government debt issued by advanced countries provides a safe, relatively lucrative vehicle for investment. For example, many pensioners in the UK rely on British government bonds, known as gilts, for an income. If the government paid back its debt and there were no more gilts, those pensioners might have to turn to riskier sources of income, such as corporate bonds (more on the pensions dilemma in Chapter 6).

Figure 3.6 shows the UK's government debt as a percentage of GDP in 1998 compared with other countries.

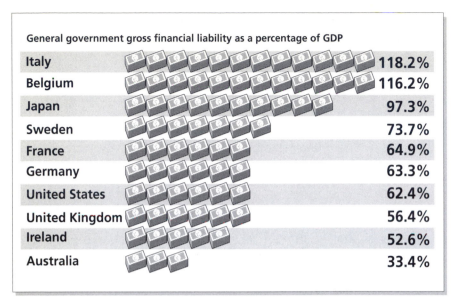

FIG. 3.6 Government debt as a percentage of GDP, 1998

Source: OECD Economic Outlook, December 1999

THE GOVERNMENT'S FISCAL RULES

In order to safeguard Britain's public services, but to prevent its debt burden from spiralling out of control, the Labour government has pledged to stick to two fiscal rules: the golden rule and the sustainable investment rule.

■ The **golden rule** says that over the economic cycle, the government will borrow only to invest. In other words, it can issue bonds and add to its debt if it is going to spend the proceeds on building more schools or hospitals. But spending on things like unemployment benefits must come out of tax revenues. In this way it can run a *total* budget deficit over the cycle, but not a *current* one.

■ The **sustainable investment rule** prevents the government from racking up too much debt in the name of investment. It says that debt will be held at a *stable and prudent level* relative to GDP over the whole economic cycle. That ratio is stated to be around 40 per cent.

Neither rule is enforceable by law, but in practice, the eagle eye of the media, the Code for Fiscal Stability and an opposition party ready to jump on the slightest mistake ensures that the government will be held to account.

If the government spends more than it receives in taxes every month, it will need to borrow money. This is called the **public sector net cash requirement**. If it collects more in taxes than it spends, it will be left with a surplus. This is called the **public sector net cash repayment**.

Using deficit to smooth out the business cycle

The government's fiscal rules talk about spending and borrowing over the economic cycle. That is not just a convenient get-out clause, inserted in case it misses its target one year. It is there because the vagaries of the business cycle have a powerful effect on public debt levels and vice versa. Borrowing can help to ease the pain of a recession, and therefore should not always be resisted.

For example, when the economy slows and unemployment rises, spending on benefits will automatically increase, helping to cushion the full impact of the recession. However, tax revenues will simultaneously decrease. There will be less collected in income tax, VAT and corporation tax as people lose their jobs and cut back on spending, and company profits fall. The net result is an increase in debt in times of trouble.

However, as the economy grows, income and corporation tax revenues will rebound, as will the money gleaned from VAT. That will not only replenish government coffers, it will also siphon off some spending power and take some inflationary bite out of the recovery. Benefit payments will also fall as more and more people find jobs, hence the net result is a fall in budget deficits – and in some cases a shift into surplus. In other words, taxation and spending have cushioned the full impact of the business cycle, and the deficit has been allowed to change to accommodate that. The budget has helped to **automatically stabilise** the economy.

Those automatic stabilisers gave the government an unexpected windfall in 1999. The surprising buoyancy of the British economy generated billions of pounds more in tax than expected. As a result, the government reported a surplus for the 1999/2000 year as a whole of around £17 billion, significantly higher than its original estimate made in early 1999 of £2 billion.

Any increase in the budget deficit due to recession is called the **cyclical** part of the deficit. Any debt still there when the economy is in full swing is called the **structural** debt.

IF YOU REMEMBER SEVEN THINGS FROM THIS CHAPTER ...

- Taxes are raised to pay for public goods such as defence, merit goods like hospitals and schools, and unemployment and other benefits. They are also a means of redistributing income.
- Taxes may be direct, like income and corporation tax, or indirect, like VAT and petrol duty.

- British government spending amounts to around 40 per cent of the total size of the economy. That is far less than the 57 per cent spent by the Swedish public sector, but more than the 30 per cent spent by the US government.

- The Internet allows people to download CDs, computer software, etc., completely tax-free. At present, the amount of revenue lost in this way is negligible, but as cybershopping increases, so will the hole in the taxman's budget.

- The government can use taxation and spending decisions to help manipulate growth and inflation. It can also use exchange rates and supply-side policies. The latter describes any measure that increases the supply of available workers and money, thereby improving the productive potential of the economy. Supply-side policies have become increasingly popular among governments in recent decades.

- If the government accumulates a mounting debt, it will increase the financial burden on future generations, transfer money from taxpayers to bond holders via interest payments, and put pressure on a country's currency, threatening the economy's well-being.

- The government's golden rule says that, over the economic cycle, it can only borrow to invest. Its sustainable investment rule says that debt will be held at a stable and prudent level relative to GDP, stated to be around 40 per cent.

ENDNOTES

1 Based on government's 2000/01 forecasts.

2 British Social Attitudes, November 1999.

3 Verdict research, December 1999.

CHAPTER 4

"WELL, IF YOU MUST KNOW IT'S A WAGE PACKET FOR 1973".

THE PRICE IS RIGHT

A guide to inflation and interest rates

" The real price of everything

is the toil and trouble

of acquiring it. "

Adam Smith (1723–1790)

INTRODUCTION

If you have ever bought a house, you will be only too aware of the bamboozling array of mortgages on offer. There are variable rates, discounted variables and fixed rates. You can lock yourself in for one year, five years or 10 years. You can choose a straightforward repayment mortgage or an interest-only one that is linked to your pension or your endowment.

Your choice of home loan (assuming it is you who decides and not a broker eager for his commission) will depend on what you think will happen to interest rates. And the path of interest rates depends on inflation.

That is why the subject gets so much attention – it has a direct bearing on your wallet. Inflation affects the value of your home and the size of your annual pay rise. It determines the cost of your weekly shopping and the amount of interest you pay on your overdraft. It influences share prices and even how much you pay in tax. On a broader level, it can affect the amount of investment in a country and therefore the amount of growth it enjoys. It is at the very heart of an economy.

66 Inflation is like sin;
every government denounces it
and every government practises it. 99

Sir Frederick Leith-Ross (1887–1968)

There is just one small problem – inflation is very hard to pin down. It is clear from Chapter 1 that there are few incontestable truths in economics. Great minds don't think alike in this subject, which is marooned in no-man's land between an art and a science. There are theories for everything and laws for almost nothing, which can make life very difficult for policymakers and everybody else.

Nowhere is that more obvious than in the case of inflation. Despite years of research, this remains one of the most enduring puzzles in economics. There is dispute about what causes it, how to get rid of it and whether it is still a problem. The only thing everyone agrees on is that it can be ruinous.

Even that is not always obvious. Inflation can be a bit like a very bad case of the 'flu – while you're suffering you struggle to do anything constructive and your daily routine grinds to a halt. But once you've recovered, the pain is soon forgotten and life returns to normal. In the same way, when inflation reached almost 27 per cent in Britain in 1975, the nation was obsessed. It was rarely out of the news as it threatened to stymie the entire country. These days, with inflation hovering around 2.5 per cent, people are more worried about the fate of their dot.com shares than the escalating size of their mortgage.

This chapter explains why it is far too soon to be complacent about inflation. It also:

- **discusses what inflation is and how it affects everybody in the country.** The chapter starts with a look at how inflation can hit you where it hurts, in your wallet;

- **looks at the causes and cures of sustained price rises.** Britain has tried just about every trick in the book to quash inflation over the years, often with disastrous results. The chapter discusses those attempts, including Margaret Thatcher's experiment with monetarism and the latest tactics used by the Bank of England's Monetary Policy Committee;

■ **gives some tips on how to spot an interest rate change.** This isn't easy. Economists get paid thousands of pounds to second-guess what interest rate setters around the world are going to do – and they still get it wrong. They don't necessarily have any special insight, they look at the same factors as everyone else. This chapter sets out what those factors are – useful if you are about to take out a mortgage or invest in a pension or the stock market;

■ **delves into the 1980s housing boom.** If you got your fingers and your bank balance burned in the 1980s housing boom, you may be wary of reinvesting in bricks and mortar. This chapter may put your mind at rest by explaining the exceptional circumstances of that boom, and by discussing whether it is likely to recur;

■ **explains how the Internet could affect inflation in future.** Web power means we can already buy cheap books, flights and CDs online, but that could be just the start. Many economists believe the net will help keep inflation at bay in the years ahead and help to drive prices on the high street lower as well. But it will probably stop short of delivering the bargains that some expect. Economics is constantly evolving, and the way it deals with the Internet is positive proof of that. Even though the likes of Smith and Keynes devised their theories well before the World Wide Web was even a dream, their theories are still relevant in today's wired world, albeit with some adjustments.

THE EFFECTS OF INFLATION

WHY YOU NEED TO KNOW ABOUT IT

Inflation is a general, sustained rise in the price level.

In April 2000, shares on the New York Stock Exchange lost a breath-taking $2.3 trillion in a single day, triggering fears of a market meltdown across the globe. The reason for the panic was a stronger than expected rise in US inflation, which stoked concerns about higher interest rates.

This highlights one reason why it is useful to know what inflation is and what causes it. There are a host of others, discussed below, but first things first. What exactly is inflation? Simply put, it is a general, sustained rise in the price level. Economists talk about it in percentages. For example, the 1.8 per cent inflation in Britain in December 1999 meant prices, on average, were 1.8 per cent higher then than they were at the end of 1998. A loaf of bread that cost £1 in December 1998 *theoretically* cost £1.02 in December 1999 (assuming nothing else changed in the meantime).

Here comes the 'but'. That percentage is a generalisation. There were vastly different price changes within it. For example, if you are a vegetarian, your weekly shopping bill probably fell during 1999 – the price of fresh potatoes plunged by 42 per cent and that of other fresh vegetables by 10 per cent. Meat-eaters didn't fare so well, however. The price of beef rose 4 per cent, while pork and bacon were up 6 per cent.

> ❝Having a little inflation is like being a little pregnant.
> # Inflation feeds on itself and
> ## quickly passes the little mark.❞

Dian Cohen (economist)

THE PRICE OF INFLATION

When newspapers and politicians talk about inflation, they use words like 'fight' and 'conquer', as if they are in pitch battle against enemy forces. It is not immediately obvious why, however. If people fully expect prices to increase and get pay rises to compensate, then no one need be any worse off. You can still buy everything you wanted to before, it is just that your wallet will be a bit fatter.

True, but the odds of everyone predicting exactly how much prices will rise in the next year are pretty bad. Highly paid economists in the City of London get their inflation forecasts wrong every month, so Joe Bloggs barely stands a chance. That unpredictability means inflation can have a profound effect on your lifestyle, in the following ways. It can:

- alter decisions you make;
- redistribute money between rich and poor;
- increase your tax bill;
- waste your time and money;
- place extra costs on businesses;
- lower economic growth.

Making your mind up

Inflation will alter any decisions you make. For example, if prices are increasing by 20 per cent a year, you may be tempted to book next summer's holiday now, while it is cheaper. Similarly, if you need a new sofa, it seems daft to wait until you have saved the money to buy one. By the time you've done that, its price will no doubt have risen. It makes much more sense to buy one now by borrowing. In other words, inflation has changed your spending plans. It has discouraged you from saving and encouraged you to borrow and spend.

The same can be said of companies, but with much bigger conse-quences. If inflation is high, firms may be less inclined to invest in new machinery or technology because the future is so uncertain. Prices are unpredictable so demand for their products will be, too. Who knows if Trendy Kitchens Ltd will sell enough stainless steel units to pay back the loan for its new factory if the prices it charges for those units rise dramatically? With inflation so high there is also a good chance interest rates will rise, making it more expensive to pay back loans. Companies may decide it is safer to stick with what they've got until the future is clearer. However, as explained in Chapter 2, investment is vital for eco-nomic growth and without it, the country will stagnate.

The great inflation gamble

Decisions are not the only things distorted by inflation. Personal finances will also fluctuate as some people get richer and some get poorer simply because prices have risen. Economists call these *redistributional costs* (although if you are the one getting richer you prob-ably won't think of it as very costly).

For example, a dose of inflation will take money from lenders and effec-tively give it to borrowers. If the price of your house doubles to £200,000 but your mortgage is still only the purchase price of £100,000, you've got a nice bonus. If you sold your house you would pocket £100,000. That may not buy you a bigger property because pre-sumably all prices have risen, but at least you are better off than someone who didn't borrow any money.

If you are drawing a pension, however, you may be at a distinct disad-vantage. Many retirees receive pensions from private company schemes which do not adjust for inflation. So if prices double within five years of retiring, real income will halve. Pensioners will receive the same amount of hard cash but that cash will buy fewer things.

Paying more in tax

Lenders and pensioners are not the only ones who stand to lose from a bout of inflation. Everyone who pays taxes could be worse off. For example, imagine you get a wage rise in line with inflation that propels you into a higher tax bracket. You are now considerably worse off. Your *real* salary hasn't increased (taking account of inflation, you still earn the same) but you are paying more tax. The government has gained at your expense. This galling side effect of inflation is known as **fiscal drag**, and has been around for centuries. As Keynes noted in his 1933 publication *Essays in Persuasion*: 'The power of taxation by currency depreciation is one which has been inherent in the State since Rome discovered it.'

It is not only governments that can hoodwink you in times of high inflation. Companies can get away with it, too. If prices are rising generally, it is easier for your local supermarket, for example, to increase the prices of some of its products over and above inflation. With so many things getting more expensive, you would be hard pushed to notice a few more pounds on the bill.

Traipsing around town

Inflation will cost you in *shoe leather* too. To make sure you are not being duped by a sudden increase in the price of socks in your local department store, for example, you will have to visit all the other sock shops in the area to check out their prices. Inflation means you have wasted both your time and money searching for competitive prices. You have literally worn down your shoes (and probably gone through your last pair of socks) traipsing around trying to find cheap goods.

Companies may also be losing out. Instead of having to innovate and improve efficiency to make higher profits, they can simply raise their prices during periods of inflation. Ultimately, firms will fall behind their competitors because they have not bothered to improve their services.

Updating menus

It is also expensive for some firms to adjust to changing prices, generating what economists call **menu costs**. Think of a restaurant that has to regularly rewrite its menu with new prices or a telecoms company that has to adapt its pay phones to take more change as inflation accelerates.

THE DOWNSIDE OF RATE RISES

Inflation's pernicious effects are not confined to what happens as prices rise. Once authorities begin to increase borrowing costs to choke off those rises, a whole new set of problems present themselves. Policies aimed at subduing inflation typically suppress growth, too, increasing unemployment in the process and triggering that boom–bust cycle that is so damaging to a country's health. That is why governments have spent the past 30 years grappling with inflation. The longer it is allowed to fester, the more radical and damaging its cure.

It is also one reason investors took fright in April 2000 at the stronger than expected increase in US inflation. Higher prices mean higher interest rates, which mean people cut back on spending and also tend to put any spare money into safe savings accounts rather than risky shares (they can now get more interest at the bank). Less demand translates into lower profits for firms in the future which makes their shares less attractive (more on that in Chapter 6). All in all, if you have an endowment policy, a pension, or own any shares, your investment could be knocked for six by an unexpected rise in inflation.

EFFECTS OF INFLATION

Distorts decisions: inflation discourages people from saving and firms from investing, damaging the long-term health of the economy.

Redistributes income: inflation shuffles wealth between all sorts of people, for example from lenders to borrowers, and away from anyone on a fixed income, such as some pensioners. If governments do not link tax bands to inflation, it can also mean workers pay more income tax.

Easier to deceive public: inflation makes it easier for firms to pass on price rises. It also discourages them from implementing new technology and improving efficiency since they can make more profits simply by raising prices.

Shoe leather costs: people waste time and money searching for bargains in an inflationary climate.

Menu costs: inflation means constantly changing machinery and price lists to reflect new, higher prices.

Lower economic growth: lower investment and saving plus action by governments to curb inflation puts a brake on economic growth and could lead to an increase in unemployment. The boom–bust cycle is set in motion and everyone suffers.

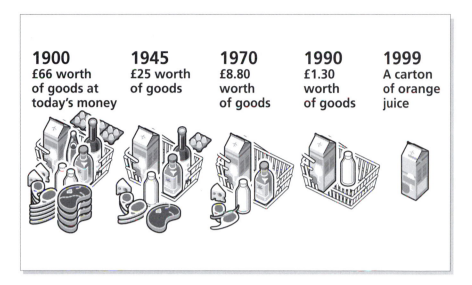

1900
£66 worth
of goods at
today's money

1945
£25 worth
of goods

1970
£8.80
worth
of goods

1990
£1.30
worth
of goods

1999
A carton
of orange
juice

FIG. 4.1 How much would £1 have bought you over the years?   Source: ONS

Figure 4.1 shows how inflation in Britain has eroded the value of money over the years.

MEASURING INFLATION IN BRITAIN

It is impossible to record the price of every single good or service in an economy. There are more than 20,000 items for sale in the average supermarket alone. Once you consider other high street shops, plus things like gym membership, holidays or getting your car serviced, it is clear there has to be a short cut to measuring inflation.

That is the job of the **National Statistics** office. Every month, it tracks the prices of more than 600 goods and combines them into the **Retail Price Index (RPI)**. First calculated in 1947, the RPI contains everything a typical Briton may buy each month, from bread to ready-made meals, gas bills, clothes, cinema tickets and pints at the local pub. The content of this huge 'shopping basket' is fixed, but the cost of it will change as the prices of all the goods in it change. That way the statistics office can estimate how average prices in the economy as a whole have moved.

There is a lot of legwork involved in compiling the RPI. Around the middle of every month, researchers visit a number of shops, mostly in person, and collect around 120,000 prices. The rest are gathered over the phone or, in the case of gas, water and newspapers, from a central point.

The next job is to give the items in the index weights to reflect how important they are in the average budget. For example, a rise in the price of beer will probably affect a household more than, say, an increase in the cost of a stamp. So alcoholic drink is given a weight of 65 – out of a total of 1,000 – and postage just one.

To make sure the index is kept up to date, the basket of goods the statistics office monitors is reviewed every year and may change as fashions change. For example, in March 2000, books and toys bought over the Internet were included in the index for the first time (albeit with a tiny weighting), as were broccoli and pre-packed salads. In return, out went luncheon meat, custard powder and tinned ravioli. Equally, the weights given to each category are scrutinised annually. Over the years people have tended to spend a decreasing proportion of their money on basics such as food while travel and leisure have eaten up a growing share of household budgets.

Once all the data have been collected, changes in prices are measured by comparing them to their levels in the previous January, and then the weights are applied to produce an overall price change. The result is an index which, when calculated from a fixed point in one year to the next, gives the annual inflation rate.

Once the government statisticians have compiled the figures they have to make them public. Financial markets are extremely sensitive to inflation data. An unexpectedly strong number can wipe millions of pounds off currencies, bonds and shares in seconds, hence it is only fair that every bank and investment house in the world has access to the figures at exactly the same time.

This is where news agencies like Reuters come in. On the appointed day – usually the second Tuesday of the month in the case of the RPI – journalists from the agencies, or 'wires' as they are known, get locked into a small room at the statistics office at around 8.45am and handed the figures. They then have 45 minutes to type the data into computers (extremely accurately; a wrong figure could lose your clients millions of pounds, not to mention losing you your job). At 9.30am precisely the data are transmitted.

Timing is vital. One second after pressing the button in London, traders in Australia, Asia and the United States can see and deal on the data. There will be an immediate, knee-jerk reaction from the markets depending on whether the figures are stronger or weaker than expected. By the time you read about the numbers in the papers the next day, they are ancient history to markets.

For more information on the RPI and other British statistics, visit the National Statistics website at www.statistics.gov.uk

COMPARING BRITAIN WITH ITS CONTINENTAL NEIGHBOURS

The RPI measure of inflation is known as **headline inflation**; in other words, it measures price changes across all goods and services in the economy. You will often see this rate reported in newspapers.

Financial markets are much more interested in **RPIX**, or **underlying inflation**, since this is the measure the Bank of England must keep under control. RPIX measures price changes *excluding* erratic mortgage interest payments. If underlying inflation is significantly higher than expected, investors may sell British government bonds or shares because of fears that interest rates may soon be raised.

A less common measure of inflation is **RPIY**, which has been published since February 1995. As well as excluding mortgage payments, it cuts out the (typically) upward effects on prices of indirect taxes, such as VAT and excise duties (taxes levied on beer and spirits).

The **Harmonised Index of Consumer Prices (HICP)** is a relatively new index which calculates inflation using methods identical to those employed in the rest of Europe. It therefore allows Britain to compare its inflation rate with those of its Continental neighbours. Should Britain decide to enter European Monetary Union, HICP would take over from RPIX as the target inflation rate.

WHAT CAUSES INFLATION?

To understand and predict interest rate changes – and to get that head start when it comes to making decisions about mortgages, savings accounts and share investments, etc. – you need to know where inflation comes from.

In many ways, its origins come back to Smith's idea that everyone acts out of self-interest. The butcher, the brewer and the baker of Smith's day all needed to earn a living and therefore made as much money as they could out of a transaction. If anything, that drive for profits has intensified since then. New technology, cheaper transport and the rise of the multinational mean firms across the globe compete for everyone's business now. If the opportunity to make more money by increasing prices beckons, it will be taken.

How does that opportunity arise? Economists divide the causes of inflation into three categories: too much demand, rising costs and too much money. These rarely appear in their purest form, but provide a useful starting point to understanding why prices rise. Psychological factors such as expectations also play a part, as explained later.

❝ Before the 1940s
prices were just as likely to fall as they
were to rise. On the eve of the First World War,
prices in Britain were almost exactly
the same as they had been at the end of the
Industrial Revolution in 1850. ❞

TOO MUCH DEMAND

Demand-pull inflation is the most intuitively appealing theory. As its name suggests, this arises when there is too much demand in an economy and not enough goods. For example, imagine a tout has got his hands on the last few tickets for FA Cup Final day. There are only 80,000 seats in Wembley (at the time of writing) but hundreds of thousands of people want to see the match. He may be able to sell tickets with a face value of £30 for more than £300 as football fans compete to buy the limited seats available.

Expand that idea to the whole economy and it is easy to see how you get inflation when times are good. When demand rises, there may not be enough goods to go around or enough factory space immediately available to make more. **Capacity constraints** kick in, bottlenecks emerge and prices rise. This is how Keynes saw inflation developing.

COSTS TOO HIGH

There are often other forces at work, too. Instead of demand *pulling* prices higher, **costs** could **push** them up. Take a football analogy again. Suppose the European cup final is being broadcast live on TV but the clubs involved have increased the price of the broadcast rights. On top of that, the cost of a satellite dish to transmit the match live has risen and the TV presenter has asked for a bonus to front the programme. In other words, the cost of televising the match has increased since last year, so the broadcaster passes that higher cost on to the viewer in the form of higher subscriptions.

Again, extend that to the economy as a whole and you get inflation.

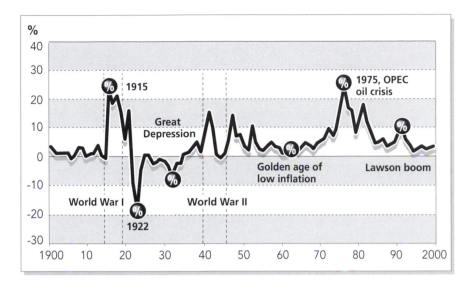

FIG. 4.2 British inflation since 1900   Source: ONS

Britain suffered a severe bout of cost-push inflation in the early 1970s (*see* Fig. 4.2). A four-fold increase in the price of oil in 1973/74 triggered a huge rise in the cost of goods, notably petrol, setting off a dangerous chain reaction. People felt worse off because of the price rises so they demanded higher salaries to compensate, which then became part of the problem. Goods were even more expensive to make, pushing up their price still further. Inflation leapt from wages to prices to wages, so that by August 1975 it had shot up to almost 27 per cent from 9 per cent two years earlier.

Higher wages and more expensive raw materials are just two ways cost-push inflation may take hold. Prices could also rise simply because companies want to increase their profits. This is obviously a risky strategy but one that could pay off in the right circumstances. If the price of cigarettes goes up, you may carry on buying them regardless. In economic-speak, demand for cigarettes is *inelastic*. It is rigid, it will not change easily with price.

The government can also play a part in cost-push inflation by increasing **indirect taxes**. These are taxes raised on spending rather than income. When value added tax (or VAT, which is levied on all goods except necessities such as food and clothing) rose to 15 per cent from 8 per cent in 1979, it added around four percentage points to headline inflation.

TOO MUCH MONEY

&&Inflation might almost be called legal counterfeiting.&&

Irving Fisher, economist (1867–1947)

Inflation comes from either too much demand (demand-pull inflation) or higher costs (cost-push), both of which are rooted in the 'real' economy. In other words, changes in tangible factors like labour and raw materials are to blame for a general price increase. These explanations are favoured by Keynesians.

Now cast your mind back to Chapter 1 and the theories of US economist Milton Friedman. He disagreed with much of what Keynes said, particularly when it came to inflation. Instead of real factors causing price rises, Friedman believed money was responsible.

Think literally here. Imagine that money really did grow on trees and every time you wanted to buy something you simply had to pop outside and pluck a few fivers off the nearest bush. If everybody did that, those fivers would soon be worthless. Demand would go through the roof because of the 'free' money and prices would have risen so much you would need a wheelbarrow full of notes to buy a newspaper.

That is an extreme and oversimplified example, but the principle is valid: if an economy is awash with money, prices will rise. Imagine the amount of money whizzing around as an economy increases. The government might spend more on things like roads and hospitals or people may borrow more from banks, effectively using money they haven't got.

Either way, money supply has increased. Everyone from households to companies to banks feels a bit richer, so there's only one thing for it – spend, spend, spend. The demand for things like holidays and cars will rise, as will that for assets like bonds or shares. This is known as the **monetary transmission mechanism**, or the route through which a change in the money supply affects the 'real' economy, the demand for and amount of goods produced. The problem is, the government and the banks can't keep on doling out money for ever, so any rise in the amount of goods made to meet the extra demand will be temporary. The only eventual outcome of an increase in the money supply is a rise in prices.

Margaret Thatcher was a firm believer in this so-called **monetarism**, making it a household word in the 1980s. The theory took a knock when her policies foundered and money growth is now just one of a number of variables the authorities keep an eye on when setting interest rates. It still attracts many followers, however, and is worth bearing in mind when thinking about inflation.

TOLERANCE

Psychological and political factors also play a part in higher prices. Inflation has been seen as a lubricant of economic growth in the past. There is nothing like a burst of house price mania to kindle the 'feel-good' factor governments crave. For that reason, Britons have been more tolerant of inflation than they might have been. It wasn't the bogeyman of the economy that it was in, for example, Germany, where rampant **hyperinflation** after the First World War saw the price of a loaf of bread rocket to 140 billion marks in 1923. It was an experience that left the country determined to stamp out inflation for ever. (The Bundesbank, Germany's central bank before the euro days, had a formidable reputation for inflation control. As former European Commission President Jacques Delors once said: 'Not all Germans believe in God but they believe in the Bundesbank.')

Expectations can also exacerbate inflation. For a long time after the exorbitant price rises of the 1970s, people were convinced inflation was a fact of life so built that into their wage demands. They asked for high pay to compensate them for what they expected would be high prices. All that did was add to cost-push inflation, fuelling the wage-price spiral.

Only recently has that cynicism abated. With the control of inflation now in the hands of the Bank of England, people are finally starting to believe price rises will be kept to a minimum. Once they adjust their wage demands down as a result, goods will become cheaper and prices will fall, turning it into a self-fulfilling prophecy. Only when that psychology is firmly entrenched, however, will we really start getting somewhere in killing off inflation.

CAUSES AND CURES OF INFLATION

Demand-pull inflation: when there is too much demand chasing too few goods in an economy, prices will be pulled higher. Cures include raising taxes to deter people from spending so much, and reducing government expenditure on things like roads and schools. ▶

Cost-push inflation: an increase in the cost of the factors of production – the resources that go into making something – pushes up the end price of goods. This can occur as a result of higher wages, higher import or raw material prices, or higher indirect taxes. Keeping this type of inflation under control therefore entails suppressing those costs, which can often be quite hard. Persuading workers to accept lower pay rises is never easy, while the price of imported raw materials is largely dictated by the whim of the currency.

Monetarism: higher prices result solely from an increase in the money supply. The monetary transmission mechanism translates changes in money supply into changes in the real economy, in other words output, jobs, etc. The only way to reduce this type of inflation is therefore to reduce the money supply.

Psychological and political factors: a misguided tolerance of price rises can encourage policy mistakes that result in inflation. Expectations of higher prices can also spark excessive wage demands, sowing the seeds of cost-push inflation.

WINNING THE BATTLE OF THE PRICE BULGE

HOW TO FIGHT INFLATION

> **"Lenin was right. There is no subtler, no surer means of overturning the existing basis of society than to debauch the currency."**
>
> J.M. Keynes, 1919

So much for the causes of inflation, now consider the cures. Britain's inflation record over the past 30 years has been decidedly patchy. Before looking in more detail at what went wrong, here is what the theory says governments should have been doing. It is all pretty logical.

Suppress demand

If you judge that prices are being pulled up by excess demand, then it stands to reason that policies should be aimed at reducing that demand. One option is to raise borrowing costs, thereby making it more expensive for consumers to take out loans and more tempting for them to save (*see* box, 'The power of interest rates', for a more detailed explanation of the effects of interest rates). Alternatively, governments could rely on fiscal policy, reining in spending on projects such as roads and hospitals, or increasing taxation to siphon spending power out of the economy.

Keep costs down

Looking at it from another angle, the key to lower prices lies in lower costs. With wages typically the biggest expense, policy will tend to revolve around curbing pay demands, hence the government's regular pleas to exercise restraint in wage bargaining – and its actual restraint in awarding public pay increases. It is therefore not just a lack of funds that stops teachers and nurses from getting generous wage rises, it is also the need to keep inflation under control.

Reduce the money supply

If you believe that the root of all inflation lies in the money supply, then unsurprisingly you should focus on keeping that money under control. Authorities could do that by printing fewer notes or imposing strict restrictions on the amount banks can lend to their customers. Either way, there will now be less money in the economy than people want. To redress the balance, consumers will either have to sell some assets, such as shares and bonds, or buy fewer things. All in all there will be less demand in the economy and inflation will fall.

THE EXCHANGE RATE AND INFLATION

The value of a country's currency relative to that of its trading partners does not just determine the cost of an overseas holiday, it can play an important role in inflation management. As a rule, *if a currency weakens, inflation rises; and if it strengthens, inflation falls.* That relationship comes up time and again, and is one reason a strong currency has traditionally been considered a good thing.

To see why, imagine sterling falls relative to overseas currencies. You can now buy, say, five francs for every pound, whereas before you could have bought 10. In other words, sterling has **depreciated**. When you go to Calais to stock up on cheap French wine, you will now be able to afford fewer cases.

Assume bottles of red table wine cost 10 francs: at the stronger exchange rate one bottle of wine would have cost you £1, but at the weaker exchange rate it will cost you £2. The price of the bottle of wine in francs hasn't changed, but the pound's depreciation has made it more expensive to you. Apply that to the economy as a whole and all imports will be more expensive when the pound is weaker. Everyone has to spend more money just to buy the same things. In other words, there is inflation.

The opposite is true when the pound rises, or **appreciates**. Overseas goods cost less in sterling, in other words, the price of imports falls, and inflation eases.

THE BEST LAID PLANS ... INFLATION CONTROL IN BRITAIN SINCE THE SECOND WORLD WAR

Politicians have tried everything to coax inflation down since the war, with varying degrees of success. Despite the best of intentions, policies have often been misguided, and sometimes downright catastrophic. Britain's post-war attempts to control inflation can be split into six broad time periods, starting with the 20 years or so to the early 1970s.

1950s to 1971: manipulating demand

In the 1950s and 1960s, thoughts about monetary policy took a back seat and were seen mainly as a by-product of other policies. Keynesian policies were in their heyday, hence priority was given to controlling demand in the economy. To that end, policymakers concentrated on two things: the rate of interest and the amount of credit, or borrowing, that was allowed.

Interest rates are important because among other things they influence the amount of investment in the economy. The higher the interest rate, the more expensive it is for firms to borrow money for new machinery, so the less likely they are to expand. As explained in Chapter 2, without investment, the economy will stagnate, so inflation will be limited.

The rate of interest also affects the amount you and I want to borrow on our credit cards, for example. If your bank charges you 20 per cent on your debt, you will be less inclined to bend the plastic than if it charged you 5 per cent. So by changing the interest rate, the authorities could exert some control over demand and hence inflation.

Governments also took a more direct hand in limiting demand by imposing strict rules on borrowing. These **lending ceilings** meant, for example, that a company that needed money to build a factory was much more likely to get a loan than someone wanting to buy a car. In this way, mortgages were effectively rationed, too.

There were also controls on hire purchase. Credit cards were introduced only in the late 1960s, so for a long time people bought larger items such as furniture by putting down a deposit and paying off the remainder in instalments. By demanding a minimum deposit and putting a maximum on the time people could take to pay back the loan, the government could influence how much people spent.

In 1966, authorities took a slightly different approach after inflation rose to 4.7 per cent from just 2.1 per cent three years earlier. The new Labour government, under Harold Wilson, imposed a **prices and**

incomes policy, which made it illegal for firms to raise prices or award pay increases. Such a radical policy seems absurd today, but since war rationing had only been abolished in the 1950s, people were more accustomed to overt government intervention.

1971–1976: inflation takes off

Things changed in 1971. The opposition Conservative party pledged to scrap unpopular incomes policies in the 1970 general election, won, and duly did, getting rid of lending ceilings at the same time.

For the next two years there was little in the way of a coherent strategy to replace them. Chancellor Anthony Barber's substantial tax cuts, a rapid increase in the money supply after borrowing restrictions were lifted, and a fourfold rise in oil prices in 1973/74 proved too potent for prices and inflation spiralled out of control. A sharp fall in the pound in 1972 exacerbated the situation by making imports more expensive. By 1975, headline inflation was a staggering 26.9 per cent. Eventually the government responded by re-introducing an incomes policy, raising interest rates and returning to tighter controls on bank lending. It seemed the lessons of the previous decade had gone unheeded and success in inflation control proved elusive.

In 1974 a new Labour government tried the carrot approach to capping prices. It negotiated a Social Contract with the trade unions, which promised to increase pensions and repeal anti-union laws in exchange for lower pay demands. The idea was to reduce wage costs, thereby reducing cost-push inflation. The deal foundered when unions failed to live up to their side of the bargain, but it was replaced by a similar, more binding contract in 1975.

1977–1985: the experiment with monetarism

The late 1970s marked a fundamental shift in economic philosophy in Britain. The rapid price rises of the previous decade prompted many economists to question the Keynesian idea that controlling demand was the key to controlling prices. Instead, it was argued, the root of all inflation lay in too much money sloshing around the economy. The country was in the mood for change and monetarists seized the day.

Politicians were anxious to find a cure for inflation that did not bring them into conflict with the unions and this theory fitted the bill. The idea was to control the amount of money in the economy instead of relying on prices and incomes policies to manipulate demand. Labour Chancellor Denis Healey duly introduced a new intermediate target in 1976 – money supply.

However, it was not until Margaret Thatcher's Conservative government in 1979 that this tack was pursued with any vigour. The
subsequent Budget in 1980 introduced a **Medium Term Financial
Strategy** which pledged to control the money supply by keeping its
growth within certain, specified bands, thus controlling inflation.

Unfortunately for the government the strategy met with limited success. Not only was there disagreement about what kind of money to
monitor, but there was also difficulty in keeping it under control. One
problem lay in the government's desire to deregulate the financial markets, in other words, to remove all the lending restrictions that had
been in place in the 1970s. Once those curbs were lifted, households
and companies began to pile on the debt, increasing the amount of
money circulating in the economy that was available for spending. In
the early 1980s, for example, the money supply grew at around twice
the rate set by the government and by November 1985 formal targeting
of money growth had been abandoned.

1985–1992: controlling the pound

The downfall of monetarism left a gaping hole in government policy
and someone had to come up with a credible alternative to fill the void
– fast. The solution, it was decided, lay in *controlling the pound*, a decision that divided the government and contributed to the eventual
eviction of Thatcher from Downing Street.

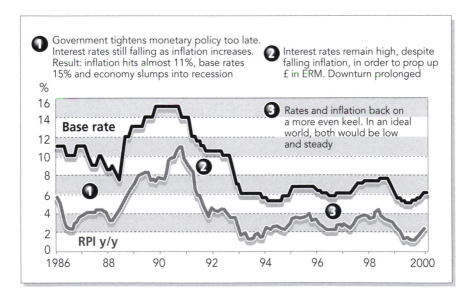

FIG. 4.3 UK interest rates versus RPI

Source: Reuters/EcoWin

Chancellor Nigel Lawson believed that informally fixing the value of the pound against the German currency, the deutschmark, would force high British inflation down to low German levels.

To see how, think of it this way. If British inflation is higher than German inflation, the pound will tend to fall. Fewer overseas investors will want to buy sterling when its value is being eroded and will probably invest in marks instead. British imports will become more expensive as the pound sinks, but exports will be cheaper, thus firms will still be able to sell their products overseas. (In a sense, this is cheating. Instead of having to cut costs to drive their prices lower, UK firms can sit back and watch the falling pound do the job for them.)

However, if the pound is informally fixed against the mark, it cannot be allowed to depreciate, so interest rates must be raised to 'persuade' investors to buy sterling, thereby propping up its value. This action of raising rates will also help stamp out the inflation, which will eventually fall to low German levels.

The other advantage of preventing the pound from weakening against the mark was that it closed the door to imported inflation (no more expensive imports), thus shoring up Britain's counter-inflation strategy.

Sadly, as with most things in economics, it wasn't that simple.

In 1987, the Chancellor declared that the pound would 'shadow' the deutschmark for the very anti-inflationary reasons outlined above. Thanks to a number of events, the pound began to rise and the Chancellor responded by bringing down interest rates to try to bring it back in line with the mark.

The problem with this response was that cheaper borrowing costs in the UK encouraged Britons to take out more loans and spend more money. Demand grew and the economy took off, driving up house prices, earnings and inflation with it. The four years of rapid growth at the end of the 1980s became known as the Lawson Boom in honour of the rotund, Conservative Chancellor who fostered it. As one City economist put it at the time: 'He seems intent on steering the economy by the seat of his pants. And in Mr Lawson's case, that offers ample scope for indiscretion.' Eventually the Chancellor had to give in and raise interest rates to choke off demand – with the result that the pound also rose, losing its link with the deutschmark.

That wasn't the end of exchange rate targeting – its biggest challenge was yet to come. In October 1990, the government took the pound into the **European Exchange Rate Mechanism (ERM)**, committing itself once again to keeping sterling close to a certain level against other currencies.

The details of the fiasco that followed belong in Chapter 7. Suffice to say for now that the policy was a spectacular failure, and the pound made a hasty and undignified exit from the system on Black Wednesday in September 1992.

1992–1997: a hybrid approach to inflation control

Once again, the pound was allowed to float and monetary policy was no longer focused on keeping sterling steady against other currencies. Borrowing costs were free to move independently, which is exactly what they did.

Between 1992 and 1997, interest rates were the primary weapon in the fight against inflation. For the first time, the (still Conservative) government adopted an explicit target for inflation, namely to keep it within 1–4 per cent. That was subsequently revised to 2.5 per cent or less. The Chancellor, who made the ultimate decision on rates after consulting with the governor of the Bank of England, looked at a combination of factors such as house prices, money supply and the exchange rate to decide policy. By and large the system was successful and inflation fell from 5.9 per cent in 1991 to 2.4 per cent in 1996, although there were blips in between.

May 1997–present day: independence for the Bank of England

The incoming Labour government, however, felt the system could be improved still further and two days after winning power in May 1997, Chancellor Gordon Brown stunned financial markets by giving the Bank of England the power to set interest rates. It was a bold, carefully orchestrated move and one that was widely welcomed as it freed monetary policy from sometimes shallow political influence and put rate control in the hands of the experts.

Until 1997, politicians had occasionally been tempted to use interest rate changes to curry favour among the voting public. It was not uncommon for rate cuts to immediately precede elections in the hope of injecting a bit of goodwill into the ballot box. But those cuts did not always make good economic sense. By taking rate control out of politicians' hands, such tempting mistakes could never be repeated, said Labour.

The government still has ultimate control over inflation in the sense that it has the power to tell the Bank of England what inflation rate it should be aiming for. At the time of writing, the Bank's **inflation target** was 2.5 per cent, with the proviso that subject to that target monetary policy must support the government's wider economic policy objectives.

In other words, it must change interest rates to make sure underlying RPIX inflation, which strips out the volatile costs of mortgage interest payments, remains at 2.5 per cent. If inflation is more than 1 per cent away from its target, in either direction, the Bank governor must write a public letter to the Chancellor explaining why. The reasoning behind this symmetric target lies in the dangers of deflation, or falling prices. As I will explain later, most economists agree that reducing inflation involves squeezing growth and jobs. By making clear that the Bank is to be as concerned about inflation falling below target as rising above target, the government is ensuring there will always be enough inflation to 'grease the wheels' of the economy.

THE POWER OF INTEREST RATES

The Bank of England's MPC relies on interest rates to control inflation. A quarter point change can be enough to change the course of the whole £800 billion economy. It does so in four ways.

Spending decisions. A change in the cost of borrowing will influence how much companies invest and how much consumers spend. If rates rise, for example, people will be tempted to save rather than spend as they can earn more by salting money away in their deposit account. Similarly, firms will be less inclined to invest at higher rates of interest because it is more expensive to borrow in order to do so. Both decisions therefore curb demand and hence inflation.

Cash flow changes. A change in interest rates will alter the amount of cash that borrowers and lenders have. For example, if rates rise and you have some money in a variable-interest savings account, you will be better off because your money is earning more. But if you have a floating-rate mortgage, your monthly payments will increase, leaving you with less money to spend than previously. This route is the most powerful and immediate way of manipulating demand in the economy and is certainly the one most keenly felt by many in the population. A recent trend towards fixed-rate home loans by a more risk-averse public has blunted this mechanism slightly.

Changes in the value of assets. A change in interest rates affects the value of assets such as houses, shares and bonds (see Chapter 6). For example, a large rise in rates could cut house prices as mortgage costs increase, or it may depress shares as alternative, risk-free investments start to appear more attractive. Homeowners and stock market investors feel poorer and will be more cautious about going on spending sprees.

Exchange rates. A rise in interest rates relative to those overseas can increase the demand for a currency and cause it to rise. This in turn will reduce the price of imports, which will not only put downward pressure on inflation but will also improve competitiveness in the economy as domestic producers will be encouraged to lower their prices to compete against cheaper imported goods.

A rise in interest rates will restrain demand, putting downward pressure on prices and inflation.

The Bank of England's website can be found at www.bankofengland.co.uk

AN INTERESTING GUIDE TO BORROWING COSTS

The next few pages tackle the nitty-gritty of interest rates. Changes in borrowing costs tend to receive a lot of media attention both for their impact on the wider economy – future inflation, investment and, ultimately, growth – and their effect on people's finances. Rate moves will alter share prices, savings rates, mortgage payments and the cost of your overdraft. But it is not immediately obvious why they are so powerful. The box above explains how something as seemingly innocuous as a quarter point change in borrowing costs can alter the course of entire trillion-pound economies.

Given their potency, it can be very useful to have an idea of when rates are going to change. The box, 'Tips on how to spot an interest rate change', gives a few pointers on how to second-guess the policymakers, giving you a head start when it comes to deciding which mortgage to take out, whether to pile on the debt or whether to invest in the stock market.

This section starts with an explanation of the logistics of interest rates – how the Bank of England reaches a decision on the issue, and how it goes about implementing that decision.

THE MONETARY POLICY COMMITTEE

Britain's inflationary fate lies in the hands of the Bank of England's **Monetary Policy Committee**, known as the **MPC**. This is a nine-member body that meets once a month to discuss whether or not to change interest rates. It is composed of five members from the Bank of England: the governor, the two deputy governors and two executive directors. There are also four external members – from academia, industry or the City, thus providing a different perspective on monetary policy. A representative from the Treasury also attends but he has no say on interest rates.

The meeting typically starts on the afternoon of the first Wednesday of the month, and finishes just before midday on the Thursday. The MPC's rate decision, which may be accompanied by a brief statement, is broadcast to the media via an electronic system just after noon. This is crucial information for financial markets and is even more eagerly awaited than government statistics. Once again it is the wire agencies, like Reuters, that are the first to break the news and they send it to dealing rooms, investment banks and newspapers around the world in seconds. This is bread and butter for clients. Send out the wrong number and you can collect your P45 on the way out. Trade in bonds, currencies and shares is often very light on the morning of a rate decision as investors stay their hands for the main event. As soon as the decision is announced, all hell breaks lose and millions of pounds are traded in minutes.

The full record of the MPC's meeting is published two weeks after the event. These minutes not only reveal which members voted which way, but also give clues as to whether any future rate changes are in the pipeline.

To date, the MPC's record has been impressive (see Fig. 4.4). During its first three years, underlying RPIX inflation averaged 2.5 per cent – bang on target – deviating only more than 0.3 percentage points either side of that rate nine times. But then again, as the Bank of England is the first to admit, it can take anything up to between 18 months and two years for the full effect of interest rate changes to be felt in the economy. So, as former Tory Chancellor Kenneth Clarke is eager to point out, part of Britain's favourable inflation performance in the latter 1990s was down to the previous government – the Conservatives.

The Bank of England's website address is www.bankofengland.co.uk

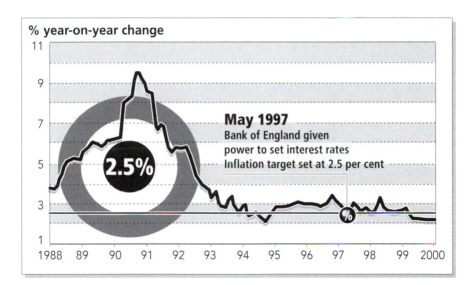

FIG. 4.4 UK underlying RPIX inflation   Source: Reuters/EcoWin

TIPS ON HOW TO SPOT AN INTEREST RATE CHANGE

Q: What sex is to the novelist, inflation is to the economist. Discuss.

A: I am not sure how I am supposed to answer this question but it may be said that both inflation and sex are characterised by a rising rate of interest.

Anonymous

Changes in interest rates will affect your mortgage, the size of your loan repayments, how much money you spend and the return on your savings and investments. They will affect the value of the pound, hence the cost of your overseas holiday, and the size of your pension.

Accurately predicting rate changes, therefore, could save you a lot of money. Here are a number of factors – in no particular order of importance – that the MPC looks at when making its monetary policy decisions.

- **The strength of demand.** By monitoring the amount of goods people buy in shops, the MPC can gauge the strength of demand, hence the chances of demand-pull inflation. Monthly retail sales figures from the National Statistics office plus evidence from consumer surveys, are therefore worth keeping an eye on.

- **Wage growth.** Wages help determine the cost of making goods and providing services. If they rise too rapidly, cost-push inflation could become a problem. Again, both official data and survey evidence on earnings are followed closely.

- **Overall growth.** Growth in the service and manufacturing sectors is carefully monitored, although the latter has less impact on rate decisions because it accounts for a much smaller part of the economy. As long as there is plenty of spare capacity around (lots of factories in the case of manufacturing, lots of solicitors, architects, bankers, restaurants etc. in the case of services), strong growth is not a problem for inflation. Therefore, GDP is always considered relative to how much space there is left in the economy to expand. Again, surveys are often more useful than backward-looking official data.

- **The pound.** Some economists have estimated that every 4 per cent rise in the pound is equivalent to a 1 per cent increase in interest rates, although this relationship is far from precise. As a general rule of thumb, the stronger the currency, the less need there is for tighter monetary policy. Knowing the pound's value against the dollar and the euro is therefore useful if you are trying to predict rate changes.

- **House prices.** The Halifax bank and the Nationwide building society release house price indices each month, giving a snap-shot of how buoyant the property market is. Rising house prices could be dangerous for inflation if they fuel confidence, encourage people to borrow more and hence drive consumption higher.

- **Producer prices.** Inflation at the wholesale level may be an indicator of future price rises at the retail level. National Statistics releases data each month on the cost of raw materials, and the prices of goods leaving factories, known as producer prices. If either of these rise, they could eventually find their way into higher prices in shops.

- **Money supply.** Since the experiment with monetarism foundered in the 1980s, money supply figures have taken a back seat in rate decisions. However, they remain a useful secondary indicator and are still monitored by the MPC.

Lastly, when you are deciding whether to take a fixed-rate mortgage or a variable one, or whether to invest in shares or bonds, it is worth considering anecdotal evidence. Official figures are often out of date, so if GDP is weak but everyone in your street has a flash new car and holiday bookings to the Caribbean are soaring, chances are growth and rates are heading higher in future.

HOW THE BANK OF ENGLAND CONTROLS INTEREST RATES

MPC members are often characterised as being *doves* or *hawks*. Doves are more inclined to give a growth chance if the decision on changing borrowing costs is finely balanced. Hawks take no risks whatsoever with inflation and tend to take a stricter line when it comes to tightening policy.

As the box entitled 'The power of interest rates' shows, by changing the cost of borrowing, the MPC can regulate demand and inflation. But there are scores of banks in Britain, each with different mortgage, lending and savings rates. Somehow the Bank of England must influence those rates – either directly or indirectly.

The Bank of England is the ultimate bank in the country – it is the place where the main settlement banks bank, i.e. they actually hold accounts there. At the end of each day, all the commercial banks in Britain (the likes of Lloyds TSB, Barclays and the Bank of Scotland) have to settle their accounts with each other. That involves electronically moving money from one bank to another depending on who has drawn cheques on whom. So if more people at the Bank of Scotland have written cheques to people who bank at Lloyds TSB, for example, the Bank of Scotland must make a net transfer of money to Lloyds TSB at the end of the day.

The banks also have to leave a positive balance in their Bank of England accounts. This is a key factor that gives the BoE control of interest rates. If banks are prevented from going overdrawn, they will be forced to borrow any money they need from the Bank of England – at an interest rate it determines.

Which begs the question – how does the BoE make sure that the banks always need to borrow money? The answer is, by keeping them short of liquid funds, so they have to borrow from the central bank at a rate chosen by the latter.

That's the rate that you hear about in newspapers, the so-called repo rate, which sets the cost of borrowing, via 'open market operations'. Essentially, the Bank buys financial instruments from the commercial banks, to supply them with liquid funds.

For example, say the Barclays account at the Bank of England is short of funds – it hasn't got enough money to pay the government and the other commercial banks at the end of the day and still have a positive balance left over. It must sell some financial instruments to the Bank. In exchange for the cash that the Bank hands over it charges Barclays a rate of interest.

Think of it as the Bank of England *lending* the commercial banks money. This is easier to understand by looking at the main financial instrument used in money market operations, gilt repos (otherwise known as a gilt sales and repurchase agreement). A gilt is just a British government bond (the government is such low risk that lending to it, buying bonds, is as good as gold. More on that in Chapter 6).

Still with me? It's almost over. Barclays then sells gilts to the Bank of England with a legally binding agreement to repurchase an equivalent amount back from the bank at a predetermined price and date. In effect a gilt repo is a cash loan with the gilts used as security.

So every day the Bank of England keeps the banking system short of money and then lends the needed funds at an interest rate that it decides. The banks agree to borrow from the BoE at this official rate because it is the cheapest money they can find (which is why it used to be called the minimum lending rate). This official interest rate, now known as the repo rate, then dictates what the commercial banks can charge for mortgages etc., while still making a profit and so forms the benchmark for all other rates in the economy.

IS INFLATION DEAD OR JUST RESTING?

Britain finally seems to be getting the hang of keeping price rises under control. During the 1970s, inflation averaged almost 13 per cent a year; in the 1980s it fell to just over 7 per cent; and in the 1990s it was just 3.5 per cent.

However, it is far too early for central bankers to pop open the champagne. Britain has had low inflation before, in the 1950s and 1960s, but that did not stop prices from going berserk in subsequent decades.

REASONS FOR OPTIMISM

There are a number of reasons to be optimistic on inflation this time round, both globally and in Britain.

- Low inflation is *de rigueur* among policymakers. Both in the UK and Europe there are clear, precise inflation targets that leave little room for deviation. The US central bank, the Federal Reserve, is equally intolerant of price rises, hence the chances of global inflation have receded.

- The will is there, and so is the way. Independence for the Bank of England has brought it more in line with its counterparts in Europe and the US, obviating the risk that political factors will compromise monetary policy decisions. Gone is the temptation to 'bribe' voters with cheaper mortgages before elections, so policy mistakes are less likely.

- Psychological factors are starting to play a role in keeping prices down. The longer the MPC keeps inflation low, the more convinced the public will be that things are going to stay that way. Workers will demand lower pay rises, so the cost of making things will be kept under control. Prices will therefore remain subdued, reinforcing the low pay demand in the first place.

CONTINUED NEED FOR VIGILANCE

Things are looking up, or rather down, when it comes to prices. However, complacency should be the last thing on policymakers' minds.

- One ever-present danger is the risk of policy errors, albeit a reduced one. Controlling inflation is a tricky business, with no hard-and-fast rules, hence vigilance is key.

- Labour market flexibility, which describes the ease with which workers can be hired and fired, or are willing to change jobs and take pay cuts, is also crucial. Any moves to restrict that flexibility could encourage higher wages and hence cost-push inflation. Labour's decision to sign Europe's social chapter, which among other things controls working hours and holiday entitlement, reinforced worker rights but also chipped away at that flexibility. The introduction of the minimum wage could have a similar impact, although the signs are that it is too low to have any lasting effect on flexibility.

■ Lack of capacity in Britain also remains a worry. Evidence on the UK's ability to make things and provide services without igniting inflation is patchy. Figures from the Department of Trade and Industry show most of Britain's top companies still invest less than their international counterparts. In 1998, for example, UK companies spent £10,200 per worker on capital compared with £15,200 spent by foreign firms. If Britain continues to under-invest it will never have the machinery, factories or technology it needs to grow faster without price rises. The good news, however, is that the longer prices remain stable, the more likely it is that investment will improve and capacity will increase.

WHAT IS THE PRICE OF LOW INFLATION?

A number of factors, such as Bank of England independence, a clear inflation target and lower price expectations, have improved Britain's inflation prospects in recent years. But before central bankers loosen the champagne corks, a word to the wise. As much as I hate to be a party pooper, this new era of low prices needs to carry a health warning – too little inflation could be bad for you.

The most obvious danger is that inflation could easily topple over into **deflation**, in other words, a sustained *fall* in the general price level. That may sound very attractive – the cost of Christmas would fall every year and your annual holiday would get cheaper and cheaper. But in reality, deflation could end up being just as ruinous as inflation.

THE DANGERS OF DEFLATION

If prices are falling because of productivity improvements, that is all well and good. For example, if new technology or better working methods mean car workers at Swindon can build more Hondas in one month, the price of those Hondas could fall. Extend that to the whole economy and people's real income will increase since they can afford to buy more things with the same salary. In other words, deflation has actually improved living standards.

Nick Leeson, the trader who brought down Barings Bank after a disastrous derivatives deal, faces the press at London's Heathrow airport in July 1999 after his release from Singapore's Tanah Merah jail. Photograph by Paul Hackett. © Reuters 1999.

Top: European Monetary Affairs Commissioner Yves-Thibault de Silguy and President of the European Commission Jacques Santer proudly display a model of a euro coin shortly before its launch in January 1999. They promised an era of stability and prosperity. Photograph by Nathalie Koulischer. © Reuters 1999.
Bottom: Just over two years and a 25 per cent fall in the single currency later, anti-euro campaigners Lord Owen and Janet Bush launch the 'No' campaign in central London. Photograph by Jonathan Evans. © Reuters 2000.

Top: UK Chancellor of the Exchequer Kenneth Clarke holds up a battered budget box before going to parliament to deliver what was to be his last budget in November 1996. Photograph by Kevin Lamarque. © Reuters 1996.
Bottom: By 1998 there was a new government, a new budget box and a new Chancellor, Gordon Brown. Photograph by Russell Boyce. © Reuters 1998.

'Steady' Eddie George, governor of the Bank of England. The man who has the casting vote on interest rates glances towards the door at the start of a Monetary Policy Committee meeting. Photograph by Michael Crabtree. © Reuters 2000.

Manufacturers worried about their jobs gather outside the 'Old Lady of Threadneedle Street' to demand Eddie George cuts interest rates, October 1998. Photograph by Russell Boyce. © Reuters 1998.

Street for sale, West London. This picture was taken in October 1998 when house prices across Britain were rising at around 5 per cent a year, and Londoners needed an average of around £130,000 to buy a home. Photograph by Paul Hackett.
© Reuters 1998.

Anti-capitalist demonstrators bring traffic to a halt outside Liverpool Street station in the City of London in June 1999. Turnout was disappointing – there were far fewer than the 10,000 protestors organisers had expected. Photograph by Ian Waldie. © Reuters 1999.

Taxes take centre stage in Britain's 1997 election battle. Soon to be Social Security Secretary Alistair Darling (top) and the Chancellor in waiting Gordon Brown highlight the 22 tax rises John Major's government introduced – a bold tactic for the Labour Party with its tax and spend legacy. Top photograph by Ian Hodgson. © Reuters 1997. Bottom photograph by Paul Hackett. © Reuters 1996.

There are elements of this kind of deflation in action today. The spread of new technology and the Internet should help nudge prices lower in coming years, while computers undoubtedly help people to produce far more in an hour than they could a decade ago. For example, a statistician somewhere has worked out that it now takes three minutes to earn enough to buy a pint of milk, compared with five minutes in 1971. The single European currency could have a similar downward effect on prices. If more than 350 million people are paying for goods in euros, price discrepancies will be more obvious and the cost of expensive goods may be forced down.

But it is not all good news. If prices start to fall because of a collapse in demand, there could be trouble. A downward spiral will be triggered where consumers will put off buying things in the expectation that goods will be cheaper in the future. This expectation will end up being self-fulfilling: people delay purchases, demand falls, firms are forced to cut prices even further, so consumers delay buying things even longer. The end result could be a depression along the lines of that in the 1930s, when prices fell and the unemployment rate in Britain more than doubled in three years, to around 22 per cent in 1932.

Deflation can be particularly painful for debtors. Just like inflation helps borrowers, deflation will harm them because the real value of debt will increase. If your fully mortgaged £100,000 home falls in value to £50,000 and you are forced to sell, you will be left with no home and a £50,000 debt.

WHERE IS THE MIDDLE GROUND FOR INFLATION?

Navigating your way through the inflation minefield is a testing task. On one side lies deflation, job loss and depression, and on the other, runaway prices and an uncertain future. The trick is to find the middle path.

Coaxing inflation down involves squeezing some life out of the economy, so at some point you must ask yourself whether the sacrifice of jobs and growth is worth it – in 'economic speak', whether the benefits of reducing inflation and keeping it low outweigh the costs.

To answer that, you need to look at what happens on the road to zero inflation. Reducing inflation usually stifles economic growth and increases unemployment.

Imagine you work in a factory that makes computers. Inflation has been running at around 10 per cent for a while, so when it comes to the annual pay round, naturally you demand a rise of at least 10 per cent to keep up.

But now imagine that the government has decided to reduce inflation by increasing interest rates. People cannot afford to borrow so much money at the more expensive rate of interest and their mortgage payments are also higher, so they have less to spend on things like computers. The multiplier kicks in (*see* Chapter 2), demand falls, and the factory cannot afford to pay you and your colleagues as much money. Unless you lower your wage demand, chances are you will be made redundant. Once that happens on a large enough scale across the country, demand for goods will fall even further because more people will be without a job and without an income.

So the downward spiral of lower growth and more unemployment has been set in motion by the increase in interest rates. The fact that people are loath to take *real wage* cuts exaggerates the scale of the downturn.

At this point, economists split into classical and Keynesian camps. True to form, the former put their trust in market forces. They say the higher unemployment resulting from the fight against inflation is only a temporary blip and the number of jobless will eventually fall back to its long-term, natural rate. With all those people unemployed, wages will soon fall to the point where firms will want to hire more workers again, so demand will start to rise again and output and jobs will soon be back to where they were before – it is just that inflation will be lower.

Keynesians, however, have traditionally said it could take more than 10 years to get unemployment down again, having sacrificed it for lower prices. They believe the process described above, where wages adjust to allow jobs to be created again, is extremely lengthy (how willing would you be to take a pay cut, even if unemployment was rising?). Therefore, they argue, the only way to increase the number in work is to stimulate the economy and fuel inflation once more.

One way to take the sting out of reducing inflation is to have a credible target for it. As mentioned earlier, if workers believe prices are going to stay put, they are more likely to accept lower wage rises and hence cost-push inflation is less of a problem. That is why the government is eager to ram home the credibility of the Bank of England's 2.5 per cent inflation target. If everyone believes that target and incorporates it into their wage demands, it should be self-fulfilling.

INFLATION AND YOUR STANDARD OF LIVING

The Retail Price Index is Britain's most popular measure of inflation. Government statisticians go to great lengths to make sure it is accurate, but it is nevertheless only an average. A headline inflation rate in December 1999 of 1.8 per cent meant that prices *on average* were 1.8 per cent higher that month than they were a year earlier. In the same period, the price of beer rose by 3.0 per cent, but the cost of wine and spirits rose by just 1.0 per cent.

So it follows that the retail price index does not necessarily reflect changes in your cost of living. Taking the example above, if you prefer drinking beer to wine, it will cost you more each month than the rate of inflation to maintain your previous standard of living. In other words, your 'real' cost of living has increased.

Expand that to the whole economy over a number of years and vast differences in living costs emerge. For example, between December 1989 and December 1999, the RPI rose by 40.8 per cent. However, food prices did not keep pace, rising by only 24.8 per cent. So if you spent a lot of your income on food and cooked it at home, your cost of living would have fallen relative to inflation.

But if you ate out all the time, you would have been relatively worse off. The average price of a meal at a restaurant in Britain leapt by 61.7 per cent in those 10 years, well above the overall rate of inflation.

If you not only cooked at home but also stayed in and watched TV, you would have been even better off. Technological progress reduced the price of audio-visual equipment by more than half between 1989 and 1999, while the cost of renting and licensing a television rose by just 26.4 per cent, much less than inflation.

Unfortunately, if you like a good night out, things have not been so economical. The price of entertainment outside the home almost doubled in the period.

Finally, the prices of alcoholic drinks, tobacco and petrol all far outstripped inflation in the period, largely thanks to hefty excise duties (taxes imposed on them by the government).

So, if you are a home-loving, teetotal, who doesn't smoke and prefers to cycle everywhere rather than drive, the cost of maintaining your standard of living will have fallen in real terms between 1989 and 1999. But if you are a chain-smoking socialite who can't cook and who loves to drive, you may want to change your lifestyle because things got pretty expensive for you at the end of the 20th century.

FIG. 4.5 British house price inflation

Source: Halifax house price index

THE 1980S HOUSING MARKET BOOM

The 1980s was the decade of money and fun, when greed was good and lunch was for wimps. Yuppies would not leave home without their Filofaxes and infinitely flexible credit cards, and 'loadsamoney' was the battle cry of the younger generation.

Nothing typified the era more than the astonishing explosion in house prices. The nation was obsessed with property. Homes in London more than doubled in value between 1985 and 1988, a time when many people made more money by buying a house than by working for a living (see Fig. 4.5). Prices in the capital were rising at around six times the pace of earnings and everyone wanted a piece of the action.

Until it ended in tears. The foundations of the boom were not firm enough and the whole shaky structure came crashing down at the end of the decade after fuelling the worst bout of inflation in Britain for more than 10 years.

A number of one-off factors conspired to drive house prices higher in the latter half of the 1980s. The psychology of the era was partly to blame, as property and share ownership became commonplace. Prime Minister Margaret Thatcher encouraged large-scale home ownership through sales of council houses at discount prices to tenants, depleting the stock of public housing and stoking inflation in one masterly stroke.

There was also an air of invulnerability. House prices had not fallen in living memory and homeowners felt invincible. The phrase negative equity, when property is worth less than the money owed on it, had not been invented yet and people borrowed with reckless abandon in the frenzied scramble to jump on the housing bandwagon.

If the will was there, a change in regulations provided the way. A relaxation of the strict rules governing borrowing fanned the house price flames as building societies were free to lend more and more. Cut-throat competition meant banks were falling over themselves to hand out mortgages, often of more than three times salaries. By the late 1980s families were spending up to a third of their income on housing costs, compared with around 13 per cent in late 1999.

A particularly badly timed tax change added a further catalyst, if one were needed. In 1988, the then Chancellor Nigel Lawson announced he would abolish a useful loophole that allowed unmarried couples to claim double tax relief on a home loan, but he stayed execution for six months. At once, there was a rush to buy before the deadline, and house prices were pushed into the stratosphere.

All this was taking place against the backdrop of swelling natural demand for homes in Britain. Divorces, later marriages and longer-living pensioners meant there were more and more single households to accommodate, but planning restrictions and building time lags meant houses were not being completed fast enough.

An added problem was that the housing market does not behave like a conventional market. It flouts the rules and has a mind of its own. Instead of demand falling off when prices rise, which is what you would expect from any well-behaved market, the opposite is often true in housing. The faster prices rise, the more people panic and buy because they are afraid of missing the boat.

The end result has been well documented. House prices rose by 15.4 per cent in 1986/87, a massive 23.3 per cent in 1987/88, and 20.8 per cent in 1988/89 (according to the Halifax house price index).

This may not have been particularly inflationary on its own, but it was what followed that caused the real problems. As the value of their homes rose, people felt considerably richer. They began to remortgage, siphoning more and more money out of their properties to spend on things like cars and holidays. As demand soared, the government was eventually forced to raise interest rates, which in turn hit those over-extended home owners particularly hard. Not only did their already considerable mortgage payments rise with the increase in borrowing costs, but the value of their property plunged, leaving them with more debts than they had assets. Negative equity was born.

When the recession of the early 1990s really bit and jobs started to go, the situation got even more desperate for a lot of people. By 1992, 1.6 million people had a property that was worth less than their mortgage and between 1990 and 1998, almost half a million households lost their homes.

It took more than 10 years for some families to rid themselves of the debt accumulated during the 1980s housing boom. Prices in parts of the country recovered to their previous peaks only in the late 1990s. According to figures from the Council of Mortgage Lenders, the average price of a house in the United Kingdom as a whole in 1996 was £69,100, still more than £1,000 less than the peak in 1989.

The moral of the tale for housebuyers is 'nest not invest'. Don't buy a house with the sole purpose of making money on it. If you are doing that, the chances are that everyone else is, too, and the market is likely to get frothy.

For now, the memory of negative equity is still fresh enough in people's minds to deter them from overextending themselves and fuelling an unsustainable house price boom. But complacency would be a mistake. Just like general inflation has the power to inhibit growth and redistribute wealth, so too do house price rises. They tend to transfer money from the poor to the rich, from those who cannot afford to buy property to those who can. Buoyant house prices may make for interesting dinner party conversation for some, but they do nothing to close the growing income divide in Britain.

E-TAILING AND THE E-CONOMY

THE NET EFFECT OF SHOPPING ON THE WEB

Anyone who underestimates the potential of the Internet does so at their peril and economists are no exception. The creation of a global marketplace via the World Wide Web could have terrific consequences for everything from growth to jobs to inflation. Exactly how large those consequences will be is open to debate. We are entering uncharted territory when it comes to the Internet, so economists have to hypothesise even more than usual.

DOWNWARD PRESSURE ON PRICES

Most agree that the World Wide Web will help to keep inflation at bay for a number of reasons.

- **Lower costs.** The Internet is a huge shop window that allows companies to display their goods at minimum expense. There are no high street rents or shop assistants' wages to pay, leaving less room for cost-push inflation. Amazon.com, the flagship Internet bookseller, has around 13 million titles stored in warehouses in the US and Britain, whereas the biggest bookshops in New York can afford to rent enough space to carry only around 180,000 books.

- **Greater price transparency.** Comparing prices on the Internet is easy, which puts extra pressure on retailers to offer you a good deal. If you want to buy a new television, for example, instead of battling your way through the Saturday crowds and visiting perhaps three or four different shops, simply surf. You will find the cheapest deal available in the time it would have taken you to get a parking space. The OECD estimates that e-commerce revenues will rise by around 1,000 per cent over the next four to five years as consumers log on to the advantages of web shopping.

- **Added pressure on conventional retailers.** High street shops are unlikely to be immune either. Competition from the Internet means they will either have to match cyberspace prices or offer services the anonymous web can't, such as personal advice from shop assistants.

- **Low start-up costs.** Setting up a website is relatively easy. If a site is proving popular with shoppers, it won't be long before someone else tries to steal some market share by doing it bigger and better. This is pure Adam Smith updated for the 21st century. The invisible hand of the price mechanism means large profits will attract more firms, which will undercut existing companies thereby eroding those profits and delivering lower prices to consumers.

The picture emerging is probably the nearest we will ever get to **perfect competition**. In this ideal world, a large number of companies produce the same thing and are able to move freely in and out of the market depending on where the profits are. Consumers have perfect knowledge about all the products on offer (one of those unrealistic assumptions that underlie so many economic models), hence will seek out the cheapest products, subjecting prices to the full force of Smith's invisible hand.

HERE COMES THE BUT...

If only it were that simple. There would be no more shopping in miserable weather, no wonky supermarket trolleys, and low, competitive prices everywhere. Alas, this happy scenario is likely to prove elusive.

Similar products sport very different price tags on the Internet, which would be impossible under perfect competition. Research has shown that prices for identical books differ by an average of 33 per cent online, while those for CDs vary by 25 per cent.[1] There are a number of reasons for this.

- **Security.** Concern about disclosing credit card details online deters many would-be cyber-shoppers from buying over the Internet. Those that do bend the plastic often do so only at well-known, reputable sites, regardless of the fact that they may be more expensive.

- **Lack of additional support.** Many web retailers do not offer the kind of after-sales support or guarantees that are taken for granted when shopping at old favourites like John Lewis. Customers cannot touch, feel, ask questions or test-run products when they are buying over the net, hence the type of good suited to cyber selling is limited. Price competition is therefore also constrained.

- **Convenience.** There is a bewildering range of choice on the Internet. A quick experiment showed that a search for book shops in Yahoo! gave up 414 sites, while one under AltaVista threw up 43,955. Personally, I'm too lazy to trawl through all those, so I usually just go straight to Amazon.com or bol.com out of sheer convenience. The books tend to cost less than they do on the high street, but I have no idea whether I could find them cheaper elsewhere on the net.

- **Loyalty incentives.** Many sites offer pre-programmed one-stop shopping or bonuses for customer loyalty, both of which will discourage people from moving around the Internet, thereby inhibiting price competition.

PERFECT COMPETITION STILL SOME WAY OFF

The Internet may not live up to the textbook definition of perfect competition, but it can still help to keep inflation at bay. As consumers become increasingly web-savvy, the balance of power will shift in their favour and prices should fall. Exactly how far is impossible to say. Web projections are largely guesstimates. At the end of 1999, Forrester Research was predicting that £3.1 billion of goods will be bought by Britons online in 2003 (annual growth of 69 per cent from 2000). Rival firm Verdict put the figure for Internet and interactive TV shopping at £7.4 billion just a year later in 2004.

The only thing we know for certain is that its influence will be unprecedented. It took 36 years for the radio to reach 50 million people, 13 years for the television, 16 for PCs and less than five years for the Internet. At the time of writing, the latest forecast from Forrester Research predicted that 24.5 million people in Britain alone would have Internet access by 2003, up from around 15 million at the end of 1999. That is a lot of people power.

The advent of the net and its impact on inflation embodies the living, breathing quality of economics. The old theories still apply, as much as they ever did, but there is now a new spin on things. The subject is still evolving and that is its great attraction. The reason it is so fascinating is that it doesn't provide all the answers on a plate. There are some good theories on inflation and some sophisticated models for dealing with it, but at the end of the day it comes down to judgement. Every economist, from the highly paid City analyst to the learned academic, has an opinion on where interest rates should be. Hopefully, having read this chapter, you will have one now, too.

IF YOU REMEMBER FIVE THINGS FROM THIS CHAPTER ...

- Inflation is a general, sustained rise in the price level. It is measured in Britain by the Retail Price Index.

- Inflation is caused by either too much demand in the economy or by a rise in the cost of resources that go into making something. It may also be caused by too much money sloshing around the economy.

- The Bank of England's Monetary Policy Committee is responsible for inflation in the UK. It must keep underlying, RPIX inflation, which excludes mortgage interest payments, at 2.5 per cent.

- The MPC monitors a variety of factors at its monthly meetings to decide interest rates, including wage growth, house prices and the strength of demand.

- The Internet could help to reduce prices by lowering costs, offering greater price transparency and putting pressure on conventional retailers.

ENDNOTE

1 Research by Smith and Brynjolfsson.

CHAPTER 5

WORKING FOR A LIVING

The changing nature of labour markets

" I think when you're working

and you pick up your wages

on a Friday you think …

that's mine.

Your sit there with pride and say

I've earned that,

the government ain't give it me.

It [makes you] proud

to work. "

Unemployed, female lone parent, Lincoln[1]

INTRODUCTION

Of all the issues covered by economics, unemployment is probably the one that strikes closest to home. Your job – or lack of it – will shape much of your life, from the people you spend your time with, to the house you can afford and the area you live in. Being in work, whether you love it or loathe it, can mean holidaying in Barcelona not Bognor, or buying a Peugeot rather than a push-bike. Being out of work can mean struggling to pay the mortgage and feeling increasingly alienated from the rest of society.

That makes it sound like work is the answer to everything. Unfortunately, for more and more it's not. Job insecurity is rife in the world's developed economies and longer working hours are taking their toll on people's health and happiness. We are deafened by calls to compete, make money and, above all, succeed. It seems mediocrity will not be tolerated in the 21st century.

In short, the laws of the labour market have changed. The job for life has disappeared and instead, we are all expected to be flexible, both in the hours we work and the jobs we do. A tidal wave of competition, from overseas and from the Internet, means relentless cost cutting has become mandatory for any firm with profit-hungry shareholders. Meanwhile, the wonders of new technology mean more and more people work in fear of being usurped by machines. Understanding a bit about economics can help you to navigate your way through this work-place minefield. It can tell you why so many people are concerned about their job security, and can suggest ways that you, the government and companies can combat that concern.

Job insecurity is just one issue addressed in this chapter. It also tackles the following:

- **It looks at why you may lose your job.** Unemployment has many causes – recession, a downturn in a particular industry such as ship-building, or a rise in wages which makes it unprofitable for firms to hire workers.

- **It considers why relative poverty in Britain is so high when unemployment is so low.** One would expect that with a record number of Britons in jobs at the end of 1999, poverty would no longer be a problem. Instead there is an enormous difference between rich and poor. This chapter considers why that is and what can be done about it.

- **It explains the economics behind a minimum wage,** and assesses its impact in Britain.

- **It explains why eliminating unemployment completely is impossible.** We can send men to the moon and make babies in test tubes but we still can't figure out a way of providing everyone who wants to work with a job. This chapter explains why. It shows how each country has a certain, minimum level of unemployment that is consistent with stable inflation, and that come boom or bust, the economy will always tend back towards that so-called natural level.

- **It looks at what the government can do to keep unemployment down.** Given that jobs for everyone is off the agenda, the next best thing the government can do is to coax that natural unemployment rate as low as possible. This chapter discusses how that may be done, and considers whether the British government's New Deal pro-gramme has been successful in this respect.

- **It considers whether the global economic rules have changed, to allow more growth at lower inflation.** You may have read in newspapers about a 'new paradigm' which describes the theory that technology has allowed countries – in particular the United States – to grow faster for longer without pushing prices higher. The chapter goes on to explore whether that is indeed the case, and whether the same theory can be applied to Britain.

- **It compares Britain's job market with that of its main competitors.** British workers earned a reputation as uncooperative, inflexible and bloody-minded in the 1970s thanks to a wave of debilitating strikes. Nowadays, they are synonymous with flexibility and value for money, helping to attract huge amounts of foreign investment into the country. But they still produce less in the average working day than most Americans, French or Germans. This productivity gap is concerning – and proving difficult to fill.

- **It takes an impartial look at whether Britain is still divided into a prosperous south and impoverished north.** If you live in the north of Britain you probably get fed up with being told how much unemployment, crime, and industrial decline there is around you. If you live in the south, you probably feel uneasy with the apparent disparity but nevertheless relieved that you are the prosperous side of the Watford Gap. This chapter considers whether these caricatures are fair, or whether there are pockets of poverty and wealth scattered across the whole country.

- **It considers the role of trade unions in the modern workplace.** Trade unions are no longer the power brokers they once were. Falling membership and loss of influence have given the once mighty lobby groups a rude wake-up call: modernise or die. The chapter ends with a look at whether unions will survive the shake-out and in what guise they may emerge.

HOW SAFE IS YOUR JOB?

WORKERS NOT SO BRAVE IN THE NEW WORLD

An unemployed person is someone who does not have a job but would like one.

Towards the end of 1999, more Britons had a job than ever before. Unemployment was at its lowest rate for 20 years and the economy was forging ahead (*see* Fig. 5.1). Inflation was down at levels last seen when The

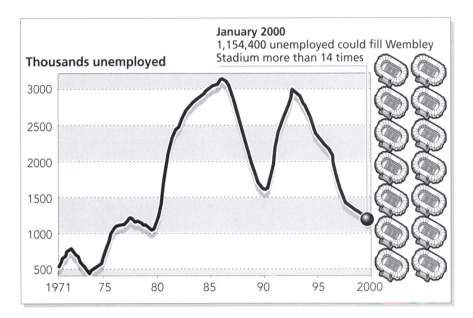

FIG. 5.1 UK unemployment 1971–2000

Source: Reuters/EcoWin

Beatles were crooning their way to number one with *I Wanna Hold your Hand* and meanwhile government coffers were positively brimming over with cash. A classic Goldilocks economy was in the making; not too hot, and not too cold, but just right. What's more, full employment had become a policy objective in Britain for the first time in more than 20 years under the watchful eye of the Chancellor, Gordon Brown. In other words, in time, everyone who wants a job should have the opportunity to get one.

It is a utopian picture, but one that belies an increasing sense of uncertainty among workers. Today's consumers enjoy lower prices, more choice and longer shop opening hours than their parents, but pay for it with job insecurity and 50-hour working weeks. The new high-tech, service economy has made the job for life redundant and our health and happiness are suffering.

❝A return to full employment was once a dream.
It is now not only a promise
but a possibility.❞

Gordon Brown, Chancellor of the Exchequer, November 1999

WHATEVER HAPPENED TO THE JOB FOR LIFE?

Research shows that job insecurity in late 1990s Britain was at its highest since the Second World War.[2] Professionals were particularly vulnerable. They went from being the most secure group of workers in 1986 to the most insecure in 1997.

Why the change of heart? Being a worker in today's world brings worries and pressures that simply weren't around 20 years ago. Here are a few, some of which you will no doubt identify with.

- **Technology.** New technology is a double-edged sword. It means 21st century man can drive a comfortable car, do his food shopping without getting off the sofa and flick between umpteen channels on the TV. But it also means job losses. The microchip has magnified fears of being usurped by machines, and relegated a growing number of workers to the low-wage, low-skill end of the job spectrum. It therefore goes some way to explaining the insecurity prevalent today.

  However, many argue the threat to jobs from new technology is simply temporary and that innovation actually stokes growth, which generates more jobs in time. As former US President John F. Kennedy said in 1962: 'We believe that if men have the talent to invent new machines that put men out of work, they have the talent to put those men back to work.' In any case, the argument goes, people will always be needed to invent, build and operate machines, and if you are technically challenged, there are jobs managing people or liaising with customers. The key is to teach people the relevant skills.

- **The hire-and-fire culture.** Flexibility is *the* buzzword in the labour market today. That means working *when* your employer wants you to – be it 20 or 80 hours a week – and doing *what* she wants you to, from photocopying to management. It also means being easier to fire and hire. In the 1980s, Margaret Thatcher clamped down on trade unions and shifted power back to the employer. Firms could sack workers more easily and mass redundancies became more commonplace. That legacy remains – severance pay for redundancies is considerably lower in the UK than in the rest of Europe – and it partly explains both the low unemployment in Britain and the high job insecurity. British workers are among the lowest paid, most flexible in the European Union, a factor which helps to attract billions of pounds of overseas investment into the country each year. That brings jobs, but it also brings the threat of job losses if competitiveness is allowed to slip. When German car maker BMW announced it was selling its Rover plant at Longbridge in the face of huge losses,

10,000 jobs were at stake at the factory alone, plus thousands more at local suppliers.

The Labour government's decision to adopt European Union job regulations in October 1998 reinstalled some worker rights, such as guaranteed paid leave and protection against working more than 48 hours a week, but many economists believe they did not go far enough. (On the other hand, many believe they went too far, strangling the labour market with red tape and eroding Britain's prized competitiveness.)

- **Cost cutting.** In today's globalised world, competition among leading firms is fiercer than ever. New technology and better communications mean businesses in Britain are fair game to rivals anywhere in the world. If shareholders think management are short changing them with foolhardy business decisions and fat workforces, they will sell to competitors quicker than you can say 'downsizing'. The end result is a relentless drive to cut costs and pare back workforces, all in the name of profit. When the Royal Bank of Scotland bought NatWest bank for £21 billion in February 2000, it was on the basis that 18,000 jobs would go over three years. This crusade to squeeze more and more short-term profit out of companies to satisfy shareholders is a major source of job insecurity. But workers could yet have the last laugh. Demotivated employees short on company loyalty will produce less and could pose problems for firms further down the line.

It is hardly surprising that job insecurity in Britain is endemic in the workplace, given the pressures of technology, the hire-and-fire culture and the persistent drive to cut costs. But is there anything that can be done about it? Should workers just sit back and take it or is there a way of bringing blood pressure and stress levels back under control?

> ❝In order that people may be happy in their work, these three things are needed:
> They must be fit for it;
> They must not do too much of it;
> And they must have a sense of success in it.❞
>
> John Ruskin (1819–1900)

CUTTING THE STRESS LEVELS

Reducing job insecurity among British workers while at the same time maintaining the country's competitive edge is a tall order. But there are things the government, businesses and you can do.

Government action

It sometimes seems that big businesses want it both ways in the globalised world – a highly skilled, loyal workforce that will put them ahead of their rivals, but one that can also be fired relatively easily if need be. We are becoming a nation of Kleenex workers – ones that can do the job in hand perfectly competently, but are disposable. That sounds pretty unfair on the average worker, but aren't we, as consumers, sometimes guilty of exactly the same hypocrisy? We want to buy cheap knickers in Marks & Spencer but we cried foul when the company awarded its underwear contract to a cut-price overseas firm, resulting in around 6,000 job losses at UK clothing factories.

The government could do a number of things to allay fears of job losses, although it must be careful not to make matters worse. Repealing the laws on redundancies could be counterproductive, as it would introduce inflexibility into the labour market when everyone else is doing the opposite. Hampering the introduction of new technology would be akin to shooting oneself in the foot, and restricting the scope for company takeovers would result in corporate inefficiency and a multitude of problems further down the road.

The best the public sector can do to relieve insecurity, therefore, is to educate and train. Making people more employable will not only make them more secure, it will also increase the productive capacity of the economy and promote stronger growth in the future. To that end, government-sponsored training courses and more money for higher education, particularly in new technology, will help to keep the workforce in jobs (a strong argument against university tuition fees).

Firm action

Businesses can also play their part in rebuilding job security through training. One idea, bandied around in the early 1990s, was for employers to provide workers with 'self-development facilities' (in other words training for another job), ensuring them a new job with a different company when the old one disappeared. Job security was dead. Long live employment security. However, with a few exceptions, the concept has been slow to develop. All those dreadful words so beloved of meeting-crazed managers such as 'multi-skilling' and 'portfolio jobs', have struggled to find their way out of the boardroom and on to the shop floor.

Another solution lies in improved corporate governance. In other words, if a company is run efficiently and is generating a healthy profit for shareholders, it is less likely to get taken over. That reduces the threat of downsizing and makes workers feel both valued and more secure.

HOW TO MAXIMISE YOUR CHANCES OF GETTING AND KEEPING A JOB IN THE 21ST CENTURY

"Work is the price you pay for money."

Anonymous

Finding and keeping a job in the 21st century can be a stressful experience. It's all very well knowing why, but it would be a whole lot more useful if economics could tell you what to do about it. As usual, the subject has its limitations. The best it can do is identify trends in the modern workplace and suggest ways of exploiting those trends to your advantage. For example, you may want to consider the following:

- **Multi-skilling.** In today's world of Kleenex careers and portfolio jobs, multi-skilling is the name of the game. Acquiring as many talents as you can and updating your skills where possible, whether through employer-run courses or government-sponsored training, will make you more employable. And the more employable you are, the less likely it is that you will be fired when cost-cutting bites.

- **Flexibility:** This is a little tougher. Firms like flexible workforces, but that could mean working unconventional hours without financial recognition in a variety of roles – the exact things that make life so difficult for the stressed-out employee in the first place. It could even entail moving home. For example, unemployment had ceased to be a problem in many parts of south-east England by the beginning of 2000, but it still blighted the lives of millions elsewhere in the country. Being mobile could therefore be key to securing a job, although as explained later, that is not always easy because of regional differences in house prices for one thing.

- **Get a job, any job.** The longer the unemployed stay outside the job market, the harder it is to find work, so getting any job at all could be a stepping stone to a better career.

■ **Pinpoint the skills needed.** Given the disappearance of a job for life, what skills should you be learning to maximise your chances of employment? Computers are the obvious choice. Personally I would rather know how to set up an Internet site and write a programme in Java than I would how to stock-take in a high street shop. I would also prefer to go into the service sector rather than manufacturing. It accounts for the bulk of output in Britain now (*see* p. 158 on Britain's industrial decline) and if anything looks set to get bigger.

POVERTY ON THE RISE, TOO

Job insecurity isn't the only headache for burnt-out, stressed-out Britons in the 21st century. Poverty is also a problem. The Joseph Rowntree Foundation, an independent, non-political body, estimates that in 1997/98 there were 14 million people in Britain living on less than half the national income (after accounting for housing costs), compared with five million 20 years ago. To put that in context, if you are a single adult, that means living on just £76 a week (after housing costs, in 2000); if you are a couple, it means paying the bills and buying food and clothes on £138; and if you are a family of five, you would have only £231 a week. It seems odd that there are so many poor people in Britain when the official statistics show a record number have jobs. (Poverty is measured in the UK in relative terms; it doesn't mean people are starving. It depends on the wealth of society as a whole, not the amount it costs to buy a certain amount of goods. It is therefore as much a measure of income inequality as actual poverty.) To address that anomaly, one needs to dig a little deeper into the unemployment figures.

❝Work is the curse of the drinking classes.❞

Oscar Wilde (1854–1900)

COUNTING THE UNEMPLOYED IN BRITAIN

Economists define an unemployed person as someone who does not have a job but would like one. Sounds simple enough, but in practice there are many ways of measuring the number of people out of work, some more flattering than others. The National Statistics office gathers two sets of unemployment data, one based on those claiming unemployment benefit, known as the claimant count measure, and one based on a monthly survey called the Labour Force Survey (LFS).

Unemployed, by international standards

The **Labour Force Survey** follows guidelines set by the **International Labour Organisation (ILO)**, an agency of the United Nations. Around 120,000 Britons are interviewed for each report, and the results are extrapolated for the whole population. The survey puts everyone aged 16 or over into one of three categories: in employment, ILO unemployed or economically inactive.

To be *in employment*, a person must work at least one hour's paid work a week, do unpaid work in a family business or be on a government training scheme.

To be *ILO unemployed*, a person must be out of work but want a job. They must have actively looked for work in the last four weeks and be available to start in the next fortnight. Anyone who doesn't fall into these two categories is classed as economically inactive, of which there are about seven million people of working age in Britain.

Adding those economically inactive back into the figures will clearly make a big difference. Labour economist Stephen Nickell estimates that if all those who don't have a job but want one are counted – including those who have not looked for work in the last four weeks – the ILO unemployment rate stretches from 6.1 per cent in 1998 to a far less impressive 12.8 per cent.[3]

One advantage of the LFS unemployment measure is that it is based on internationally agreed definitions, and so allows cross-country comparisons. Another is that it is not affected by changes in regulations governing unemployment benefit.

Unemployed and drawing benefit

…Unlike the **claimant count** measure, which is based on those collecting unemployment benefit. This is the most familiar jobless tally in Britain and the one that usually appears in newspapers. It is also one of the most inaccurate. Umpteen changes in those deemed eligible for unemployment benefit over the years mean it should be considered with a healthy dose of cynicism. Between 1981 and 1988, for example, almost half a million people disappeared from the unemployment tally because of spurious definition changes by the Conservative government. Some 50,000 people were wiped off in March 1986 alone when a two-week time lag in counting the unemployed was introduced. The figures were flattered, yet not one single job was created.

WHAT THE STATISTICS DON'T TELL YOU

66 Statistics can be made
to dance to any tune you want to play. 99

William Davis, author

Counting the unemployed is harder than you might imagine (*see* box, 'Counting the unemployed in Britain'). Many people do not fall into an obvious category, like the housewife who would like to have a job but isn't looking for one on a daily basis, or the partner of a working spouse who cannot claim unemployment benefit but would nevertheless like the opportunity to work.

Neither measure of unemployment used in Britain – the claimant count or the ILO measure – is comprehensive. The former has been manipulated so many times by anxious politicians that its accuracy must be questioned. The latter shunts millions into an economically inactive category, flattering the headline figure enormously. And neither gives an idea of exactly *who* is unemployed, or how much those who have a job get paid. Both these factors, discussed below, can help to explain the rise in relative poverty in Britain in the past 20 years.

■ **The spread of unemployment is extremely uneven.** The proportion of households in Britain where no adults have work quadrupled from 4 per cent in 1968 to more than 17 per cent in 1996.[4] To compound the problem, the share of households where every adult is in work has also risen, resulting in a growing polarisation between rich and poor families. For example, it seems ludicrous that so many people work longer and longer hours, putting in 70-hour weeks on a regular basis, yet so many others don't have a job at all. The problem is partly one of skills, or rather the lack of them, and partly that drive to cut costs.

■ **Some are more likely to be unemployed than others.** The headline unemployment figures you read about in newspapers fail to give a picture of *who* is unemployed. Although there is no one type of person queuing up for a dole cheque, some people are more likely than others to find themselves down at the benefit office. Men of all ages in Britain have higher unemployment rates than women, particularly those aged over 50 and those with no qualifications. Economic inactivity among men has also increased markedly in recent years. According to the Labour Force Survey, they now number more than two million among men of working age, up from around 400,000 20 years ago.

- **More part-time jobs.** It is not just the distribution of jobs that has contributed to the increase in poverty, the quality of those jobs is also important. There are more part-time positions in Britain now, predominantly in the service sector and predominantly filled by women. That is obviously good news for those entering the work-force but not so welcome if the jobs being lost are full-time positions previously held by the sole breadwinner in the family.

- **Low pay, no pay.** Britain has the dubious honour of having a high proportion of low-paid workers among its population. Those jobs most likely to pay a pittance, notwithstanding the introduction of the minimum wage, include hairdressers, waiting staff, cleaners, child carers and security guards (the box below has more on the minimum wage). So even if people do have jobs, they may still be struggling to break free from the poverty trap if those jobs do not provide a living wage.

THE LOWDOWN ON THE MINIMUM WAGE

Britain has had a **minimum wage** since April 1999, bringing it into line with most of the industrialised world, including the US, France, Japan and New Zealand. It started life at £3.60 an hour for adults and rose to £3.70 in October 2000. Those aged 18 to 21 initially received £3.00 an hour, rising to £3.20 in June 2000. It gave an estimated two million people a pay rise and helped to narrow the gap between men and women's wages (which is still scandalously high). It meant an almost 5 per cent pay increase for many chefs, cleaners, bar staff, hairdressers and care workers and, contrary to the gloomy predictions of the staunch free-marketeers, there hasn't yet been a knock-on effect up the pay scale as workers try to maintain differentials.

But before the government chalks it up as another New Labour triumph, a word of warning. Things happen slowly in £800 billion economies and it is far too soon to declare the policy a success. For a start, many unions believe the minimum wage is still too low. It is equivalent to 43 per cent of average earnings in Britain, higher than the 31 per cent in Japan but significantly lower than the 57 per cent in France and 54 per cent in Australia. They also decry the 'low wage apartheid' suffered by the young.

Then there is the question of how minimum wagers will survive a downturn. If the government cannot bring the British economy to heel and the bust that typically follows boom rears its ugly head again, all those workers who used to be extremely cheap but now command a minimum wage may find themselves out on their ear

▶

as profits are squeezed. Real-wage unemployment (discussed a bit later), which has so far failed to materialise, could yet arise, although it would be difficult to distinguish it from cyclical unemployment in a recession.

Then there are the fears of an inflation spiral. Again, as yet a false prophecy from the gloom merchants, it could still kick into action if the labour market gets much tighter and bargaining power shifts back to workers.

It is too early to judge the success or otherwise of the minimum wage with any assurance. But while the jury is out, the chances are they will return a favourable verdict. The problem for the government will be to keep it that way. As is often the case, New Labour finds itself between a rock and a hard place. There is a traditional commitment to help the low-paid and marginalised members of society, but on the other hand parties rarely win elections these days without the backing of big business, and they are the ones picking up the tab for this policy. At the end of the term in office they are also the ones who tend to prove most persuasive.

The Low Pay Commission, the body responsible for advising the government where to set the minimum wage, has a website at www.lowpay.gov.uk

GETTING PEOPLE BACK ON THE JOB

WHY TRY TO GET PEOPLE WORKING?

> ❝Unemployment is of vital importance,
> # particularly to the unemployed.❞

Edward Heath, 1980

Low pay and the rise of the part-time job both contribute to wide income inequalities in Britain. So does unemployment, hence getting more people into work will be a big step towards narrowing the gulf between the haves and the have-nots.

Unemployment is one of the biggest single sources of unhappiness in Britain. Figure 5.2 shows its rise and fall over the past century. In an average year, around 1.8 million people in the UK lose their jobs involuntarily. Some are more at risk than others, but when it comes to counting the cost of not being in work, no one is immune. As the

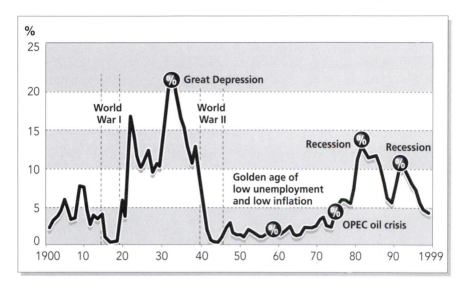

FIG. 5.2 100 years of UK unemployment

Source: ONS

French philosopher Voltaire observed in the 18th century: 'Work banishes those three great evils, boredom, vice and poverty.'

Without jobs, the unemployed will not only suffer emotionally and psychologically but also financially. Apart from losing income while out of a job, the average person re-entering work will earn almost 10 per cent less than in their previous employment. That is if they can find work. The longer someone is unemployed, the harder it is to break back into a job as skills and training suffer and the stigma of unemployment worsens.

Then there is the cost to the community of widespread job loss. There is evidence that crime and vandalism rise in areas of mass unemployment and if the breakdown of the labour market is severe enough, whole communities can die as shops close and areas become run down.

The effect is not just confined to the immediate area of the job losses. Anyone who pays taxes will be worse off as more is spent on unemployment benefit from a smaller pool of revenue (fewer people in jobs means less income tax and less spending which in turn means less revenue from indirect taxes such as VAT). Finally, there is the loss to the economy as a whole. Unemployment is a terrible waste. All those people drawing benefit could be making goods or providing services and helping the economy to grow. They could be recycling their income back into the country by demanding more goods and sparking more production.

Given that unemployment comes with such a high price tag, it makes sense to try to reduce it as far as is economically sensible. Before exploring how that may be done, it helps to consider why you may find yourself unemployed in the first place.

WHY MIGHT YOU LOSE YOUR JOB?

> 66 The rate of unemployment is 100 per cent
> if it is you that is unemployed. 99

Anonymous

People are unemployed for all sorts of reasons. They may be the victim of cost-cutting, they may struggle to get a job after having children, or they may have a skill that is no longer in wide demand. However, as far as economists are concerned, everyone without a job falls into one of five categories: cyclical, classical, seasonal, frictional or structural unemployment.

- **Cyclical or demand-deficient unemployment.** This is how Keynes characterised a large chunk of unemployment. He believed that many people did not have jobs because there was not enough demand in the economy to sustain full employment. The answer, therefore, was for the government to create that demand by spending more or lowering taxes.

  Cyclical unemployment is prevalent during recessions. For example, in the early 1990s, the collapse of the housing market in Britain and the sudden rise in interest rates meant people could not afford to buy as much as they used to. Demand fell, so firms didn't need as many workers and unemployment shot up from 5.4 per cent in the summer of 1990 to over 10 per cent three years later. Economists call this type of unemployment involuntary; there is little those out of work can do to get a job.

  If you were unemployed in Britain in the late 1990s, it was unlikely to be for cyclical reasons. The economy had chalked up seven and a half years of growth by then, suggesting that demand was relatively buoyant.

Therefore there must have been other reasons that 5.9 per cent of working-age Britons did not have a job (according to the ILO definition). These are considered below.

- **Classical unemployment.** As usual, pitched against the Keynesians are the classical economists, who look to the market for an explanation of unemployment. They believe that people price themselves out of a job by demanding high wages. If workers allowed wages to fall until it became profitable for firms to hire them, unemployment would decline. This tallies with the classical call to curb the power of trade unions, which they believe force earnings above the so-called market clearing level (in other words, that level where everyone has a job). Some economists thought the minimum wage would do the same thing when it was introduced in April 1999, but within the first 18 months, at least, those fears proved unfounded.

  Unlike demand-deficient unemployment, economists call classical unemployment voluntary. That sounds harsh, but it means that in theory, workers who don't have a job could do something about it – lower their wage demands.

- **Seasonal unemployment.** You may be seasonally unemployed if the demand for your labour varies with the time of the year. For example, if you are a Red Coat at Butlins, or if you pick apples for a living, work will doubtless tail off in winter. Seasonal unemployment is common in the tourist, agricultural and construction sectors.

- **Frictional unemployment.** No matter how healthy the economy is, there will always be a pool of workers who are in between jobs. If you are a school leaver, it will take time to find work. Similarly, if you are a mother returning to employment after having children, you may not find a job immediately. The frictional unemployed are an inevitable part of the labour market.

- **Structural unemployment.** If there are more workers than are needed in an individual sector of the economy, they are said to be structurally unemployed. Chances are, if you did not have a job at the beginning of the 21st century, this is the category you fell into. Some Rover workers became structurally unemployed when BMW sold its Longbridge plant to the Phoenix consortium, while unemployed coal miners, shipbuilders and textile workers are similarly categorised. This type of unemployment tends to be concentrated in regions and as such can also be blamed partly on a lack of labour mobility, the reluctance or inability of workers to move around the country in search of work. It also tends to be concentrated in the industrial sector, where workers have particular skills which are increasingly overlooked in the rush to become a service economy.

TYPES OF UNEMPLOYMENT

Cyclical or demand-deficient: when there is insufficient demand in the economy to sustain the required number of jobs. This type of unemployment typically occurs during recessions and is termed involuntary.

Classical: when wages are too high, pricing people out of a job. Can occur in boom conditions and is therefore considered voluntary. Some economists feared the minimum wage would push the lower paid into classical unemployment.

Seasonal: occurs when demand for labour varies with the time of the year, for example in the tourist or agricultural sectors.

Frictional: those jobless who are in between work and are likely to find employment soon. Sometimes known as search unemployment, this is also considered voluntary.

Structural: occurs when demand for labour is less than supply in a particular sector of the economy. Structural unemployment has bedevilled British industry as manufacturing has declined in importance. It is largely responsible for a perceived north/south divide in the UK.

WORKING OUT A SOLUTION TO UNEMPLOYMENT

> ❝Lord Finchley tried to mend the 'lectric light himself;
> it struck him dead and serve him right;
> it is the business of the wealthy man
> to give employment to the artisan.❞
>
> Hilaire Belloc (1870–1953), quoted in *The Times*, October 25,

Now you know why people are unemployed, consider what might be done about it. Suggested solutions to the problem differ, depending on who you talk to.

WHY CAN'T UNEMPLOYMENT BE WIPED OUT COMPLETELY?

A country's unemployment rate will never fall to zero. It is impossible for every single person to have a job at the same time because the flip side of low unemployment is high inflation. As more people find work, wages get pushed higher – if you are desperate for an extension and every single builder in your area, bar one, is booked up for months, that builder can charge you over the odds for the work. As that effect spreads to the whole economy and wages rise, prices rise too until the situation becomes unsustainable. Before unemployment has a chance to reach zero, the bust follows the boom as interest rates are jacked up and dole queues lengthen again. In other words, inflation acts as a restraint on economic policy. It puts a floor under unemployment.

That floor is known as the **natural rate of unemployment**. Simply put, this says that while there may be an inverse relationship between inflation and unemployment in the short run, in the longer run the jobless rate will always gravitate towards a certain level. So during a recession, for example, unemployment may be higher than its natural rate, but once recovery sets in, it will fall back again. Similarly, the government can reduce unemployment below its natural rate in the short run but in the long run the number of jobless will simply climb back up and inflation will be higher. At the natural rate, inflation will be stable; prices will rise by exactly the same amount each year. Therefore it is sometimes called the **non-accelerating inflation rate of unemployment**, shortened to **Nairu**.

The natural rate of unemployment is made up of frictional, seasonal, structural and classical unemployment. It's all the unemployment that is still there even if the economy is in full swing (hence excludes demand-deficient unemployment). The natural rate is also the **full employment** rate. That doesn't necessarily mean that everyone has a job, only that everyone who wants one does. For example, unemployment may still be 4 per cent, but if that is the lowest it can go without sparking inflation, it is the full employment rate.

Clearly, the lower that natural, full rate, the better. If more people can be employed without prices taking off, the economy will grow faster and everyone will benefit. It therefore stands to reason that government policy should be focused on reducing all the frictional, seasonal, structural and classical unemployment there is in the economy. They can do that using **supply-side policies**. As you may recall from Chapter 3, that involves improving the supply of workers, making them more employable or willing to work.

It is difficult to put a precise figure on Britain's long-run natural rate of unemployment. In this sense it is a misnomer. There is nothing natural or inevitable about it. It changes all the time, largely depending on supply-side factors. Britain's natural rate is thought to have been somewhere around 9 per cent for most of the 1990s but probably fell in the last three years or so of the decade to under 7 per cent, or maybe even less.

Before discussing the different approaches to reducing unemployment it is a good idea to have a quick read of the box, Why can't unemployment be wiped out completely? If that sounds too much like hard work, here is a summary. Unemployment cannot be eliminated entirely. While there is an inverse relationship between the number out of work and inflation in the short run, economists believe there is some *natural* level of unemployment to which the country will inevitably return in the longer run. It doesn't matter what is done to stimulate the jobs market in the interim. This natural level is the rate of unemployment at which inflation is stable, hence its alternative, rather more cumbersome name, the non-accelerating inflation rate of unemployment, or Nairu for short.

The natural level of unemployment is made up of classical, seasonal, structural and frictional unemployment, in other words, all those who may still find themselves out of a job even if the economy is going full tilt.

Policies to reduce unemployment come in two guises:

- stimulating demand, which will help to reduce demand-deficient unemployment in times of recession;
- reducing all the other types of unemployment – classical, seasonal, structural and frictional – that make up the natural level. That will allow more jobs with stable inflation – clearly a better option in the longer run.

DEMAND MANAGEMENT HAS ITS DAY

In the 1950s and 1960s governments put their faith in Keynesian demand management. The deep depression of the 1930s had made the public desperate for a policy to reduce unemployment and Keynes' theory that higher government spending would do the trick was gratefully adopted. As the great man himself said in 1930: 'If we just sit tight there will be still more than a million men unemployed six months or a year hence. That is why I feel that a radical policy of some kind is worth trying, even if there are risks about it.'

For a while those risks seemed minimal. Demand management worked a treat and unemployment in the period averaged only 1.7 per cent. But by the mid-1960s governments were increasingly frustrated at not being able to achieve both low unemployment and low inflation. Strict demand management was abandoned and a hybrid policy followed for the next 15 years or so, during which unemployment rose, inflation increased and the trade account suffered.

SUPPLY-SIDE POLICIES TRIUMPH – AGAIN

When Margaret Thatcher came to power in 1979 the British public were fed up with strikes and sky-high inflation and were in the mood for change again. Employment was abandoned as a government objective, in the belief it would tend to its natural level no matter what, and low inflation became the priority. The Chancellor at the time, Nigel Lawson, famously – and rather pompously – declared in 1984: 'It is the conquest of inflation and not the pursuit of growth and employment which is or should be the objective of macroeconomic policy.' In other words, don't bother using interest rates or government spending to reduce unemployment, use them solely to reduce inflation. The rest will then fall into place. A bold statement considering there were more than three million people without work in Britain at the time.

Meanwhile, the government used supply-side policies to try to make the labour market more efficient, in other words, to try to bring down the natural level of unemployment. These were discussed in Chapter 3, so will be mentioned only briefly here:

- **Improve information to those searching for work.** This will reduce frictional unemployment. In May 2000, there were 1.7 million Britons out of work (on the ILO measure), while vacancies at job centres numbered more than 350,000. Since they account for around a third of vacancies across the country (many firms advertise in the national press or rely on recruitment agencies), that means there were about one million unfilled jobs in Britain at the end of the millennium. The Labour government has launched a website to disseminate more job information with the aim of reducing frictional unemployment.

- **Cut unemployment benefits.** Classical economists recommend reducing or withdrawing benefits after a limited amount of time to give the jobless a greater incentive to find work quickly. This will also reduce frictional unemployment. Within three years of coming to office in 1979, the Conservative government cut the link between benefits and average earnings. Since then, they have only been indexed to the typically lower RPI inflation rate.

- **Government grants to lure investment and jobs.** Keynesians suggest pumping government money into areas of structural unemployment, to tempt businesses and therefore jobs back into the region. Classical economists however would rely on market forces. They say land and labour will be cheaper in run-down areas and so firms are more likely to set up there to save money.

■ **Education and training.** As usual, equipping workers with the right skills will reduce unemployment. If shipbuilders, for example, find that riveting work is in short supply in modern Britain, they might retrain in information technology. By making themselves employable again, they have increased the supply of skilled labour on hand, thus keeping wage demands lower and inflation down. To that end, the Labour government introduced its New Deal jobs programme shortly after winning the 1997 election (*see* box, 'New Labour's New Deal: Is it working?').

■ **Curb the power of trade unions.** Thatcher's assault on trade unions in the 1980s was motivated by a desire to make labour markets more flexible. Industrial relations had long been recognised as a problem in Britain. Over 4.3 million working days were lost to strikes in the 1978–79 'winter of discontent', which ensured there was little resistance from the public to union reform. A number of acts were passed that made it harder for unions to strike and made collective pay bargaining much more difficult. Without fear of reprisal, firms found it easier to hire and fire people and could also negotiate lower pay rises.

■ **Reduce income tax.** Classical economists believe that by reducing tax rates, people will have a greater incentive to work harder. *See* Chapter 3 for a more detailed explanation.

HAVE WE GOT A BRAND NEW ECONOMY?

THE CHANGING RELATIONSHIP BETWEEN INFLATION AND UNEMPLOYMENT

Amid all this talk of stress, job insecurity and poverty, there is one, potentially very bright, spot in the labour market that bodes well for the years ahead. That is the possibility that a greater proportion of the population could have jobs in the future, without igniting inflation. In other words, Britain's natural rate, or Nairu, could fall.

A look at the data suggests this may be happening already. Unemployment in Britain spent much of the summer of 1999 around a 20-year low, but instead of triggering a rise in inflation, the headline rate actually fell, at one stage to its lowest rate for 36 years. Apart from allowing the welcome possibility of more jobs in Britain, a lower Nairu also has implications for monetary policy. Whereas interest rates may have been raised in the past when unemployment fell too low in the belief that inflation was around the corner, a new set of rules could spell lower borrowing costs (and therefore mortgages) for everyone.

Explanations behind a possible fall in Britain's natural rate of unemployment are fourfold: globalisation, the Internet, the decline in trade union membership, and a phenomenon called the new paradigm.

- **Globalisation.** Greater international competition has forced wages lower in Britain than they might otherwise have been. (As usual, that has an ambiguous impact. On the one hand, it means workers are poorer, but on the other, it means more have jobs. Which is preferable?) Factors behind the fall in pay include cheaper imports (thanks to the strong pound and the ability of less developed countries such as Thailand and Korea to produce goods for less money), which mean workers in Britain cannot afford to demand high wages if they want to keep their jobs. Greater foreign investment in the UK has also played a role. Anecdotal evidence suggests that in many industries the threat of an overseas firm relocating a factory abroad has had a significant effect in keeping a lid on wages. Every time Nissan or Toyota threaten to close car assembly plants in the UK, for example, it is a subtle reminder of the need to stay competitive and be co-operative.

- **The Internet.** Price wars in retailing due to the spread of the Internet have also helped drive inflation lower without triggering a rise in unemployment (*see* Chapter 4 on e-tailing and the e-conomy). The greater price transparency offered by the web means canny shoppers can hunt for bargains more easily, keeping inflation down.

- **Decline in union membership.** One-off improvements in the efficiency of the labour market have allowed the Nairu to fall. A decline in union membership is the most obvious of these. Almost half of all workers belonged to unions in 1980 compared with around one in three now. Strike activity was much higher 20 years ago, too: in 1980 almost one million working days were lost due to strikes compared with just 30,000 in 1998. That decline in union influence, plus a gradual tightening of the benefits system, has helped keep a lid on wages and encouraged more people back into the workforce, so helping to lower the Nairu.

- **The new paradigm:** There has been great debate among economists that the actual relationship between inflation and unemployment has altered thanks to new technology. In other words, a given change in wages (which make up the majority of the cost of making something) no longer leads to as large a change in unemployment. This has been dubbed by some as the 'new paradigm' theory; you might have seen it in newspapers recently.

The new paradigm debate began in the United States, which has seen unemployment fall to 30-year lows of around 4 per cent, plus average economic growth of 3.6 per cent a year between 1992 and 1998 – all against a background of virtual price stability. One would usually associate long-term GDP growth of more than 2.5 per cent or unemployment of less than 6 per cent with growing pressure on prices. One explanation for this paradox would be a fall in the Nairu.

However, before we get carried away and predict a return to the golden post-war era of low unemployment and low inflation, a word of warning.

There are signs of growing skill shortages in Britain and recruitment difficulties, both of which could push wages and hence inflation higher in future. There is also evidence that firms need fewer and fewer unskilled workers, partly due to competition from abroad and partly thanks to new technology. Those workers will struggle to find jobs in the new cut-throat environment and unemployment could rise.

As ever in economics, the middle ground beckons. It seems highly probable that Britain's natural rate of unemployment has fallen in recent years, which is good news for everybody: more jobs and less inflation, hence, ultimately, lower mortgages. However, it seems just as probable that we will not see a return to the extraordinarily low jobless rates of the 1950s and 1960s. As far as economics has any rules, that period looks set to go down in history as the exception.

After years of having a dismal reputation in labour market circles, Britain is enjoying a purple patch in job creation that is fast becoming the envy of its Continental neighbours. The unemployment rate on the ILO measure in the UK in November 1999 was 5.9 per cent, significantly lower than the 9.0 per cent in Germany and 10.4 per cent in France (*see* Fig. 5.3). The painful labour market reforms started in the early 1980s appear to be paying dividends.

WORKING IN EUROPE

In fact, rather than losing promising young talent overseas, Britain seems to be on the receiving end for once. With nigh on four million unemployed in Germany and more than two-and-a-half million in the dole queues in France, more and more young Europeans are taking the brain train to the UK in search of work. In 1998, more people moved to Britain than in any other single year in history, surpassing the influx experienced through invasion in Europe and two world wars. Figures from the National Statistics office show that of the 402,000 new arrivals in 1998, 224,000 were job seekers from other EU countries.

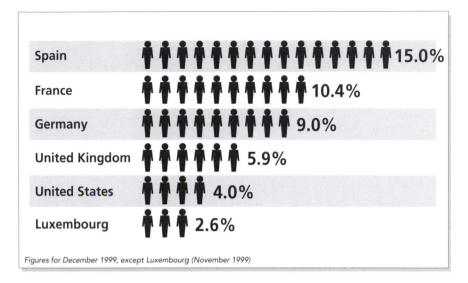

Spain	🧍🧍🧍🧍🧍🧍🧍🧍🧍🧍🧍🧍🧍🧍🧍	15.0%
France	🧍🧍🧍🧍🧍🧍🧍🧍🧍🧍	10.4%
Germany	🧍🧍🧍🧍🧍🧍🧍🧍🧍	9.0%
United Kingdom	🧍🧍🧍🧍🧍🧍	5.9%
United States	🧍🧍🧍🧍	4.0%
Luxembourg	🧍🧍🧍	2.6%

Figures for December 1999, except Luxembourg (November 1999)

FIG. 5.3 International ILO unemployment rates, 1999   Source: ONS

NEW LABOUR'S NEW DEAL: IS IT WORKING?

On the way to winning the general election in 1979, the Conservatives splashed posters all over Britain proclaiming 'Labour isn't working'. Twenty years later it was a completely different story. A record 27.5 million people had jobs at the end of the 20th century after two-and-a-half years of Labour rule and full employment was back on the political agenda for the first time since the 1970s. The party that was created by the workers was finally living up to expectations.

But dig a little deeper and Britons look less industrious. There may have been an historically low 1.7 million unemployed (on the Labour Force Survey measure) at the end of 1999, but there were also another five million people of working age who simply did not want a job. Add in the fact that many firms were crying out for staff – there were around one million job vacancies across the country, the most for almost 30 years – and something had clearly gone wrong. The jobs were there, the problem for the government was persuading people to take them.

The answer, according to New Labour, lay in the New Deal, a £5 billion initiative to wean Britons off welfare and into work. Funded by a windfall tax levied on privatised utilities, the programme is designed to equip the unemployed with useful skills, then make it extremely difficult for them to refuse jobs. Goodbye welfare, hello 'workfare'.

It was initially aimed at 18–24-year-olds who have been unemployed for at least six months. However, since its nationwide launch in April 1998, it has been extended to cover others alienated by an inability to find work: the long-term unemployed over the age of 25, lone parents, the disabled and those over 50.

▶

The young unemployed – still the flagship part of the programme on which its success or failure rests – go through a four-month 'gateway' period during which they have interviews with personal advisers and receive help with job chasing. If they still have not found work at the end of this period they face four choices: full-time education and training, a job subsidised by the government, work on an environmental taskforce, or a voluntary job. Returning to benefit is *not* an option.

Has it lived up to its ambitious promises? The short answer is that it is too early to say. The longer answer – and economists can always give a long answer – is that the initial figures look promising, but not overwhelmingly so.

An independent study commissioned by the government found that by the end of 1999 around 140,000 young people had found work through the programme, more than half of the government's target of 250,000. But most of those would have found a job anyway thanks to a growing economy and a falling jobless rate in general. The study concluded that just 30,000 New Dealers would still be on the dole if the government had not rescued them – not quite so impressive. So next time you hear a politician trumpeting the marvels of 'welfare to work', you should take it with a pinch of salt.

In general, however, the report was upbeat. It concluded the New Deal would be close to self-financing as the extra activity generated led to higher government revenue (more workers mean more income tax and less social security spending, as well as more VAT and excise duty etc. as spending increases). It predicted that around half a million people could benefit from the New Deal over four years, half of whom should move into jobs – exactly the number the government initially set out to help.

However, there are plenty of detractors of the New Deal who say the scheme is a colossal waste of money and no more than a cheap trick to massage unemployment figures lower. They say it does not actually increase the supply of skilled labour – only a nationwide training programme would do that – it simply recycles workers.

But there is also a deeper worry that goes beyond political point scoring. The New Deal takes away the right to say no. Refuse to take part and your benefits will be stopped. That does not concern some, who argue that everyone who is capable of working has a responsibility to do so whether they like it or not. Others warn it is the start of a slippery slope towards US-style workfare where draconian rules mean women can have their children taken into care if they lose their workfare job. In San Francisco, workfare street-sweepers get one-third union rates and have their benefits docked for 30 days if they are 10 minutes late for their 6.30am shift.

For all the speculation, the ultimate success of the New Deal will depend on making the jobless more employable, thus keeping wage pressures down. If the government can do that, and so reduce the Nairu, it will be on its way to finding work for everyone.

(The government has a New Deal website at www.newdeal.gov.uk that contains more detailed information on the schemes on offer.)

BRITAIN: A TALE OF TWO NATIONS

ARE YOU BETTER OFF IF YOU LIVE IN THE SOUTH?

About 150 years ago Victorian novelist Elizabeth Gaskell popularised one of the most enduring stereotypes in British history when she wrote of the stark contrast between the dark, satanic mills of the industrial north and the comforts of country life in the affluent south. The social portrait in her 1855 novel *North and South* has been a thorn in politicians' sides ever since.

Prime Minister Tony Blair insists the cliché is beginning to wear thin; that there are pockets of wealth and poverty all over the country regardless of their proximity to Watford. Given Labour's ambition to be the 'one-nation' party, a cynical person might put that claim down to wishful thinking, so a good look at the facts is called for. The National Statistics office provides data on every region in Britain and some of the figures make for uncomfortable reading – if you are an unskilled manual worker from Tyneside you may want to look away now.

THE BARE FACTS

Wealth across Britain varies hugely. Statisticians measure it using gross domestic product per head, in other words, the amount of output produced per person. For example, if you lived in the South-East in 1998, you were about 17 per cent more wealthy than the average Briton, while Londoners enjoyed a generous 30 per cent more wealth than others.[5] North Easterners were less fortunate: GDP per head there was only 79 per cent of the British average, while that for residents of Yorkshire and the Humber was 88 per cent (*see* Fig. 5.4).

Almost every other statistic you look at tells a similar story. The north of the country suffers more crime, higher unemployment and inferior earnings. But as usual, things aren't that simple, this time for two reasons – house prices, and an uneven spread of wealth within both regions.

While Londoners may earn more than, say, Liverpudlians, the cost of living in the capital is also much higher. A teacher working in Islington, north London, for example, had to fork out around £150,000 for a modest one-bedroom flat in the area in 1999, enough to buy a three-bedroom family home in St Helen's. The education authority's London weighting cannot compensate for such a vast gulf in house prices.

Secondly, Tony Blair's claim that parts of the north are just as wealthy, if not more so than the south, has some truth. The North-West as a whole is much poorer than the 'cappuccino' economy of the South-East, yet

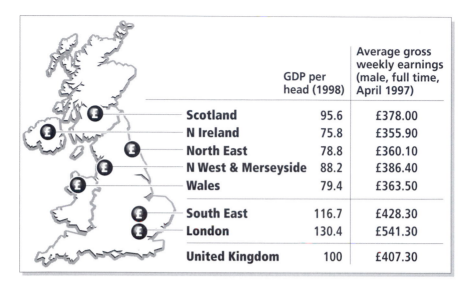

	GDP per head (1998)	Average gross weekly earnings (male, full time, April 1997)
Scotland	95.6	£378.00
N Ireland	75.8	£355.90
North East	78.8	£360.10
N West & Merseyside	88.2	£386.40
Wales	79.4	£363.50
South East	116.7	£428.30
London	130.4	£541.30
United Kingdom	100	£407.30

FIG. 5.4 Life in the North and South of Britain   Source: Government Statistical Service

Cheshire is in many ways better off than Kent. Leeds is positively brimming with lawyers, while parts of London have the largest tracts of unemployment and deprivation of anywhere in the country. As Nicholas Higgins, the humble toiler in a northern factory in Gaskell's novel, observed: 'North an' South have each getten their own troubles.'

WHY SHOULD IT BE GRIM 'OOP NORTH?

The bottom line, however, is that in general terms, the north is still poorer than the south. The reason comes down simply to jobs – more specifically, the decline of Britain's manufacturing industry, traditionally located in the north of the country.

The demise of British industry

In the immediate aftermath of the Industrial Revolution in 1850, Britain was the undisputed world leader in manufacturing. Thanks to technological innovations in textiles, iron-making and the steam engine, the UK accounted for around 40 per cent of world trade in manufactures by the 1870s. Unfortunately that lead did not last long. The old rival France was slipping behind, but there were new threats from Germany and the United States, where a second industrial revolution based on electricity, organic chemistry and the combustion engine was to cost Britain its industrial pride (*see* Fig. 5.5).

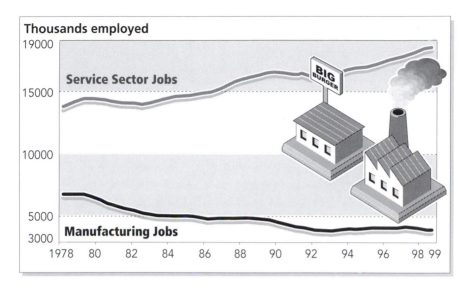

FIG. 5.5 The decline of smokestack Britain: manufacturing vs service sector jobs

Source: Reuters/EcoWin

Many factors have been blamed for the decline of smokestack Britain:

- The country was committed to out-dated methods as a hang-over from the first Industrial Revolution.
- Britain's Second World War victory ironically robbed it of the incentive (and financial help) to rebuild industry from scratch.
- Closed overseas markets gave foreign firms the sanctuary to form powerful positions in the new industrial world.
- There has been a lack of adequate technical education, particularly compared with Germany.
- Finance for industry was often harder to come by in Britain compared with Germany and the US.
- Britain's late arrival in Europe may be partly to blame for its loss of industrial prowess.
- Government reluctance to inject more competition into industry to encourage greater efficiency could also have played a part.
- The dominance of trade unions for many years may have deterred some firms from investing in Britain.

A catalogue of woes

The end result has been a shocking decline in industrial competence. By 1973 Britain's share of world exports of manufactures had shrunk to around 9 per cent from almost 24 per cent in 1929. Meanwhile, Germany and Japan were racing ahead: the former's share had grown to around 22 per cent from just over 15 per cent and the latter's to 13 per cent from 4 per cent.

Britain has fared little better since. It took industry 10 years to recover from the recession of the early 1980s. The nation's car industry is now all but foreign owned and its textile output has contracted by almost half since 1979. Employment in manufacturing overall has withered from 27 per cent of the workforce when Margaret Thatcher came to power in 1979 to 19 per cent today, with most of those jobs disappearing from the north of the country. Former coal miners and shipbuilders have had to turn their hands to answering phones in one of Britain's mushrooming call centres while former engineers work in B&Q as they wait for their pensions to mature.

Monetary policy exacerbates the problem

It is not just the collapse of manufacturing that has perpetuated the split; monetary policy has also contributed. Interest rates tend to be set for the whole economy, and manufacturing is only around 20 per cent of that nowadays – the service sector accounts for more than 70 per cent. With manufacturing concentrated away from London, many businesses in the north feel policy is at best unhelpful, at worst damaging. When the Bank of England's Monetary Policy Committee began raising interest rates in September 1999, Britain's manufacturing sector was still firmly in the doldrums. Higher borrowing costs plus the higher pound hit industry both at home and in terms of demand for exports, a double whammy it struggled to survive.

House prices widen the divide

The well-documented chasm between house prices in the north and south of the country must also carry some of the blame for preserving the divide. Infamous tales of estate agents offering 'buy two get one free' house deals in Greater Manchester in 1999 coincided with a frenzy of house buying in London that propelled prices up by more than 25 per cent in some areas. With homes in the capital going for more than double those in, for example, Tyne and Wear, it is little wonder unemployed Geordies were not getting on their bikes and jumping on the 'Tebbit Express' south in search of work. (Conservative politician Norman Tebbit once famously said: 'I grew up in the 1930s with our unemployed father. He did not riot, he got on his bike and looked for work.') Economists call this inability to move in search of work *labour immobility* or *inflexibility* and as long as it persists, there will always be some kind of regional segregation in Britain.

BRIDGING THE NORTH/SOUTH GAP

Imagine you had to come up with a policy that banished the north/south divide in Britain once and for all. If your solution would be to spend billions of pounds in grants and tax incentives to encourage firms like BT or IBM to relocate in the north, then you are probably instinctively Keynesian. If you think that would be an irresponsible waste of taxpayers' money, you are more likely to be a classical economist.

Over the years, politicians have tended to hedge their bets, in typical fashion, and use bits of both philosophies. Since manufacturing industry began to decline, arguably in the 1920s, until the early 1980s the British government handed out a variety of incentives to firms to locate in high unemployment areas. There have been grants for new investments, tax relief schemes, subsidies on employment, spending on infrastructure such as motorways and factories, and strict rules on start-ups in low unemployment areas.

But this is an expensive strategy. Between 1972 and 1983 it cost the government around £35,000 to create every extra job in the assisted regions – and there were half a million created. The policy was abandoned by 1984 and the Conservative government introduced more selective regional help. A die-hard classical economist would have stopped regional assistance altogether and relied solely on market forces. High unemployment areas, goes the argument, have cheaper land and labour which will attract inward investment regardless of the extra incentives on offer. Both Keynesian and classical economists would promote training, the former funded by the government, the latter by private firms.

Finally, to shore up your regional policy, you could make housing in high employment areas more affordable. By building, say, one million more new homes in the South-East, for example, you may persuade an unemployed Yorkshireman to leave the Dales and move to Kent. Going down this road however could cause you all sorts of problems with the Nimby (not in my backyard) contingent of middle England. A concerned voter from Maidstone may be all in favour of reducing unemployment in Doncaster in theory, but if it entails 50,000 new estate houses going up around the corner he may not be so keen on the idea.

Greater labour mobility is one of the secrets behind the United States' success in reducing regional unemployment differences. Affordable housing and Americans' willingness to move inter state in search of work means different jobless rates across the country rapidly smooth out. Britons, on the other hand, are significantly less adventurous.

According to one estimate, 60 per cent of British adults live within five miles of where they were born, a higher proportion than in the 19th century. Gaskell would have been astonished.

TRADE UNIONS, PAST, PRESENT AND FUTURE

FIGHTING BACK AFTER THE THATCHER YEARS

British trade unionists are in danger of becoming a dying breed. After a history spanning more than 175 years they are fighting for survival in the modern workplace where the growing number of part-time, temporary and service sector workers provide lean pickings for recruiters. Membership has plunged by 40 per cent in the past 20 years from 13 million in the 1970s to around seven million today, with young people the most reluctant to sign up: a typical trade unionist is 46, 12 years older than the average British worker.

The choice is therefore clear: unions must modernise or die. It won't be easy, however. As Ernest Bevin, former head of the Transport and General Workers union and later minister for labour, remarked in 1927: 'The most conservative man in this world is the British trade unionist when you want to change him.'

WORKER POWER TO MAKE A COMEBACK?

There are tentative signs that unions are poised to enjoy something of a renaissance. Growing job insecurity, worker distrust of management and a recognition by unions that the war against capital was self-defeating and futile have revived interest in the movement. The haemorrhaging of members appears to have been stemmed and unions have recognised the need to go on an aggressive recruitment drive. Many have merged to create more powerful organisations and have pledged to work in partnership not conflict, with business. While their role in the darkest days of the 1970s was largely seen as negative by the public (the 1978–79 'winter of discontent' was a public relations disaster), they now have a much more constructive part to play in the economy. They negotiate training for workers, mediate in disputes and ensure health and safety standards are upheld. In a sense they are going back to their roots: one of their main functions more than 100 years ago was to provide workers with sickness insurance. These days it is the promise of another type of insurance – legal back-up in a workplace dispute – that is one of the main reasons for signing up.

Finally, a rising backlash against globalisation could provide trade unions with their greatest recruitment opportunity in years. Growing worker discontent at the huge profits and sheer power of the world's multinationals could translate into potent union firepower in time. Some even speculate that this trend towards mega companies and their mega bucks could shake the foundations of capitalism, just as Karl Marx predicted in the 19th century. Back then, Marx argued that as workers were exploited, they would feel increasingly alienated by their rich employers and would end up banding together and forcing change. His memorable call for the 'workers of the world to unite' could yet be heeded.

THE RISE AND FALL OF BRITISH TRADE UNIONS

The unions' proud history gives some idea of why change is difficult, but also why they have no choice. They owe much of their existence to Britain's industrial heritage and its deterioration has deprived them of a fertile source of members.

Unions were legalised in 1824 with the repeal of the Combination Act. This law had prohibited workers from banding together to influence wages, which were, in theory, fixed by the state. Those who joined in a strike during this time could have been imprisoned for three months.

Once unions were freed from the stigma of criminality they grew in both influence and number. Their early years were spent protesting against the appalling conditions in the factories of industrialising Britain, where women and children were pushed into tubs of cold water to keep them awake during their interminable hours of labour. However, government distrust of workers remained. In 1834 the union movement was dealt a severe blow when six farm labourers from the Dorset village of Tolpuddle were transported to Australia for trying to organise a union. They had been prosecuted under an old law that prohibited the administering of unlawful oaths, which had featured in the union's initiation ceremony.

The movement grew in stature over the remainder of the century and in 1868 the Trades Union Congress (TUC), the umbrella group for unions in Britain, had its first meeting in Manchester. Six years later the first trade unionist was elected to parliament, but he was heavily reliant on the organisational support of the Liberal Party. So in 1900, the TUC and a number of socialist societies formed the Labour Representation Committee, which, six years later, was converted into the Labour Party.

Between 1906 and 1914 membership almost doubled and relations between workers and employers became more turbulent. Things were particularly fractious between mine workers and owners, and when the latter sought to impose a wage cut in

1926, the result was the first and only general strike in British history. It collapsed after just nine days.

The turning point in modern-day industrial relations came in the 1980s with Margaret Thatcher's merciless attack on union power. Strikes were crippling British industry and some say the former prime minister's greatest achievement was bringing the unions to heel. According to the ILO, Britain lost almost 540 working days for every 1,000 employees between 1971 and 1975 thanks to strikes. That compared with 48 in Germany and 187 in France (although Italy managed to outdo the Brits with a stupendous 1,064).

Among other things, the Conservative government passed laws banning secondary picketing, enforced secret ballots for strike action and withdrew social security benefits from the dependents of striking workers. When the miners walked out in protest at pit closures in 1984, Thatcher was ready, and their crushing defeat heralded the end of an era of union militancy.

On top of the legislative changes and Britain's industrial decline, unions have been the victim of a shift in psychology. The idea of collective action has been replaced by individualism which, along with the perception that unions are in danger of being a spent force, has deterred people from signing up. The power of unions – their ability to win better pay deals for members and improve working hours and conditions – depends on a number of factors. Their membership, their perceived militancy and the demand for the service their workers provide are all key (if union members are highly skilled, firms are more likely to acquiesce to pay demands because of the cost of retraining replacements).

This decline in trade union power has played a crucial role in fostering the low-unemployment, low-inflation environment in Britain at the end of the 20th century, but it has also contributed to growing wage inequality. Without the force behind them, low-paid workers have suffered, although it remains to be seen whether the minimum wage can help redress the balance.

IF YOU REMEMBER SEVEN THINGS FROM THIS CHAPTER …

- New technology, a hire-and-fire culture and greater international competition has led to a significant increase in job insecurity in Britain.
- Employees are being encouraged to learn many different skills in order to maximise their chances of staying in work. Job security has been replaced by employment security.
- Inflation puts a floor under unemployment, preventing it from declining to zero.

- The rate of unemployment at which inflation is stable is called the natural rate, or the Nairu, and it is made up of classical, seasonal, structural and frictional unemployment.

- The best way of reducing unemployment is to use supply-side policies to coax more people back into the workforce, thereby reducing the natural rate.

- When the government talks about reaching full employment, it does not mean that everyone will have a job, but that everyone who wants to work will have the opportunity to do so.

- There is ample evidence to suggest that Britain's north/south divide is alive and well, partly thanks to the spread of unemployment across the country. House prices exacerbate the gap.

ENDNOTES

1 From *Voices Within and Without, Responses to Long-term Unemployment in Germany, Sweden and Britain*, by Jochen Clasen, Arthur Gould, Jill Vincent, Bristol: Policy Press, 1998.

2 According to research by the University of Cambridge, August 1999.

3 In *The State of Working Britain*, edited by Paul Gregg and Jonathan Wadsworth, Manchester University Press, 1999.

4 The Family Expenditure Survey, 1968–96.

5 Based on National Statistics figures from 1998.

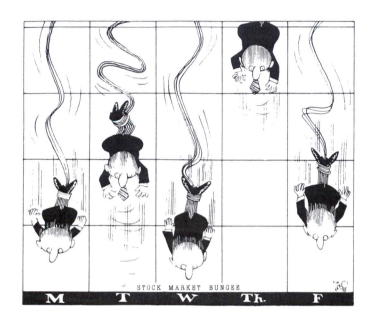

CHAPTER 6

FINANCIAL MARKETS

Where economics meets
your money

The market,

whether stock,

bond or super,

is a barometer of civilisation.

Jason Alexander, *Philosophy for Investors*

INTRODUCTION

To the uninitiated the words 'financial markets' have an almost mythical quality. They conjure up a mysterious world where people in suits make vast sums of money by watching their computer screens. Words like p/e ratio, yield and market capitalisation hold the key to untold riches which can be won and lost in a matter of hours.

But like everything else in this business, things are not as complicated as they seem. Financial markets suffer from a classic case of jargonitis. Cure them of that and they are simplicity itself.

For starters, what do newspapers really mean when they talk of 'financial markets'? They are usually referring to the stock market, where companies' shares are traded, the bond market, where government and corporate debt is traded, or both. Markets are where anyone from an Internet start-up firm to the United States' government can raise money.

They are where economics comes to life.

Thinking in terms of the circular flow of income mentioned in Chapter 2, markets act as a kind of bridge between savers and investors, providing an easy route for money to flow from the former to the latter, and back again. Without them, that exchange of money would probably dry up.

To see why, imagine you have £10,000 to invest. You may like the idea of taking a stake in, say, a web design firm. But if there is no market that will allow you to trade that stake when you need your money back, you will probably be reluctant to part with your cash. Few people like the idea of committing their savings indefinitely, and a market is there to make sure they don't have to.

This chapter unmasks financial markets for the simple creatures they are.

- **It discusses what bonds are**. Not the James, premium or Brooke variety, but loans which allow governments and companies to borrow huge sums of money from the public. If you pay into a pension, have an endowment mortgage or put money into a unit or investment trust, you probably already own British government bonds. In other words, the government has borrowed *your* money to help build the country's schools and hospitals;

- **It looks at the different varieties of bonds on the market**. There is a dazzling array of bonds on the market, each with slightly different characteristics. This chapter takes you through the main ones and explains who buys them, why their yields are important and what determines their price;

- **It considers why bond prices move**. Why do I care? I hear you ask. Because the state of the bond market could affect how well you live in retirement or when you can pay off your mortgage. Annuities in Britain – annual income from pensions – fell in the late 1990s partly because of the bond market. This chapter explains why and suggests ways you can make sure your retirement is more luxury cruise than lawn bowls;

- **It considers why share prices move**. When it comes to making headlines, bonds have got nothing on the other main vehicle for raising money – shares. A wave of lucrative privatisations in the 1980s spawned a generation of capitalists who saw the stock market as their ticket to ride. You could double your money just by filling out an application form on the back of a British Telecom prospectus. With their intoxicating mix of greed and fear, equity markets became synonymous with easy money and fast lifestyles. This chapter won't tell you how to make your million on the stock market, but it will tell you what shares are, where they are traded and what affects their price;

■ **It offers some pointers on how to spot a stock market bubble;**

■ **It explains what derivatives are**. This chapter ends with a quick look at the more complicated financial instruments such as derivatives. It explains what they are, using futures and options as examples, and winds up with the incredible story of the infamous trader Nick Leeson and his role in bringing down Britain's oldest bank, Barings.

Economics, with its theories on inflation and growth and its forecasts for interest rates and public debt, is a central theme throughout the chapter. It is the bedrock of all markets.

THE NAME'S BOND, GOVERNMENT BOND

'The only part of the so-called national wealth that actually enters into the

collective possessions of modern peoples is their National Debt.'

Karl Marx (1818–1883)

WHAT IS A BOND?

When the government wants to borrow money to pay for, say, a new hospital, it can't just go to Barclays or Lloyds like the rest of us and ask for a loan. It needs billions of pounds, and the only way it is going to get its hands on that sort of money is by issuing a **bond**.

A bond is a form of loan that usually carries a fixed rate of interest and lasts for a specified period of time (hence its alternative name, a fixed-income security). Take a simple example. Say the government needed to borrow £5 billion to build a new motorway. It could issue 50 million bonds, each with a face value of £100 so that no one lender has to fork out the total amount needed.

In exchange for the money, the government promises to pay lenders 10 per cent interest every year – in other words, £10 per £100 bond – for 20 years. When that 20 years is up, it will repay the original £5 billion borrowed. Once bonds have been issued they can be traded in the second-hand, or secondary, market, where their price will vary according to a number of factors (I'll go into them a bit later).

The British government has never failed to make an interest payment on a bond, or to repay the principal borrowed. Its debt is as good as gold, hence the nickname for British government bonds is gilts, short for **gilt-edged securities**.

Governments aren't the only ones who issue bonds. Companies and banks also use them to raise money. However, unlike the public sector, a firm cannot simply print money or increase taxes if it is having trouble paying back its debt, hence corporate bonds usually carry a higher rate of interest to reflect the fact that they are riskier than their government counterparts.

Bonds are a form of loan. They usually carry a fixed amount of interest and must be repaid after a fixed period of time.

BRITAIN'S NATIONAL DEBT

At the end of March 1999, the British government owed almost £300 billion in the form of outstanding gilts. The country's National Debt, the total amount it owed including things like national savings and foreign currency debt, totalled almost £420 billion in 1998, about 50 per cent of GDP. That sounds like an awful lot of money, but when you compare it with countries like Japan, whose debts are approaching a staggering 125 per cent of GDP, it doesn't look quite so bad.

What is worrying, however, is the amount it costs the government to service its debt. In 2000/2001, the government expected to spend £28 billion of public money in interest on its loans, its fourth largest single expenditure after social security, health and education.

The British government first started borrowing money in 1694 when it took out a £1.2 million loan to help finance a war against France. The financiers who lent the money were given a charter to form a bank as a result, which later became the Bank of England.

Other loans followed and by 1697, when the war with France ended, the National Debt had risen to £15 million. It leapt again after the First World War to £7.5 billion and again after the Second World War, to £21 billion, an enormous 252 per cent of GDP. In other words, government debt was two-and-a-half times the size of the British economy.

Periodic bouts of high inflation in the 1970s and 1980s pushed the nominal debt even higher (*see* Fig. 6.1), although economic growth during that time ensured it never again reached such lofty levels against GDP.

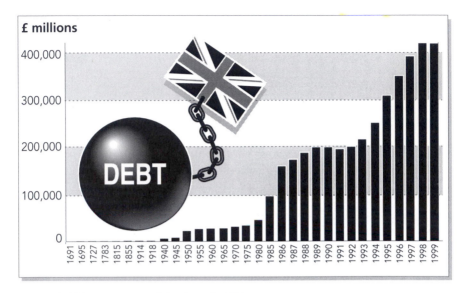

FIG. 6.1 British government debt since the 17th century   Source: Debt Management Service

WHEN INTEREST RATES RISE, BOND PRICES FALL...

> The yield on a bond is the amount of interest it pays relative to its market price. Yields fall as bond prices rise and vice versa.

The golden rule of bonds is that when interest rates in the economy rise, bond prices fall and when interest rates fall, bond prices rise. That is about all you need to know to understand the market.

For example, say interest rates in Britain fell to 9 per cent from 11 per cent. Suddenly the return on that 10 per cent motorway bond looks pretty attractive, so investors will start buying it and its price will rise. If you keep a close eye on the economy and can predict when rates are going to fall, you could make a tidy sum buying bonds before everyone else cottons on and drives up their prices.

The same rule applies to the yield of a bond (the amount of interest it pays relative to its market price). As the price of a bond rises, its yield will fall and vice versa. Why? It's just maths.

As mentioned earlier, bonds usually pay a fixed rate of interest (known as a coupon), which is calculated on face value. So if you bought £100 worth of that 10 per cent motorway bond, you would receive £10 a year in interest, regardless of what happened to the price of the bond in the secondary market. The yield, on the other hand, would change.

Imagine the bond is now worth £110 (there may be a dearth of supply which forces up prices. More on that later). Your £10 interest now constitutes just 9.1 per cent of the bond's value. The yield has gone down as the price has gone up.

YIELD CURVES AND A BRITISH ANOMALY

Bonds are issued for different periods of time, depending on when the borrower wants to repay the loan. They are classed as short-dated if they have seven years left to run, medium-dated if there are between seven and 15 years to go until maturity, and long-dated if there is anything over 15 years left.

Maturity is one of a number of factors that can affect a bond's interest rate, or coupon. A long bond will generally carry a higher coupon to compensate for uncertainty. A 30-year bond may see all of its value wiped out by inflation by the time the principal has to be repaid, hence it must offer a higher return to investors to persuade them to take on that extra risk. In that sense, a long bond may be a proxy for *inflation expectations*. If investors think inflation will remain low for some time, they will be willing to accept a lower interest rate on a 30-year bond.

Different coupons plus different prices for bonds mean yields vary markedly. Again, applying the inflation expectations rule, logic would say 30-year bonds yield more than five-year ones. If you plotted a graph of bond yields, starting with the shortest maturity and ending with the longest, you would expect it to be upward sloping (*see* Fig. 6.2).

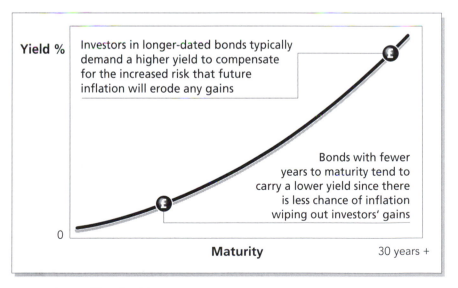

FIG. 6.2 A typical bond yield curve

As usual, there are plenty of exceptions to this rule. Take Britain. Towards the end of the 1990s, gilt yields at the shorter end rose above those at the longer end. Usually this would signal the onset of recession – interest rates are high to fight inflation, paving the way for a sharp downturn in growth in future.

However, the economy was reasonably healthy, suggesting there had to be another explanation. It could have been that investors believed the Bank of England would keep underlying RPIX inflation at 2.5 per cent in future. Inflation expectations had been scaled down, reducing the yield on long bonds. In addition, fewer long bonds were being issued because healthy government finances had reduced the need to borrow money. The law of demand and supply says that will drive up the price of longs, hence their yield will fall.

NAVIGATING THE BOND MINEFIELD

There are numerous types of bonds that your pension fund or unit trust may invest in. Here are the main ones, classified by issuer, characteristic and maturity.

WHO ISSUES BONDS?

- *Governments*: government bonds with publicly quoted prices date at least as far back as long-term Venetian loans, called *prestiti*, in the 13th century. These days, most governments issue bonds to raise finance. Those in developed economies such as the US, Japan and Europe are the most creditworthy and can therefore raise money at the cheapest rates.
- *Companies*: companies sometimes raise money in bond markets instead of issuing shares. These are known as corporate bonds and their prices and interest rates are determined by how creditworthy the issuing company is. So-called **rating agencies** like Moody's and Standard & Poor's assess how likely the borrower is to default on its debt and assigns it a mark accordingly. In the case of the latter, a AAA rating is the highest accolade, suggesting the company's debt is only slightly more risky than US Treasuries. Unilever's bonds fall into this category, as do Nestlé's, the name behind Milky Way and Smarties. A CCC denotes considerable uncertainty about the ability to repay a loan, hence bonds with this rating are also called junk bonds. They represent high risk but deliver a high return. The lower the rating, the more expensive it will be for a firm to borrow money. There are almost $10,000 billion of non-government bonds on the market.

- *Supranationals*: these are agencies which raise money in the world's capital markets to fund investment in developing countries. Examples include the World Bank and the Asian Development Bank. They are usually considered extremely creditworthy and command relatively low coupons.
- *Banks*: banks may issue bonds for the same reason as companies: because it can be a cheaper way of raising finance than issuing shares. They may lend out the proceeds as mortgages or other loans, charging a higher rate of interest than they are paying on the bonds.
- *Eurobonds*: when firms issue bonds in foreign currencies, they issue eurobonds. These fall outside the jurisdiction of any one country. Contrary to what their name suggests, these are often denominated in dollars. Major eurobond issuers are large international corporations and governments.

MAJOR TYPES OF BONDS

- *Conventional bonds*: these pay a fixed coupon or rate of interest and are repayable on a fixed date. About three-quarters of gilts fit into this category and most corporate bonds.
- *Index-linked*: bonds whose interest and principal payments are adjusted for changes in the RPI index, making them inflation-proof. These became popular in Britain after the high inflation of the 1970s.
- *Undated bonds*: these comprise about 1 per cent of outstanding gilts and, as their name suggests, have no redemption date, so it is up to the government when to pay them back. Some outstanding undated gilts were originally issued in the 19th century, some in the early 20th century to finance the First World War.
- *Floating rate bonds*: again, pretty self-explanatory. These are bonds whose coupons vary according to current short-term interest rates, rather than being fixed like conventional bonds.
- *Strippable bonds*: sadly, not as intriguing as they sound. Strips is the acronym for Separately Traded and Registered Interest and Principal Securities (contrived? No). Stripping a bond means breaking it down into its individual cash flows which can be traded separately as zero-coupon bonds.
- *Convertible bonds*: these give the investor the right to convert the bonds into either other bonds or, in the case of corporates, into shares at some point in the future.

BONDS ACCORDING TO THEIR AGE

- *Shorts*: bonds with up to seven years left to run.
- *Medium-dated bonds*: bonds with between seven and 15 years left to run.
- *Long-dated bonds*: bonds with more than 15 years to go. In theory these can go up to any duration (China recently issued a 100-year bond), but in practice 30 years tends to be the maximum.

WHO BUYS BONDS?

The global bond market is colossal. In 1997 there were $24,100 billion of bonds from developed economies for investors to choose from.

Who are those investors? The answer is: *you* are. By putting your money into a pension fund or taking out an endowment, you are supplying a steady stream of cash to governments, companies and banks around the world. You are unlikely to buy a whole bond by yourself – although you could buy a gilt by filling in a form at the post office – but by pooling your money with thousands of others you can take a profitable stake in the market (*see* Fig. 6.3).

Pension funds

During your working life you will probably make regular contributions into a pension fund to provide yourself with an income when you retire. There are two types of schemes: the *defined benefit* pension and the *defined contribution*. As their names imply, the former provides a guaranteed, specific pension related to the number of years of service and salary reached, the latter provides an income dependent on the level of contributions made and the fund's investment performance. Falling gilt yields and less favourable tax laws have sparked a move by firms in recent years to defined contribution funds.

Pension funds tend to like bonds with longer maturities to match their long liabilities. They also prefer assets that carry lower risk so tend to plump for

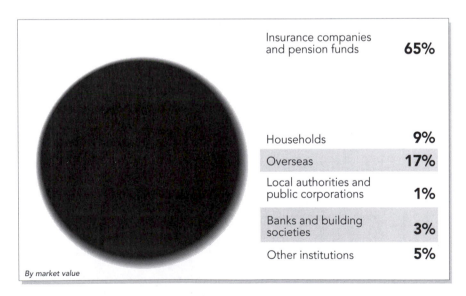

Insurance companies and pension funds	**65%**
Households	**9%**
Overseas	**17%**
Local authorities and public corporations	**1%**
Banks and building societies	**3%**
Other institutions	**5%**

By market value

FIG. 6.3 Who buys gilts?   *Source: Debt Management Service*

gilts rather than corporate bonds. In 1999, there was about £800 billion under management in pension funds in Britain, about 20 per cent of which was invested in bonds. Some 70 per cent was invested in equities, with the remainder split evenly between cash and property. (For the latest data on pensions, Phillips and Drew has a website at www.phillipsdrew.com)

Life assurance companies

Life assurance firms sell a variety of long-term investment products such as personal pension plans and endowment policies. The insured pays regular contributions to a fund over a number of years, typically 10 or more, then receives a guaranteed lump sum at the end.

In the case of an endowment it may be without profits, in which case the final sum will be known and agreed at the outset, or with profits, where a basic sum is guaranteed plus any bonuses depending on how well the fund in question has performed. (The Association of British Insurers has a website at www.abi.org.uk)

Investment and unit trusts

Both unit and investment trusts enable small investors to pool resources to gain the benefits of diversification – the principle of mutual investment.

Unit trusts are funds of money run by a professional manager who follows guidelines set out in a trust deed. Investors can sell their stakes in the trust at any time, in which case the manager would have to sell some investments to repay the unit holder. Each investor is entitled to a pro rata share of the value of invested funds.

First formed in 1868, investment trusts are slightly different in that they are limited companies that issue their own shares and use the proceeds to invest in other companies. So anyone who buys a share in an investment trust automatically buys a diversified investment. These shares are listed on the stock exchange and can be bought and sold just like any other equity. There are more than 350 investment trusts operating in Britain with combined assets of more than £60 billion.

The majority of money in unit and investment trusts in Britain is invested in equities. (The Association of Unit Trusts and Investment Funds has a website at www.investmentfunds.org.uk)

Other bond holders

Other investors in bonds include overseas governments and domestic banks. The latter may buy gilts, for example, to use as collateral for borrowing or as a top-quality investment to shore up their balance sheets.

Private individuals can also buy British government bonds by filling in a form at their local post office and sending it to the Bank of England (for more information on buying gilts, visit the Debt Management Office website at, www.dmo.org.uk). Unlike in the United States however (where buying Treasury bills is relatively commonplace), not many people in Britain invest directly in government bonds. Tax laws and cultural differences mean they prefer the higher risks and higher returns offered by the stock market.

> ❝There are two fools in every market; one asks too little, one asks too much.❞
>
> Russian proverb

WHY DO BOND PRICES MOVE? (AND HOW TO KEEP AN EYE ON YOUR PENSION)

Bonds can generate a return for investors in two ways: by producing a stream of income from the regular interest payments or by rising in price on the secondary market. Pension funds are more concerned about the former since they have long-term liabilities to fulfil, but many shorter-term investors are chasing the latter. The maxim 'buy low, sell high' applies just as much to bonds as any other investment.

Unfortunately, you can't have your cake and eat it in the bond market. If prices rise, the shorter-term investor will cash in by selling bonds and realising a capital gain, but the pension fund will see yields, hence the return on its investment, fall. So if you are nearing retirement you may want bond prices to fall and yields to rise to provide you with a generous annuity.

What determines bond prices? In other words, what will affect the size of your pension or the bonus on your endowment? There are four main factors: credit ratings, the economy, technical factors and politics.

■ *Credit ratings* are key. If a corporate bond gets upgraded (a rating agency thinks the issuer is more creditworthy) its price will rise and its yield will fall. Pensioners will lose, but short-term investors will gain. Examples include successful Internet start-up companies which have graduated from high-risk investments into the mainstream, such as Colt Telecom, a provider of high bandwidth data.

■ *The economy* also plays a crucial part in determining bond prices. If the market thinks interest rates are about to rise – maybe because inflation has crept higher or wage growth has risen – bond prices will fall (remember the golden rule, when interest rates rise, bond prices fall and vice versa). In most cases investors won't wait for the actual rate rise but will sell bonds in anticipation of it. Again, rising rates and yields will be good news for those relying on bonds for their income, but bad news for those hoping to make a capital gain.

■ *Technical factors* will also affect bond prices. If the supply of gilts falls for example (healthy public finances may mean there is less need to borrow) but demand stays the same, prices will rise. Conversely, if the corporate bond market is flooded with issues of a similar maturity and credit rating, prices may fall. The state of other markets will also affect the demand for and price of bonds. For example, if share prices were to tumble, investors might pile out of equities and put all their money into the relatively safe bond market. Again, the trick is to spot when the stock market crash is about to happen, cash in your profits there and transfer them to the bond market before everyone else does (*see* box on p. 186 for tips on how to predict a stock market crash).

■ Finally, *politics* will also impact on government bond markets. In the run-up to European Monetary Union, the growing realisation that Italy would join the single currency drove prices in its government bond market sharply higher. Fixed-income securities backed up by the might of Germany and France are much more popular than ones backed by a profligate, politically volatile government like that in Italy.

THE PROBLEM WITH PENSIONS – WHY BONDS MATTER TO YOU

Now you know what bonds are, who issues them, who buys them and why their prices change. But they still don't seem particularly relevant to everyday life. Why can't you just ignore them and leave City traders chasing six-figure bonuses to worry about them?

You could, after all, that's why you pay commission on your pension or unit trust. However, if you want peace of mind in later years, you should be aware of a potential problem developing in Britain's pension industry.

Yields at the long end of the bond market – a key determinant of the size of your annuity when you retire – had fallen sharply by the middle of 2000 for three reasons: reduced supply of bonds thanks to healthier government finances, increased demand for gilts due to pension regulations, and lower inflation expectations.

This decline in yields made it more expensive for employers to guarantee workers a certain income in retirement, hence there was a marked shift from defined benefit to defined contribution pension schemes. Leaving the moral questions of that move aside, it could mean many workers will end up being disappointed with their pensions unless they raise their contributions to reflect lower potential returns. So just as companies turn their attention to the younger generation, and early retirement becomes increasingly attractive to both employers and workers, your pension may limit your options.

However, before you squirrel away every penny you have for retirement, some potentially good news. If Britain were to join the European single currency, a whole new range of government bonds would open up for pension funds to invest in, thus alleviating the squeeze at the long end of the market. At the moment, currency risk means large-scale investment in overseas bonds is unwise. If those bonds were no longer counted as overseas, things would look very different for pensioners.

SHARE AND SHARE ALIKE

'October. This is one of the peculiarly dangerous months to speculate in stocks.

The others are July, January, September, April, November, May, March, June,

December, August and February.'

Mark Twain (1835–1910)

WHAT ARE SHARES?

A share represents ownership in a company. It gives the holder the right to receive a portion of company profits.

There is something incredibly exciting about shares. Maybe it's the tantalising prospect of picking a winner and seeing your money multiply in front of your eyes, or the thrill of pitting your wits against the market and beating it. The stock market is like the thinking man's lottery, the grown-up version of Monopoly.

Whatever the lure, it has 12 million people in Britain in its thrall. That is how many own some of the 12,000 shares listed on the London Stock Exchange in 1999. What exactly do those people own?

A share is just what its name suggests: part ownership of a company that entitles the holder to a portion of profits – and losses. If a firm needs more money to expand or replace defunct machinery, it has five options. It can reinvest profits from previous years, go to the bank for a loan, approach venture capitalists for money, issue a bond, or issue shares.

The most common type of share (also known as equity or stocks) is the **ordinary share**. This gives the holder the right to vote on a company's future (usually on a one-share, one-vote basis) and receive a **dividend** (a proportion of the company's profits). Ordinary shareholders are the very last people to get their money back if a firm goes bust. So if the price of a share falls and you hold it until the bitter end, you will probably end up with nothing.

Preference shares are also fairly common. These entitle the investor to a fixed dividend, decided at the time of issue. Preference shareholders are ahead of their ordinary neighbours when it comes to both dividends and creditors, but they do not have voting rights.

Securities that looked much like modern shares were issued as early as the late Middle Ages in Italian city states. These days, you can take a stake in most shops on an average British high street by buying their shares. The staples such as Tesco, Sainsbury, Marks and Spencer and Boots are listed, as are smaller shops like chocolate-maker Thorntons, Whittard of Chelsea (makers of the brightly coloured plates and bowls that are *de rigueur* for first-time home buyers) and Clinton Cards. Their share prices can vary hugely: high street thoroughbred Marks and Spencer shares plunged to 230 pence (shares are always expressed in pennies, not pounds) from 600 pence in just two years.

Most shares in Britain are traded on the London Stock Exchange. To get an idea of the general mood on the LSE, commentators often talk about the FTSE 100 index, or footsie (*see* Fig. 6.4). Literally the Financial Times Stock Exchange index, this comprises the 100 biggest shares listed on the LSE, accounting for around 70 per cent of total market capitalisation (a measure of the value of shares, this is the number of shares on the exchange multiplied by their price). By noting how much the FTSE rises or falls in a day, investors can gauge whether the market as a whole has done better or worse.

Newspapers also talk about the FTSE All Share index, which encompasses the majority of the shares listed on the London Stock Exchange. This index typically mirrors the FTSE as the same shares dominate each measure.

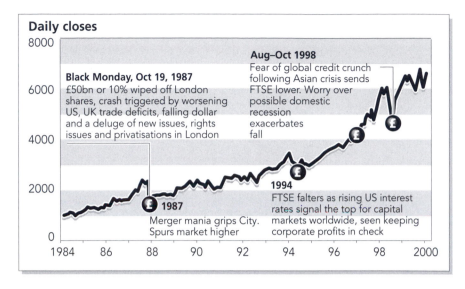

Daily closes

Black Monday, Oct 19, 1987
£50bn or 10% wiped off London shares, crash triggered by worsening US, UK trade deficits, falling dollar and a deluge of new issues, rights issues and privatisations in London

Aug–Oct 1998
Fear of global credit crunch following Asian crisis sends FTSE lower. Worry over possible domestic recession exacerbates fall

1987
Merger mania grips City. Spurs market higher

1994
FTSE falters as rising US interest rates signal the top for capital markets worldwide, seen keeping corporate profits in check

FIG. 6.4 FTSE 100 Index

Source: Reuters/EcoWin

66 Speculation is really only

another name for foresight. 99

J.R. McCulloch (1789–1864)

PREDICTING SHARE PRICES

Why do share prices move? That's the $64,000 question. If you knew the answer to that you'd be a zillionaire. Just think, if you had spent £1,500 buying shares in the Internet service provider Freeserve when the company initially floated in July 1999 at a price of 150 pence, you could have sold your stake for almost £9,000 at the beginning of February 2000 (although if you had hung on until the end of April, your stake would have fallen back down to around £3,500).

Alternatively, if you had spent your money on Halifax shares when they were going for 921 pence in April 1999, your £1,500 would have dwindled to less than £700 by February 2000.

Hindsight is a wonderful thing, but without it, shares can seriously damage your wealth.

It is impossible to predict every movement in a share's price, but by keeping an eye on some key factors, you at least stand a chance of avoiding disaster. (Although if you took Mark Twain's advice, the only way to ensure that is to stay out of the stock market altogether. As he once wrote: 'There are two times in a man's life when he should not speculate: when he can't afford it, and when he can.') Those key factors are:

- a company's actual performance versus its expected performance;
- the general economic climate;
- the mood of investors.

Company performance and expectations

When you buy a share you are buying part of a company, so it stands to reason that when that company does well, its share price will rise, and when it does badly, it will fall. Company news is the bread and butter of the stock market. Just as inflation figures are vital for currency and bond markets, profit data is key for share prices.

Profit *forecasts* are almost as important as the actual numbers. If a company posts a healthy surplus but warns that things don't look so rosy in the months ahead, the share price will fall as analysts scale back their estimates of future earnings. Equally, if a firm delivers disappointing results but predicts that things will pick up in future, the share price could rise.

Conversely, news of expansion plans could bolster a share price. When satellite TV firm BskyB announced in February 2000 that it was to spend £250 million on boosting its Internet presence, its share price jumped almost 20 per cent in one day.

Takeover bids can have a similar Midas quality. When the Bank of Scotland launched a surprise bid for fellow bank NatWest in September 1999, shares in the latter jumped to more than 1400 pence from 1046 pence in one day. The Bank of Scotland offered to buy NatWest shares for what amounted to more money than they were worth at the time (as measured by market capitalisation), claiming it could increase profits and improve efficiency. (The Bank of Scotland eventually lost its bid for NatWest to rival Royal Bank of Scotland after shareholders judged that the latter would make a better job of running a merged company.)

There are numerous other factors that affect a company's prospects and hence its share price. New product launches, changes in the boardroom, R&D announcements and investigations by competition authorities are just a few. In short, shares react to anything that comes as a surprise to the market. If they know about it already, it will be factored into the price and investors won't be interested. A glance at the business section of a newspaper will give you a good idea of what the market keeps an eye on.

General economic climate

Company news is not the only thing that can affect a share price. Stocks move every day regardless of whether a firm has released any results, sacked its managing director or announced an ambitious Internet strategy. There are other influences nudging prices up and down all the time, one of which is the general economic climate.

Shares are more likely to advance against a vibrant economic backdrop. It stands to reason – if unemployment and inflation are low, people can afford to spend more on the high street, which will push company profits and share prices higher. They will also be more inclined to take a punt on the stock market when they feel richer, thus providing an extra fillip to shares.

Causality between the stock market and the real economy runs both ways. Take the inexorable rise of the US market in the 1990s. It is no coincidence that the record highs on Wall Street, where US shares are traded, coincided with the longest economic expansion in US history. Strong consumer demand fuelled company profits, which drove equity prices higher. That increased the wealth of the share-holding population, which in turn fuelled demand. And so on. Wall Street was pumping money on to Main Street and vice versa.

The tendency for a strong stock market to boost consumption is called the **wealth effect**. If share prices rise, consumers may sell part of their portfolio and spend the proceeds. The same rule applies to other assets such as houses. When their prices rise, people feel wealthier, borrow more money against their homes and spend it. In other words, rises in asset prices feed through to the real economy. Central banks keep a close eye on potential wealth effects as they are powerful, if indirect, means of fuelling inflation.

Changes in interest rates can also affect share prices. As a rule, an increase in rates will depress shares for three reasons. Firstly, they make interest-bearing assets such as savings accounts more attractive and so encourage shareholders to sell their stakes and tuck their money in the bank. Secondly, rising rates are often a precursor to a slowdown in growth, which will choke off company profits and send shares lower. Thirdly, higher borrowing costs make it more expensive for firms to pay off their loans, again adversely affecting profits and hence share prices.

Mood of investors

Shares are owned by thousands of people, each with a slightly different opinion on where prices are heading and when to bail out. That is what

The Tories fight back. Shortly before the 1997 election, Prime Minister John Major and Chancellor Kenneth Clarke attack Labour's tax and spend plans … four months later it was a case of 'I told you so'. Shadow Chancellor John Redwood criticises Labour's first 100 days in power, highlighting 17 tax rises. Photographs by Paul Hackett. © Reuters 1997.

The men that move markets. Dollar traders do the deals that determine how much your pound is worth overseas. This day in February 1999 was a good day for them – the Bank of Japan had just reduced interest rates, sending the yen down against the dollar. Photograph by Eriko Sugita. © Reuters 1999.

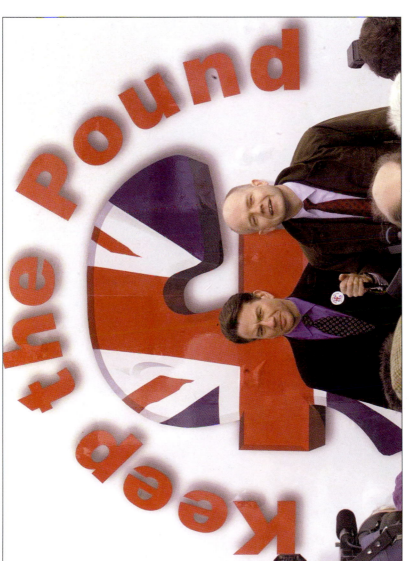

UK Conservative leader William Hague and Shadow Chancellor Michael Portillo field questions from residents of St Albans as they launch their 'Keep the Pound' campaign in February 2000. Photograph by Ian Hodgson.
© Reuters 2000.

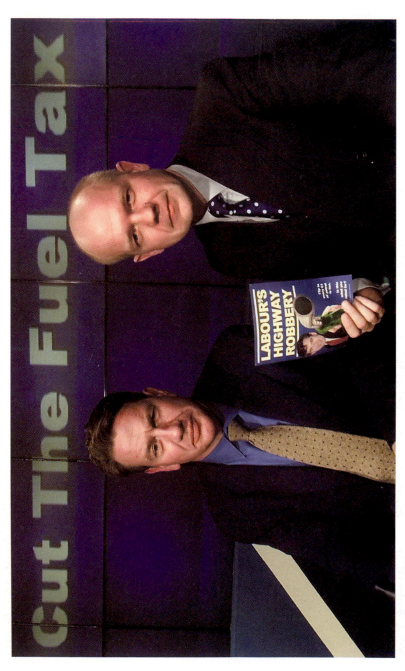

Britain's Shadow Chancellor Michael Portillo and Conservative leader William Hague weigh into the fuel debate by announcing plans to cut petrol taxes by 3p a litre. They were later out-trumped by Labour's pre-budget report which delivered a cut in tax on low sulphur fuel plus a reduction in car tax, which added up to 4p off petrol. Photograph by Dan Chung. © Reuters 2000.

The end of sugar rationing in February 1953 sparks a rush to stock up on sweets from this West London shop.
Photograph © 2000 Getty Images, Inc.

Economics underlies another election, this time in 1959. Harold Macmillan, British prime minister between 1957 and 1963, increases the Tory majority with the slogan 'You've never had it so good'. The campaign is based on a belief in an affluent society. Photograph © 2000 Getty Images, Inc.

Shepherd Street in Central London is swamped by rubbish in February 1979 after bin men go on strike. Economic chaos helps sweep Conservative leader Margaret Thatcher to power soon after, marking the beginning of a radical change in policy. Supply side economics, privatisation and tax cuts are the new order. Photograph © 2000 Getty Images, Inc.

Picketing miners, South Yorkshire pit, March 1985. Trade unions are at their zenith, soon to be crushed by Margaret Thatcher's far-reaching reforms, which included secret ballots and bans on secondary picketing. Photograph © 2000 Getty Images, Inc.

makes investing in the stock market so fascinating and unpredictable. The best way to gauge the general mood of investors is to keep an eye on the newspapers. The more negative stories there are about a company, warning of impending doom, the more likely it will happen. Around 10 million newspapers are sold in Britain every day. If they are all predicting the demise of Hot Air Ltd, chances are it will soon turn into a self-fulfilling prophecy.

> A bull market is one in which prices are rising or are expected to rise. On average, they last about four years. A bear market is one in which prices are falling or are expected to fall. They generally last about a year.

You have come to the end of your whistle-stop tour of what moves share prices. Company news is clearly key, with impending mergers, profit forecasts, expansion plans and staff changes all exerting powerful influences. Then there are the more intangible factors such as the economic backdrop and the future path of interest rates. Finally, there is the really unpredictable part: trying to second guess what everyone else thinks is going to happen.

Over the past 25 years economists have churned out hundreds of studies examining the effects of all these factors on shares and each has come to the same conclusion: you cannot beat the market and you will make only your stockbroker rich by trying.

> ❝No price is too low for a bear
> # or too high for a bull.❞

Proverb

WHERE ARE SHARES TRADED?

Shares are traded in a market, in other words, anywhere buyers and sellers can slug it out to find the optimum price for something. Markets are melting pots of information which lie at the very heart of capitalism.

Shares can be exchanged in *real* markets. Just like you can haggle over the price of an antique face to face with a stallholder in London's Portobello Road, dealers can yell at each other on a trading floor to secure the best price for a share or bond for their client. The New York Stock Exchange still operates on this basis (at the time of writing).

However, most financial markets these days are virtual, where buying and selling happens in cyberspace. Stock markets in London, Germany and most other developed economies use computers rather than people to match trades, as do the burgeoning number of Internet share dealing sites.

In fact, the web provides an ideal platform for share dealing. It hasn't been this easy to buy equities in Britain since the heady days of privatisation in the 1980s. Simply log on, select your stock and place your bets ladies and gentlemen. But what exactly are you letting yourself in for?

BUBBLE TROUBLE: HOW TO SPOT A STOCK MARKET CRASH

When Sir Isaac Newton lost a fortune in the South Sea Bubble in 1720, he declared: 'I can calculate the motion of heavenly bodies, but not the madness of people.'

Therein lies the trouble with bubbles. They bring out the insanity in investors. While the money is rolling in, people feel invincible, convinced it will be different this time. It never is.

Bubbles are periods when asset prices, like those of houses or shares, rise at an ultimately unsustainable rate. Once they burst, any previous gains are wiped out by a subsequent violent reversal.

Perhaps the most bizarre one of all time was the tulip mania that swept the Netherlands in the late 1630s. Tulip bulbs, newly arrived from Turkey, became wildly fashionable and their prices soared. At the height of the frenzy, exotic varieties sold for the price of an elegant town house in Amsterdam. A year later, the bubble had burst and bulbs were worthless.

Sadly, almost 400 years later there is still no convenient checklist of bubble symptoms investors can rely on to protect them from losing everything. The best economists can do is to cut through the hype and analyse the fundamentals of each boom.

Concerned stock market investors should consider the following. Bubbles typically have three characteristics: a fundamental element, a suspension of reality, and a steady stream of cheap money.[1]

Take the first factor. Something has to kick-start the boom and get money flowing into the market. The most likely contender is an improvement in technology that appears to promise inflated future company profits and so justifies higher share prices. If inflation in an economy is low and growth is high, investors become convinced that firms have found a way of producing more goods for less money. In other words, productivity has increased.

Problems arise when the second element makes an appearance. If investors overestimate the growth in productivity they will pile more and more money into shares, convinced of higher future returns, thus inflating stock prices above 'normal' levels. A suspension of reality means absurd equity market valuations (like abnormally high prices to profits ratios, or **p/e ratios**) are conveniently ignored. For example, in February 2000, the Internet company Interactive Investor had a p/e ratio of 81,395. That meant that, based on its earnings at the time, shares would generate the amount they cost by the year 83,395. In those circumstances, some kind of shake-out looked inevitable.

A crucial factor is emerging: inflation is still low, despite higher economic growth. In which case, maybe the punters are right. Maybe a productivity miracle has taken place and higher share prices are justified. But what if the low inflation is for other reasons. For example, it may be that a strong currency is keeping a lid on import prices, disguising dangerously strong domestic demand.

In any case, as long as prices appear to be under control, the authorities will keep interest rates relatively low, paving the way for the third criteria for a bubble – cheap credit. Investors borrow more, get further into debt, and fall faster when the bubble bursts.

Why will that bubble burst? Again, there are no hard and fast rules. It could be that the external forces holding inflation down abate and authorities begin to raise interest rates. That will prompt a re-evaluation of growth and profit prospects and share prices will start to fall. Alternatively, interest rates in other countries may rise, offering investors a better return elsewhere. They may sell their shares in one country and move their money abroad. If investors have over-extended themselves, they will panic once selling starts and the fall in prices will be exaggerated.

Each bubble is different. What signals bust in one won't even feature in another. But there are warning signs. A prolonged period of low inflation, low interest rates and strong growth, a running down of savings, an increase in consumer debt and ludicrous stock market valuations are just some. The rest is common sense. When a garden plant costs as much as a town house, it could be time to bail out.

WHAT DOES A STOCK MARKET DO?

A stock market performs two basic functions. It makes it easier for companies to issue shares because investors know they can sell their stakes in the time it takes to make a phone call, and it provides a mechanism for **takeovers** and **mergers**. Stock markets allow multi-billion-pound companies to be bought and sold as easily as most of us would buy a car. If markets are at the heart of capitalism then takeovers are what keeps the blood pumping.

"The market is totally impartial."

Anonymous

Takeovers: capitalism at its best or its worst?

Takeovers are one of the few business stories that make it on to the front page. They have the three vital ingredients for a gripping read: money, greed and power.

Fans of the hostile bid say the threat of acquisition forces a company to be efficient, giving shareholders and customers a better deal. If a business is poorly run its share price will fall, leaving it vulnerable to predators. Another firm can come along and offer what amounts to a higher price for the shares, usually in the form of cash plus the promise of stock in the new, merged company. If it can convince shareholders that it can cut costs and run the company better than the incumbent management, it will get enough votes to take control.

Detractors of the process, however, say it breeds dangerously short-sighted attitudes. When the shareholder is king, long-term investment may suffer in the single-minded pursuit of higher profits now. They also argue that takeovers do not necessarily result in better companies. If two firms in the same sector merge, competition could suffer and consumers could be worse off (although there are authorities that are supposed to safeguard against this).

And what about the thousands of jobs that are sacrificed in the name of cost-cutting? When the Royal Bank of Scotland won its bid to take over NatWest, it promised to cut 18,000 jobs in the industry. That may be economically efficient but is it socially responsible?

The hostile takeover culture thrives in Britain and the United States, where ownership of equity is fragmented and the shareholder rules. It is a different story on the Continent, however, where unsolicited bids are rare. In France, a lot of firms are family-controlled, and in Germany, banks own large chunks of company stock. Up to now they have been relatively passive shareholders, preferring to foster a culture of long-term investment and stability. But that attitude is becoming increasingly equated with inflexibility, a taboo concept in today's globalised world.

The first sign of cracks in fortress Germany came with the takeover of Mannesmann by Britain's Vodaphone-Airtouch in February 2000. The deal, the largest of its kind in the world at the time, created Europe's biggest telecoms company with a global customer empire of 54 million people. It also opened the door to other mergers in Europe, providing a rich hunting ground for the acquisitive multi-national.

However, cultural barriers could prove hard to conquer. The French, for example, are notoriously reluctant to embrace foreign ownership of domestic companies. A case of *liberté, égalité et fraternité* – as long as you're not from Britain or the US.

TRADING PLACES: THE LONDON STOCK EXCHANGE

Looking back

The **London Stock Exchange** was founded in 1801 but its origins go back to the closing years of the 17th century. A fledgling market where shares in newly formed joint stock companies could be bought and sold took root in London's coffee houses around the Royal Exchange in what was to become the financial heart of the capital.

The creation of a permanent National Debt in 1694 spurred growth by paving the way for government paper to be issued and traded like shares. As the Industrial Revolution gathered pace, the London exchange extended its reach both overseas and at home. By 1850 it was the leading institution of its kind in the world, blazing a trail in technological developments such as ticker tape, which was introduced in 1872 at a rate of six words per minute.

By then more than 20 stock exchanges had grown up around the country. These continued to operate independently of London until their amalgamation in 1973 (which was also the first year female members were admitted to the London market).

The 20th century was a prosperous one for the LSE. The total value of listed shares grew to around £5,000 billion from £5.4 billion in 1899. It was not a smooth ride, however. The reputation of the exchange was damaged by a speculative boom in 1928, and its business further curtailed by the worldwide financial crisis of 1929–31.

Things took a turn for the better in the 1950s and 1960s and the exchange flourished. However, by the 1980s, as competition with markets in other countries mounted, it was clear that the LSE had to modernise or die. The days of the exchange as a gentlemen's club were numbered.

On 27 October 1986 Big Bang catapulted the LSE into the modern age. Trading went from being face to face on a single market floor to being performed via computers and telephones from separate dealing rooms across the country. All firms became both brokers and dealers, able to buy securities from or sell them to clients without the need for a middle man.

Almost a year later, on 19 October 1987, the new system was stretched to the limit when shares plunged on what became known as Black Monday. A spate of multi-million-pound privatisations had left the UK market bloated and vulnerable to a correction. When a series of interest rate rises and poor trade figures in the US sent Wall Street tumbling, London duly followed suit. Within a fortnight the LSE had shed more than a third of its value and in the months that followed an estimated 5,000 jobs were lost in the City's securities houses as firms faced the longer-term implications of Big Bang.

▶

With hindsight, many economists say Black Monday was 'the crash that never was'. Just two years later the FTSE index was back at pre-plunge levels and the fall did little to dent consumer confidence or economic growth. In fact, the country went on to experience one of its biggest booms in history.

The years since Big Bang have been spent trying to harness new technology in the fierce battle between worldwide exchanges for market share. In June 1995 the LSE launched AIM, the Alternative Investment Market, where smaller, more innovative companies are listed.

In April 2000, the LSE took a step towards modernisation when it demutualised, in other words, separated its ownership from its membership. The move allowed the exchange to extend its commercial freedom and paved the way for flotation. It also made it a target for a possible takeover. At the time of writing, it was still independent, following an abortive merger with its German counterpart, the Deutsche Borse.

Looking ahead

The LSE and other traditional stock exchanges face a gruelling battle for survival. Their most powerful rival – and, ironically, their biggest weapon – is technology in the form of electronic communications networks (ECNs). These are computerised trading platforms that allow big investors like pension fund managers to deal directly with each other, bypassing the traditional exchanges.

In the US, where ECNs have been around for longer, they had seized more than 30 per cent of the equity market from established players like the New York Stock Exchange by the beginning of 2000. In Britain, the system that poses the biggest threat to the traditional exchange is Tradepoint, an electronic stock exchange jointly owned by large broking houses such as Merrill Lynch and Deutsche Bank. Its biggest selling point is that it allows big stock market investors to buy and sell shares from all over Europe, and pay for them, all on one network. In today's globalised world, that is the future.

It is not only the ECNs that are poaching business from traditional exchanges. The Internet is also a growing force, particularly for the small investor. It allows them to buy shares from companies cheaply online without the need for a physical market (hence the rise of the so-called day trader who makes a living out of online share trading). It is also an incredible font of information, providing profit records, share prices and complicated market calculations for anyone intrepid enough to trade without the advice of a stockbroker. In short, everything you need to invest in the market is at your fingertips. But be warned. Trading online as a small investor is not for the faint-hearted. Markets are ruthless and will take your money quicker than you can say 'that was my life savings'.

Useful websites

The London Stock Exchange website is at www.londonstockex.co.uk

In the UK, www.deal4free.com allows investors to trade share price movements rather than the shares themselves.

The site at www.sharepeople.com allows investors to trade in shares and invest in unit trusts online.

Other Internet-based share dealing sites include www.schwab.com and www.e-trade.com

The Financial Services Authority, at www.fsa.gov.uk, is responsible for regulating investment in Britain.

> 66 There is nothing so disturbing
> to one's well-being and judgment
> as to see a friend getting richer. 99

Charles Kindleberger, economist

DERIVATIVES

WHERE ECONOMICS MEETS ROCKET SCIENCE

'When I first stepped out on to the trading floor, I could smell and see the money.'

Nick Leeson (in his book, *Rogue Trader*, 1996)

A derivative is a financial instrument derived from an underlying stock or asset. Derivatives are used by hedgers and traders.

A derivative is a complex financial instrument whose value is determined by the change in price of an underlying asset. They may be traded in extremely complicated ways, using strategies with weird and wonderful names like butterflies, condors, Christmas tree spreads, Bostons and Scouts. I will stick to the more mundane varieties, explaining what calls, puts and futures are, giving examples of each and suggesting who might use them.

Derivatives shot into the headlines in 1995 when 28-year-old trader Nick Leeson used them to such deadly effect. His lavish bets on the Japanese share market backfired and ended in the downfall of Barings, one of Britain's oldest banks. I will finish this chapter by recounting that infamous story, a cautionary tale that highlights the darker side of markets.

HEDGING AGAINST THE FUTURE

The derivatives market is like one big casino where everyone is betting against everyone else, trying to hit the jackpot. Two types of investors use derivatives: hedgers and traders.

Hedgers use them to cover an exposed position, in other words, to protect themselves against potential future losses in financial markets. They may use them to guard against future interest rate rises if they have large outstanding loans, or to protect themselves against adverse currency movements if they conduct a lot of business overseas. The latter may be done using a **currency future**. This is best explained by example.

Suppose you own a fashion company in Britain and win an order to supply 500 coats to a department store in Paris. You agree a price of 1,000 francs a coat, which you will receive on delivery in six months' time. At the time of the agreement, one pound will buy 10 francs, so you are getting £100 a coat. Given that it costs you £80 to make each one, that will leave you with a tidy profit of £10,000.

However, disaster strikes and the French currency weakens, so it now takes 15 francs to buy one pound. You are now receiving only £66.67 per coat, leaving you with a net loss of £6,666 on the 500 coats. That is where the currency future comes in.

When the initial price for the merchandise has been agreed, a prudent business manager would buy a currency future. This would give him the right to buy 500,000 francs worth of pounds (500 coats at 1,000 francs each) in 12 months' time at an agreed rate of 10 francs to the pound. So a year later when the French currency has weakened, he simply receives 500,000 francs from the department store and instead of converting it at the market rate into £33,333 he converts it into £50,000 as planned. The company is saved.

Of course, if the franc had strengthened in that six months the British company would have been better off without the currency future. However, many companies would prefer not to take that risk. By buying a currency future they know exactly how much money they are going to make regardless of what goes on in the foreign exchange market.

A future is an agreement to deliver a set quantity of a certain commodity at a pre-agreed price on a date in the future. That commodity could be anything from pork bellies to currencies to a share index like the FTSE 100.

TRADING DERIVATIVES FOR PROFIT

Traders, on the other hand, use derivatives for the sole purpose of making money. Instruments like calls and puts (explained below) allow small bets to be placed on what will happen to the price of things like shares, with the potential for huge gains – or losses. This is because of gearing.

Consider the following example. Imagine it is January and shares in Tesco cost £5. Given the supermarket chain's plans to build an online customer base and expand its business, you think that price could rise in the next six months. But you are broke after Christmas and you cannot afford to buy any shares at the moment. So you buy a June **call option** instead. You spend, say, 10 pence per share, securing the right, but not the obligation, to buy Tesco stock at £5 at any time over the next six months.

If you are right and the shares rise to £5.50, you can *exercise* your option. You can buy the shares at £5 each (having already spent 10 pence on the call) and immediately sell them for £5.50. You have made 40 pence on your original 10 pence stake, a gain of 400 per cent. The shares, on the other hand, have only risen by 10 per cent. That is gearing.

Naturally, if you had been wrong and the share price had fallen to £4, your call option would have been worthless. What is the point of buying the shares for £5 when you can get them on the normal market for less than that? When the option expired in June you would have lost your original stake of 10 pence a share.

The opposite of a call option is a **put option**. In other words, the right (but not the obligation) to sell an asset at a certain price at a predetermined time in the future or at any time leading up to that date. Take the Tesco example again. Imagine you already own Tesco shares and you think they are fully valued at £5. In other words, there is a good chance the price will fall in coming months. You would buy a June put option for, say, 10 pence a share that gives you the right to sell your stock for £5 between now and then. If the shares slip to £4 you will exercise the option, making 90 pence a share (assuming you buy them back immediately at the market price). If they don't fall, your put will expire worthless.

In both cases there is a predetermined maximum amount you can lose – the amount it cost you to buy your put or call. The scope for gains, however, is huge, which is what makes derivatives so attractive to investors.

If you were on the other end of those transactions, you would be in a much riskier position. Anyone who writes options could lose a stack if the market goes against them. For example, imagine you write a call option giving someone the right to buy Tesco shares at £5 at any time in the next six months, and you charge 10 pence per share for doing it. If the shares rise to £7 and the option is exercised, you will have to buy the stock on the market for £7 and sell it for £5. You have lost £2 per share (minus the 10 pence you charged in the first place), around 20 times your original stake.

It is easy to see how people can get themselves into trouble using derivatives if they bet on the market the wrong way or if they simply do not understand the risks. Many think they are inherently unstable for these very reasons, and have the potential to bring about worldwide financial collapse. Tales like that of Nick Leeson and the millions of pounds he lost trading derivatives in Singapore have fuelled the concerns and prompted tighter control of derivative markets.

Derivatives like calls, puts and futures are traded in markets such as the Chicago Board Options Exchange, or the London International Financial Futures Exchange (Liffe). Options can also be traded *over the counter*, meaning they are tailor-made for each investor and priced accordingly.

NICK LEESON: THE MAN WHO BROKE THE BANK

Nick Leeson was just 28 years old when he achieved notoriety in 1995 as the rogue trader who brought about the collapse of Barings, one of Britain's oldest banks. This venerable institution had been around since the 18th century and had played an important role in financing the Industrial Revolution. With such a noble history, many thought it was invincible.

Leeson began his Barings career in London as a settlements clerk in the back office, managing the paper trail generated by traders. He was ambitious, and when the opportunity to go to Singapore came, he grabbed it.

Once there, he worked as a clerk on Simex, the Singapore International Monetary Exchange. He earned a good reputation and was soon promoted to trader. By 1993, he was the general manager for Barings futures in Singapore. At first he was a raging success. In just seven months to July 1994, the Singapore trading activities made a profit of $30 million, almost 20 per cent of the entire Barings Group profit for the whole of the previous year.

However, in January 1995, someone in the bank appeared to introduce a disastrous new trading strategy. They started to sell put and call options on the Nikkei 225 Index, the Japanese equivalent to the FTSE. The money they earned from writing those options was allegedly put into an unauthorised trading account numbered 88888.

By writing both put and call options at the same exercise price, Barings was creating a 'straddle'. This meant that the options would be taken up only if the Japanese stock market moved outside a certain range. As long as it was stable, the bank could simply pocket the money it made by writing the options and walk away with an easy profit.

You guessed it. Japanese shares were anything but stable. By the middle of January the Nikkei had drifted down to the bottom of Barings' no-pay-out zone. The bank was still ahead, but only just. Then on 17th January an enormous earthquake shook the Japanese industrial centres of Kobe and Osaka. By the end of the month the Nikkei had fallen out of Barings' stability zone and the bank was facing losses in the region of £380 million.

But it didn't end there. The puts and calls still had time to run and as long as the market kept falling, the bill for Barings kept mounting. By this time the whole market had got wind of the bank's problems. Barings had lost an amount possibly exceeding £800 million, more than the bank's entire available capital. Time was called and the bank went under. If it hadn't been for the fact that Dutch bank ING bought the remains for £1, its fate would have been sealed.

IF YOU REMEMBER SIX THINGS FROM THIS CHAPTER …

- A bond is a form of loan. It usually carries a fixed rate of interest and must be repaid after a fixed period of time. British government bonds are called gilts.
- Bond prices move on credit rating changes, on movements in their supply and demand and on broader economic factors such as interest rates.

- A share represents ownership in a company. It gives the holder the right to receive a portion of company profits. The most commonly held shares are ordinary shares and preference shares. The former carry voting rights but are at the end of the queue if a company goes bankrupt.

- Share prices move on a company's performance, particularly versus expectations, on the general economic climate such as growth and inflation rates, and on the general mood of investors.

- A bull market is one in which prices are rising or are expected to rise. A bear market is one in which prices are falling or are expected to fall.

- A derivative is a financial instrument derived from an underlying stock or asset. They are used by hedgers to protect against possible future losses in financial markets, and by traders as a tool for speculation.

ENDNOTE

1 Based on work by James Grant, editor of a New York-based financial newsletter.

CHAPTER 7

Garland
WITH
ACKNOWLEDGEMENTS

"IF HE LET GO OF THE STRING, HE WOULD FALL – *BUMP* – AND HE DIDN'T LIKE THE
IDEA OF THAT, SO HE THOUGHT FOR A LONG TIME…"   *(WINNIE-THE-POOH)*

BEST OF BOTH WORLDS

Getting the most out of trade

"If a foreign country can supply us

with a commodity cheaper

that we ourselves can make it,

better buy it off them

with some part of the produce

of our own industry,

employed in a way

in which we have some advantage."

Adam Smith, *Wealth of Nations*, 1776

INTRODUCTION

Imagine life in Britain without overseas trade. There would be no fresh Florida orange juice for breakfast, no mid-morning cup of Colombian coffee and no glass of Bordeaux in the evening. There would be no cheap televisions from Asia, no cut-price video recorders from Japan and little in the way of videos to watch on them anyway. Life would be more expensive and much more limited.

Yet free global trade often gets a drubbing in the press. It gets blamed for the destruction of the environment, for Britain's shrinking manufacturing industry, and for the loss of thousands of jobs. 'Why don't we *make* anything any more?' has become an all too familiar lament.

It is not immediately obvious whether free trade is good or bad. It gives us all more choice in the food we buy, the clothes we wear and the cars we drive, but it also means job losses in some industries that are incapable of competing with cheap imports. It presents us with a real dilemma.

The trouble is, trade is no longer just about goods, it's about people. It's about who gets to build ships and design cars in the 21st century and who is left answering telephones in a call centre. It's about whether farmers can survive a European boycott of British beef, and about whether unskilled workers will get paid less and less in the face of relentless international competition.

This chapter addresses all those issues, and more.

- **It considers why countries trade.** As patriotic citizens, we often feel a responsibility to buy goods made in our home country, support our own jobs. Economics suggests that loyalty is misplaced. It argues that each country is better off concentrating its resources on what it is good at, and importing everything else it needs.

- **It explains what globalisation is all about, and whether it is a cause for concern.** Violent protests against globalisation have become increasingly frequent of late – it seems the World Trade Organisation cannot congregate these days without the nearest McDonald's getting demolished. This chapter explains what the phenomenon is all about, and discusses whether we should be concerned at the rise of the mighty multinational.

- **It looks at the advantages and disadvantages of free trade.** Trade could mean you can afford to buy more clothes, a slicker computer and a faster car. But it could also entail job losses. This chapter discusses the darker side of free trade and weighs up the arguments for and against it.

- **It considers whether trade deficits matter.** Britain spent three-quarters of the last century with a deficit on its trade in goods and services account. That sounds like something to be ashamed of. It sounds as if the UK was consistently incapable of providing everything its people needed. However, trade deficits often are not as bad as they seem. This chapter discusses why, and explores what governments can do about them if they get out of hand.

- **It discusses what makes a currency move.** Exchange rates can move for a host of reasons, and every time they do, the cost of your annual overseas holiday changes. This chapter gives a few tips on when to buy your spending money before you head for foreign climes.

- **It tells the story of the pound's disastrous foray into the European Exchange Rate Mechanism.** When sterling was shunted out of Europe's currency grid in 1992, the government was humiliated, not to mention rendered a good deal poorer. This chapter looks into the whys and wherefores of Black Wednesday.

- **It considers whether governments let manufacturing industry down when they refuse to manipulate their currency.** A strong pound has caused all sorts of problems for British industry, increasing the price of exports and forcing manufacturers to cut either costs or profit margins. This chapter considers whether the government should do more to help struggling manufacturers, or whether it is right to leave the value of the pound to the foreign exchange markets.

WHY DO COUNTRIES TRADE?

Countries trade if they have an absolute or comparative advantage over other nations in making goods.

There was a time in Britain when anything plastic seemed to have 'Made in Taiwan' imprinted on its bottom. Somehow it made more sense to make goods like cigarette lighters thousands of miles away and transport them across two continents than it did to churn them out of a factory in the UK. That seems a little puzzling. Lighters are simple to make, need hardly any raw materials and retail for about a £1. Surely we must be capable of manufacturing them ourselves. Yes, we are. But if we do that, why stop there? Why not make ashtrays and matches and expand into pipes and tobacco and then even further afield into clothes, luggage, furniture or anything you care to name?

It would be impractical to try to make everything Britons need. It makes more financial sense to concentrate on the things we are good at, such as medical research and financial services, and use the money from that to buy everything else. As Adam Smith put it more than 200 years ago: 'It is the maxim of every prudent master of a family, never to attempt to make at home what it will cost him more to make than to buy...What is prudence in the conduct of every private family, can scarce be folly in that of a great kingdom.'

WHEN TRADE IS ABSOLUTELY ADVANTAGEOUS

Smith's logic is clear – it is ludicrous to make something yourself when it is cheaper to buy it from someone else. In this way, trade is obviously advantageous between countries that are very different. Spain has lots of olive groves but Sweden has none, so it makes sense for the former to sell olive oil to the latter. Spain is said to have an **absolute advantage** over Sweden in olives.

This regional diversity goes some way to explaining why countries trade, but it does not provide all the answers. For example, Britain is perfectly capable of making clothes, and indeed has a (somewhat depleted) textile industry to prove it. Yet two-thirds of the clothes sold in UK shops are imported. By the same token, the US has a thriving car industry driven by the likes of Ford and General Motors, yet also imports billions of dollars worth of Japanese vehicles every year. Even more puzzling, what if the US is more efficient and better placed than every other country in the world at making every single good? It would be totally impractical to supply the whole globe with everything it needs, and not import anything itself. It is still worth its while to trade, this time because of **comparative advantage**.

WHEN TRADE IS COMPARATIVELY ADVANTAGEOUS

The theory of comparative advantage says it is still worthwhile for two countries to trade even if one can produce everything more cheaply than the other. The easiest way to think of it is to use the example of a lawyer and a secretary. Imagine that the best lawyer in town is also the best typist in town (in economic-speak, she has an absolute advantage in both activities). It would be foolish for the lawyer to give up her precious time studying legal documents, which earns her far more money and therefore gives her a huge comparative advantage, to do the typing, in which she has no comparative advantage. From the secretary's point of view, she is worse than the lawyer at both jobs, but her relative disadvantage is least in typing. It makes most sense for the lawyer to pay the secretary to do the typing, so each can concentrate on her relative talents.

Applying that to countries, Britain may be better than France at producing both aircraft and apples, but its comparative advantage in the former is considerable. It can make more money by specialising in high-tech aerodynamics than it can by spreading its resources between both products. It can build up a skilled workforce and invest money in the latest technology while at the same time reaping **economies of scale**, which means that the greater the scale of production, the less it costs to make one extra good. All in all, it makes more sense to concentrate British resources on making aeroplanes and to import Golden Delicious from France.

FREE TRADE VERSUS PROTECTION

TRADING YOUR WAY TO WEALTH

> 66(Protectionism) is …
> # the sacrifice of the consumer to
> ## the producer – of the end to the means.99

Frederic Bastiat (1801–1850)

Most people take the benefits of global trade for granted. If you fancy a banana, simply pop round to your local shop. Likewise, if you want a crisp salad with Italian tomatoes and Spanish peppers, or a cup of tea, probably from China, nip down the road to the supermarket.

Free trade gives us all more choice. It also delivers lower prices. Cheap labour in developing countries translates into affordable clothes in Britain, relatively inexpensive electrical goods and even cheaper cars (if you are prepared to buy a Lada). However, it also means that British textile workers are losing their jobs, that shipbuilding is a dying craft in the UK and that former welders, riveters and skilled machinists are now answering telephones in call centres.

That is the dilemma of free trade. We all wear two hats – as consumers we want more value for money, as workers we want to protect our livelihoods. We relish buying bargains yet feel angry and concerned when factories close and British jobs are lost.

Like most other things in life, there must be a compromise. The problem is finding it. There are two diametrically opposed views in the debate, the **free trader** and the **protectionist**. The former believes more trade means more choice to consumers, lower prices, more wealth and more growth. She believes the path to prosperity lies in allowing goods freedom to move across borders.

Her arch-rival, the protectionist, says that can only lead to job losses, environmental terrorism and the inexorable rise of the multinational to the detriment of elected governments. She thinks countries should safeguard themselves by putting obstacles in the path of trade, thus preventing imports from flooding into the country.

Only one can be right. Both put forward powerful cases, which are considered below, starting with the protectionist view.

GLOBALISATION AS THE ROOT OF ALL EVIL

Globalisation is the removal of all barriers that stand in the way of free trade of goods, services, information and money both within and between countries.

Lying at the heart of the protectionist cause is the belief that free trade makes powerful multinational companies richer at the expense of everybody else. Unfettered access to a global market means General Motors' annual sales are greater than the entire Norwegian economy. Ford generates more income than Saudi Arabia. In fact, 52 of the 100 largest global entities are corporations and only 48 are countries. Such staggering figures send shivers down the spines of protectionists.

They believe this phenomenon called **globalisation** is driving a wedge through society, bankrolling a rich few and impoverishing the rest. This rather ugly word describes the breaking down of barriers both within and between countries, and can occur in three ways.

- It could be in the *cultural sense*. A ready supply of pasta, curries, noodles, sushi etc. in your local supermarket is the most obvious manifestation.

- Or the *technological sense*. Advances in transport mean it is often cheaper to make things in low-wage countries like India and ship them to the wealthy west to sell. The Internet has also contributed significantly to globalisation, allowing people to communicate across continents quickly, inexpensively and with the minimum of fuss.

- Alternatively, it could be in the *economic sense*. In the past, punitive taxes on imports, in other words tariffs, often made it unprofitable to freight goods from developing countries to industrialised ones. Any profits were wiped out by import duties. But a gradual erosion of those duties, a move away from protection towards free trade, has changed all that.

All three factors have facilitated the rise of the multinational, that unwieldy, gargantuan creature that spans countries and cultures and means that McDonald's opens a new restaurant somewhere in the world around every six hours.

These fears about globalisation spilled over into violence in November 1999, when thousands of rioters went on the rampage through the streets of Seattle in protest at a World Trade Organisation (WTO) meeting that was being convened there. They blame the WTO – the international body responsible for promoting free trade – for job losses, growing inequality, environmental damage and progressively powerful multinationals. Their arguments are considered below.

Globalisation and jobs

Take the first concern, job losses. Just about every increase in international trade has generated losers (in 1946 only 5 per cent of world GDP was traded internationally, now it is around 25 per cent). Britain's car and textile industries are prime examples. In 1954 there were just over 850,000 people employed in the UK's textile industry. Cheap imports, thanks to lower labour costs overseas, and a reduction in tariffs means there are now about 240,000. The Union of Textile Workers estimates that number is shrinking by 500 a week.

If you think your job is safe because you sit behind a desk instead of on a production line, think again. The Internet means people can trade currencies, shares and bonds from anywhere in the world, for example. If it wasn't for the fact that London is an exciting, culturally diverse place to live, with excellent business facilities and back-room support, City traders could well have been displaced by their Frankfurt counterparts long ago.

It is therefore indisputable that jobs in certain parts of the world have been lost because of growing international trade (although if workers in poor countries benefit as a result, surely that is for the greater good?).

Globalisation and inequality

The second concern is that free trade is spurring greater inequality, an issue already touched on in Chapter 5. The facts here are unassailable. The gap between rich and poor has widened both within developed countries like Britain and the US and between poorer countries like Thailand and Ethiopia (the Far East, for example, has been much more effective in harnessing growth than sub-Saharan Africa). Whether this has been because of free trade or in spite of it is a moot point, however, and one which is addressed later.

Environmental damage

Protectionists say that free trade encourages competing multinationals to ransack the environment in the name of profit. For example, threats to the Amazon rainforest may be receding now, but huge swathes have been destroyed to provide land for profitable beef farmers, etc.

The power of multinationals

A fourth concern is that politicians are losing their power to govern, and that they are being bullied by aggressive multinationals into policies against the public interest. Nobody likes the idea of being dictated to by unaccountable, wealthy businessmen whose sole aim is to make money. However, hard evidence that this is the case is difficult to come by. In fact, many economists believe multinationals spread wealth, work and better living standards (discussed later).

Exceptional reasons to put up trade barriers

Protectionists say that all these concerns present valid reasons to put up trade barriers. Other, more textbook, grounds include the **infant industry argument** and the **anti-dumping** measure.

Many young firms face higher costs than their long-established competitors because they cannot reap the rewards of economies of scale, for example, or they have to climb a steep learning curve. Tariffs can be temporarily imposed to deter foreign competitors and give domestic producers room to flourish. For example, Germany used trade barriers to protect its engineering industry in the late 19th century, allowing it to catch up with and eventually surpass Britain following the latter's lead in the Industrial Revolution.

Secondly, a country may impose tariffs to protect itself against **dumping**. For example, a firm may deliberately sell its goods overseas at a loss either to rid itself of excess stock or to drive firms in its key export markets out of business. Japanese companies have been accused of such unscrupulous tactics in the European video recorder market. This type of protectionist strategy appears to be becoming increasingly popular. In 1999, 328 anti-dumping investigations were initiated globally, significantly higher than the 232 in the previous year.[1]

PUTTING UP THE BARRICADES

'In matters of commerce the fault of the Dutch

Is offering too little and asking too much.

The French are with equal advantage content

So we clap on Dutch bottoms just 20 per cent'

From a despatch by George Canning, former British minister of foreign affairs and prime minister, to the British ambassador in the Hague, circa 1820s.

There are all sorts of ways countries can prevent imports from entering their shores and taking market share from domestic producers, some more surreptitious than others. Listed below are six tactics used by governments over the years.

■ **Tariffs.** A tariff is a tax imposed on imports. Not only does it raise money for governments, it also increases the price of imported goods and so reduces demand for them. Domestic producers look cheap by comparison and demand for their products increases. For example, suppose the ready supply of cheap labour in China means they can make stainless steel saucepans and ship them to Britain for less money than a factory in Sheffield can manufacture them. If the UK were to impose a tariff on Chinese saucepans high enough to make them more expensive than their Sheffield counterparts, people would be more inclined to buy British and the country's steel industry would be in better shape. Global tariffs have tended to fall over the years, but that masks a rising tide of 'non-tariff' policies such as those talked about below.

■ **Quotas.** A quota is a physical limit on the quantity of a good imported or exported. If the supply of, say, CD players from Japan entering Britain is restricted, that will leave domestic producers with a greater market share.

■ **Voluntary export agreements.** In the 1970s and 1980s Britain relied heavily on agreements with other countries about how much they could export to the UK. For example, Britain had a deal with Japanese car manufacturers that they would not take more than 10 per cent of the UK car market. Such agreements are technically illegal now although that has not prevented them from re-emerging recently.

■ **Non-competitive purchasing by governments.** Governments spend millions of pounds each year on defence, hospital equipment and roads, etc. Many award contracts to domestic firms, even if they quote higher prices than overseas businesses, so as to promote home-grown industries. Britain's annual defence procurement budget is around £10 billion – plenty to support a shipyard if need be.

■ **Safety standards.** Countries sometimes use strict rules on safety as a reason for not importing overseas goods. For example, the French government refused to lift its ban on British beef along with most of the rest of the EU in 1998 because of concerns over mad cow disease. In a similar stand-off, the EU has banned hormone-treated beef imports from the US for the past decade on the grounds that it poses a potential cancer risk.

■ **Customs delays.** A simple but effective way of deterring imports is for customs officers to delay their entry into a country.

The problem with imposing any of the penalties above is that retaliatory action is almost guaranteed. A dispute between the EU and the US over bananas is a perfect example. The US imposed almost $200 million in sanctions against EU exports in 1999 in protest at what it said were unfair rules governing international trade in bananas, the world's most traded fruit. At the time, the EU imposed strict quotas and high tariffs on bananas from efficient producers in Latin America, while allowing free access to those from a handful of small African, Caribbean and Pacific countries, many former European colonies. Such tit-for-tat trade wars can impair global growth and escalate into damaging political rows.

"If we will not buy we cannot sell."

William McKinley (1843–1901)

GIVING A FREE HAND TO TRADE

Protectionists can argue a persuasive case, but most economists say they are wrong. Theory suggests trade between countries is a good thing, for a number of reasons.

■ **Lower prices.** Trade allows specialisation and therefore economies of scale so goods can be produced for less money. International competition also spurs greater efficiency. In other words, all of a country's resources, be they human, natural, industrial or financial, can be used to best effect. On top of that, tariffs raise prices for consumers. For example, the WTO estimates that import restrictions and customs duties mean UK consumers pay around £500 million more per year for their clothing than they otherwise would.[2]

■ **More choice.** Without trade, our choice of food, cars, clothes, anything you care to name, would be a lot narrower.

■ **Greater growth.** There is strong evidence that trade boosts growth, which in turn raises living standards and erodes absolute poverty. For example, the OECD says that in the past decade, countries that have been more open to trade have achieved double the annual average growth of others. It estimates that recent moves in Australia to remove artificial barriers to trade have, in effect, put A$1,000 in the hands of each Australian family.[3]

Trade and jobs

But what of protectionists' claims that free trade threatens the livelihoods of many in advanced countries? Low-wage, poorer nations have indeed been able to undercut the likes of Britain and the US in certain industries and snatch market share. But it is important to keep things in perspective.

For one thing, this tactic allows impoverished nations to earn money and develop their economies. It could be argued that cheap labour is their greatest asset, and they are simply making the most of their comparative advantage, as any country would.

Secondly, it is not just trade that has stolen jobs. The OECD estimates that in the case of the United States, trade was responsible for less than 6 per cent of the drop in manufacturing employment between 1978 and 1990. Other factors such as technological change, domestic competition and shifts in demand have played a much more significant part.

In fact, trade actually supports many jobs, both in the developed and the developing world. For example, the OECD calculates that one in four jobs in Ireland depends on exports, while in Canada it is one in three. In poorer countries such as Turkey, there is evidence to suggest wages paid by foreign firms are often higher than those paid by local businesses, while workforces at multinationals have expanded much faster, too. How can multinationals be all bad when they bring so much wealth to impoverished countries?

However, if it is your job at stake, it is of little comfort to know you are in the minority. The problem in free traders' eyes therefore becomes one of better provision for the unskilled, disaffected in society through improved labour and social policies, not through resorting to protection. For example, when BMW announced it was to sell off its troubled plants in Britain, the government offered millions of pounds for retraining local workers, the idea being to divert labour towards more profitable areas.

Free trade and inequality

Many believe that far from increasing poverty among developed economies, free trade is actually their ticket out of deprivation. The World Bank estimates that the number of people living on less than $1 a day in

East Asia fell from 720 million in 1975 to 345 million in 1995, a period of huge growth in both trade and the economy.[4] In addition, there is evidence that some of the most impoverished countries in the world are also the most closed, for example, Myanmar, Rwanda and Algeria.

Free trade and national sovereignty

What about the worry that free trade diminishes the power of governments and threatens national sovereignty? Protectionists believe global rules for trade and investment mean countries have less say over environmental and health and safety issues, for example.

Free traders, however, argue the opposite. They believe liberalisation actually increases a country's power by making it wealthier, improving its competitiveness and insulating it from external shocks. They see countries' decisions to abide by WTO rules as exercising their sovereignty, not relinquishing it.

FREE TRADERS WIN – IN THEORY

When it comes to economic theory, free traders win, hands down. Trade promotes growth, lowers prices and gives consumers more choice. Clearly protectionist concerns about inequality and the environment should not be dismissed, but building tariff walls around countries is arguably not the answer. Supply-side policies aimed at nurturing a skilled, flexible workforce and at encouraging a modern, high-tech investment base could be far more effective in the long run.

In any case, a completely free trading world is likely to elude even the most ardent supporters of globalisation. Someone, somewhere will always rely on either tariff or non-tariff barriers to protect their industry, prompting retaliatory action from aggrieved trading partners. As US senator Henry Clay said in 1832: 'The call for free trade is as unavailing as the cry of a spoiled child for the moon. It never has existed; it never will exist.'

There is also arguably a natural limit to globalisation that will prevent money and goods from moving unchallenged around the globe. Humans like to belong somewhere, creating a psychological need for patriotism. A tendency for people in the UK to 'buy British' or boycott Golden Delicious apples during the beef row with France shows there will always be barriers to trade, regardless of the official rules.

The heated debate on free trade versus protectionism is not going to go away. If anything it will escalate as globalisation spreads and the backlash against it intensifies. Hopefully, you will know now which side of the tariff wall you want to sit on.

THE BALANCE OF PAYMENTS

A country's balance of payments account records everything that comes into a country – all the goods, services, investments and loans – and everything that goes out. It is split into a current account and a capital and financial account.

The current account

The current account records all the goods and services a country sells abroad, its **exports**, and all those it buys from overseas, its **imports**. If exports exceed imports, the current account is in surplus, but if imports are greater than exports, it is in deficit.

The current account's **trade in goods balance** is where products such as cars and food – things you can actually see and touch – are recorded. This is sometimes called the visible balance and it gives a snapshot of how much we rely on other countries to keep us stocked up with all the cars, computers, hi-fis etc. that we need. Britain's trade balance has been in deficit since 1983.

Services such as banking and insurance are recorded in what used to be known as the invisibles balance but now has the unwieldy title the **services, investment income and current transfers balance**. Also included here are things like royalties on music, books and films. Television series such as *Cracker* and *Prime Suspect* have been particularly lucrative for Britain in what are very competitive markets. Exports have outpaced imports in the invisible account in every year since 1966.

The capital and financial accounts

The financial account records all the money that flows into and out of a country, be it for investment, borrowing and lending or grants. It is split into four categories:

1 *Portfolio investment*, which records every share and bond that is traded between Britons and foreigners. Much of the money invested is short-term, hot money, for example, when investors put money in a sterling deposit account purely to take advantage of high interest rates. Other money, such as that invested in equities or bonds, is longer term.

2 *Direct investment*, which records any investment made by Britons abroad and investment by foreigners in Britain. For example, if Lloyds Bank were to set up a branch in Paris, it would be recorded here.

3 *Other investment* records, among other things, all currency transactions between Britons and foreigners and all loans. For example, if a UK importer needed dollars to pay his US supplier, he would sell pounds on the foreign exchange market and buy the US currency. That deal would be registered in this section.

4 *Reserves*, which are large piles of foreign currency held by the central bank in case of emergency. This pool of money can be used to prop up the domestic currency if it is coming under pressure.

The **capital account** is slightly different in that it records *transfers* of capital for which nothing is received in return, for example the forgiveness of overseas debt. This is also where the buying and selling of things such as copyrights (as opposed to the income from those copyrights, royalties, which are recorded in the current account) and football players is noted. For example, when Manchester United bought Jap Stam from the Netherlands, it was recorded as a negative in the capital account (nothing personal, I'm sure).

A country's current account will always be offset to an equal degree by its financial and capital accounts. So if the current account is in deficit – as it was in Britain between 1986 and 1996 inclusive – the capital and financial accounts must be in corresponding surplus.

PAYING FOR TRADE

HOW DOES A COUNTRY PAY FOR A CURRENT ACCOUNT DEFICIT?

Britain is one of the most open economies in the world. About 30 per cent of GDP comes from exports, and it imports the equivalent of just over 30 per cent too, so it is an important sector. It is also a volatile one (*see* Fig. 7.1). In the past 20 years, the UK's current account has yo-yoed from surplus to deficit and back again. It ended the 20th century sharply in the red – 1999 saw a thumping £12.8 billion deficit on the current account, equal to 1.4 per cent of GDP.

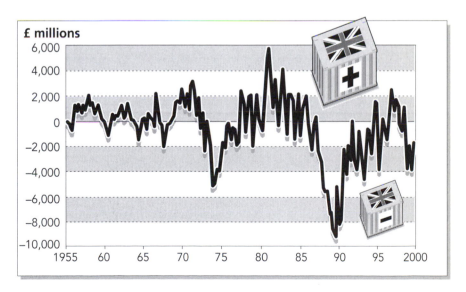

FIG. 7.1 UK current account balance since 1955   Source: Reuters/EcoWin

How did Britain finance that deficit? If a country buys more goods and services from overseas than it sells in return, it has to pay for the shortfall somehow. Just as you must pay for a car when you buy it, either straight away or by taking out a loan, so a country must pay for its imports, either straight away or by borrowing money from overseas. Both will be recorded in the capital and financial accounts, which track all the money flowing into and out of a country.

Consider what happens when Britain borrows from overseas to pay for its current account deficit. This may be in the form of overseas investors buying British government bonds, or buying shares in British companies. Both those transactions will show up in the portfolio investment section of the financial account (*see* box on page 212). When a Japanese firm builds a car plant in the Midlands, it is also effectively lending the country money, which shows up in the foreign direct investment section of the financial account.

If British firms pay for their imports straight away, a company will simply buy the foreign currency it needs on the market and hand over the dollars, yen, etc. to its trading partner. That transaction will show up in the other investment section.

DO CURRENT ACCOUNT DEFICITS MATTER?

Thirty years ago, large current account deficits caused enormous problems. For one thing, exchange rates were fixed and so could not adjust to help bring shortfalls back into balance as they can now (more on that in a moment). And even when currencies were allowed to float freely against each other, strict restrictions on how much money could be taken into and out of the country caused the British government enormous headaches. In 1976 Britain was forced to go cap in hand to the International Monetary Fund for a loan, partly because of a growing current account deficit. It was an ignominious period in British history and one which governments have been eager not to repeat.

No, they don't matter

These days, a current account deficit is a lot less worrying. It sounds like a bad idea, and indeed is often portrayed that way in newspapers, but in many ways it is harmless. Here are a few reasons why you should not lose too much sleep over it:

- **Confusing the ends with the means.** A current account deficit means a country is importing more than it is exporting. That sounds like a waste – it sounds like other nations are making money out of our demand, by supplying us with the goods we need. But that is a commonly held fallacy. Think back to the law of comparative advantage. As long as a country is buying its goods from the cheapest possible source, and maximising its own wealth by concentrating its energies on what it is good at, then everyone will be better off. It doesn't matter who makes what, or who buys from whom, as long as everyone is producing goods as efficiently as possible.

- **The market will restore balance, eventually.** The market is a powerful force. In a world of floating exchange rates, currencies will adjust so as to restore current account balance – in the long run – suggesting deficits are no more than temporary phenomena. For example, imagine Britain has a £10 billion deficit. Exports are considerably less than imports so, other things being equal, the pound will fall (overseas firms will demand fewer pounds to pay for fewer exports, and domestic firms will demand more overseas currency to pay for more imports). A weaker pound makes exports cheaper and imports more expensive, boosting demand for the former and cutting it for the latter. In time, the deficit will start to fall.

- **It depends how the deficit is financed.** A look at the financial account will show you how the deficit is funded. If there is a lot of overseas investment coming into Britain, as opposed to a lot of short-term, speculative money, it suggests that the finance behind the current account deficit is secure. Investors are not going to pull out at a moment's notice and leave the country in the lurch.

- **A deficit may be a sign of strength.** A current account deficit means that imports are outpacing exports. Rather than being a sign of weakness, that could signal both strong consumer demand and robust economic growth. For example, the longest expansion in US history, which began in March 1991, made it impossible for domestic producers to satisfy national demand and imports rocketed. In 1999, the current account deficit was a colossal $340 billion, almost 4 per cent of the US economy. Because investors still had an insatiable appetite for US assets such as shares and government bonds, that yawning shortfall was manageable. The dollar remained strong and the deficit was relatively easy to finance. If you owned US Internet shares or Treasuries, you effectively funded the US current account deficit.

Yes, they do matter

Thought about in this way, current account deficits sound pretty innocuous. Yet they often seem to be a source of consternation for governments. To see why, consider the following.

- **The market panics.** This scenario is to be avoided at all costs. Take the US experience again. If everyone who bought US bonds or shares started to get worried about the size of the £340 billion deficit and could see no immediate sign of it shrinking, they might take fright and dump their dollar assets in the belief they were never going to get their money repaid. (Market sentiment can be very fragile – if everyone sells dollars because they think there *might* be a disaster, there inevitably *will* be a disaster.) The dollar would plunge, suddenly making imports very expensive and possibly precipitating a sharp interest rate rise to ward off inflation. Given the amount of debt Americans hold at present, that could severely curtail demand and therefore economic growth.

- **A deficit could signal domestic problems.** A large current account deficit could be a warning of trouble ahead. For example, it could mean consumer demand and therefore inflation is getting out of control. In 1989, at the peak of the boom in Britain, the UK current account deficit was a shocking £23.5 billion. Not long after, interest rates were hoisted to choke off rising prices and the economy was nose-diving into recession. Secondly, a poor export performance could signal a lack of competitiveness. Inefficient factories and unskilled workers may be the root cause of poor exports and therefore a current account deficit, suggesting further investment and training is needed if the country is to hold its own on the world stage.

BRITAIN'S TRADE SECRETS

Did you know that in 1999 Britain exported frozen chicken feet to China (where they are considered a great delicacy) and sold 126 tons of sand to Saudi Arabia for use in foundries and golf course bunkers? Among the more bizarre imports into the UK were holy water from Saudi Arabia and a consignment of elephant's milk.

A rifle through Britain's trade accounts reveals more about national idiosyncrasies than you might think, and gives a fascinating insight into how British tastes have changed over the last century. For example, it appears that while the UK has always been a nation of tea drinkers, it has only recently acquired a taste for coffee. In 1900, Britain imported 2.75 kilos of tea per head of the population – only slightly less than the 2.97

kilos per head shipped in in 1998. However, coffee imports amounted to just 0.32 kilos per head in 1900, a fraction of the 2.79 kilos bought in 1998, equivalent to a heart-racing 1,400 cups per person.

It is not just caffeine that has got the Brits hooked – alcohol is equally tempting. At the turn of the last century, the UK imported 1.7 litres of wine per head a year. In 1998 it imported 15.6 litres, or the equivalent of almost 21 bottles per person.

While the 4.3 million paper declarations collected each month by customs and excise throw up a host of intriguing insights into British life, the bigger picture is not quite so pleasant. During the 20th century, the UK recorded an annual surplus on trade in goods and services on just 25 occasions. In goods alone, it managed surpluses in just six of the 100 years. If it had not been for the almost continual surplus on the services account – which has been in the black every year since England took home the World Cup in 1966 – things could have been pretty bleak.

HOW TO CURE A CURRENT ACCOUNT DEFICIT

Current account deficits are not particularly dangerous, provided the afflicted countries are solvent and have a strong, stable currency. However, as explained above, if they are left to build up indefinitely, markets could turn ugly and trigger a nasty chain reaction that ends in higher interest rates and slower growth. (This is a particular risk for more unstable countries deemed less creditworthy.) Hence governments may consider implementing the following strategies to eliminate an external deficit.

■ **Reduce the exchange rate.** Governments can hasten current account adjustment by artificially reducing the exchange rate (thereby making exports cheaper and imports more expensive). In a fixed exchange rate system, a country could simply devalue its currency – reduce its value relative to other currencies. Under a floating system, however, it is much harder. As discussed in Chapter 3, it is futile to try to coax an exchange rate lower when it does not want to weaken. This strategy is therefore hard to implement with any certainty. Britain has managed it in the past, however, albeit by default. When the pound was forced out of the Exchange Rate Mechanism in September 1992, it fell 15 per cent against the German mark in just a couple of weeks. Exports rose in time and the current account deficit went from £10 billion to £1.5 billion within two years.

■ **Deflate.** One way to curb demand for imports is to put a damper on the whole economy. By raising interest rates or increasing taxes, authorities can choke off total demand, reducing the appetite for overseas goods in the process. Looking at the Lawson boom from a different angle, when demand got out of control, the Conservative government increased the cost of borrowing sharply, which tipped the country into recession and slashed the current account deficit from £23.5 billion in 1989 to £8.4 billion in 1991.

■ **Put up barriers to trade.** Imports could be curtailed by imposing tariffs, quotas or any other protectionist measure. Apart from being politically difficult these days, particularly for the 135 members of the World Trade Organisation, it could spark retaliatory action, make protected industries uncompetitive and reduce overall economic growth. Economists do not recommend this strategy.

■ **Currency controls.** Back in the days when overt government intervention was more acceptable, authorities could restrict the amount of money that flowed into and out of a country, thereby exerting an influence over the current account. For example, in the late 1960s, when Britons went on holiday abroad, they could take only a certain amount of money out of the country with them. Apart from the fact that modern-day sun-seekers would find such restrictions absurd, EU regulations would now prevent it.

Britain is highly unlikely to resort to any of these tactics to redress a current account imbalance. The Chancellor, Gordon Brown, has ruled out manipulating the exchange rate in order to boost industrial exports (*see* box, 'Manufacturers and the pound') and has repeatedly vowed to wipe out economic boom and bust, which excludes the second strategy. The final two options are more or less ruled out in today's free-trading world. That leaves just one choice: the trusty supply-side route.

■ **Supply-side policies.** This is far and away the best way to reduce a current account deficit. By improving the efficiency of a country's export sector, more goods can be made and sold for less money, boosting demand on a long-term basis, not simply for the duration of a weak currency or a deflated economy. Supply-side policies could include encouraging more investment, improving education and training, and making labour more flexible and more productive. The only trouble is that they all take time.

MANUFACTURERS AND THE POUND: HAS GOVERNMENT LET INDUSTRY DOWN?

'If we try and affect (the pound) artificially, we may find the cure is worse than the disease. We have to be very careful. I think devaluation of the pound would be a mistake.'

Prime Minister Tony Blair, February 2000

'There is no point in having a strong pound if it is ripping the guts out of British manufacturing.'

Bill Morris, general secretary of the Transport and General Workers Union, March 2000

British manufacturers have been fighting for survival for more than half a century and have the scars to prove it. But even by their battle-weary standards, the late 1990s were particularly bruising. Their export markets shrank after the Asian crisis knocked global growth off course and their borrowing costs mounted as the Bank of England raised interest rates. But most frustrating of all, the prices of their exports soared in world markets thanks to the relentless rise of the pound.

In January 2000, sterling hit its highest level for 14 years against the currencies of the UK's main trading partners. For no other reason than the strength of the pound, British exports were a third more expensive in their overseas markets than they had been four years earlier. With those kinds of price rises, the only way firms could retain their market share was by slashing costs, which they duly did, shedding 100,000 jobs in the sector in 1999 alone.

Meanwhile, the government did little to help.

In its former life, the Labour Party saw a weak pound as a panacea to Britain's industrial problems. If UK manufacturers were not competitive in world markets, simply weaken sterling until they were. Nowadays the philosophy could not be more different. Both the Chancellor Gordon Brown and the Prime Minster Tony Blair ruled out coaxing the pound lower in order to throw struggling manufacturers a lifeline. Instead, Brown called for a 'stable and competitive pound' in the medium term, which, for manufacturers, loosely translates as, shape up or ship out.

Was the government being too harsh? Was Labour abandoning industry in its hour of need, or would an attempt to weaken the pound have done more harm than good as both Blair and Brown said?

The hard economic facts are on the government's side. Past endeavours to target the exchange rate have invariably ended in tears. Currency manipulation is often as futile as King Canute's attempts to halt the tide, and even on the rare occasions that it works, the effects can be counterproductive. An excessively weak exchange rate may cheapen exports, but it also makes imports more expensive, thus fuelling cost-push inflation and sowing the seeds of the dreaded boom-and-bust cycle. What manufacturers gain in a respite from higher prices, they soon lose in a tangle of high inflation, low investment and slower growth.

That leaves just one realistic option – use supply-side policies to improve efficiency, allowing exporters to compete in world markets regardless of the exchange rate. That may mean more investment in new technology, more training for workers and more job losses – a tall order for any firm. The British Chambers of Commerce, a lobby group for British industry, said that manufacturing costs in the UK rose by 11 per cent in 1999, almost entirely due to the rise of the pound against the euro (which had been the real problem. Sterling had been fairly steady against the dollar). Productivity, the amount of output produced per worker, rose by 5 per cent in the same period – less than half the rate needed just to make up for the pound's increase alone.

British manufacturers face tough times. The pound is a hard taskmaster and many firms are leaner and fitter than before as a result. They are learning to live with the strong currency. Ironically, that could bring a whole new set of problems. If Britain were to join the euro, it would have to do so at an exchange rate consistent with recent levels. If the pound stays strong, that could mean sterling gets locked in for ever at a punitively high rate. All hope of a depreciation would evaporate – something that manufacturers can at least cling to at present.

MAKING SENSE OF THE POUND

One of the questions I get asked most as an economic journalist (after 'how much money should I invest in the stock market?') is 'when should I buy my holiday money?'. The value of the pound can swing wildly in very short periods of time, making a significant difference to how much your annual break costs.

If you had taken a city break to Berlin at the end of September 1992, it would have cost you about £500 to buy 1,250 marks of spending money, provided you had got it the day before you left. However, if you had been organised and bought the same number of marks a few weeks earlier, before Britain's sharp exit from the European Exchange Rate Mechanism, it would have cost you about £440.

Sterling plunged almost 15 per cent against the German mark within a couple of weeks of the ERM debacle (*see* Fig. 7.2). That move was exceptional, but it nevertheless illustrates how gyrations in the exchange rate can have a substantial effect on your wallet.

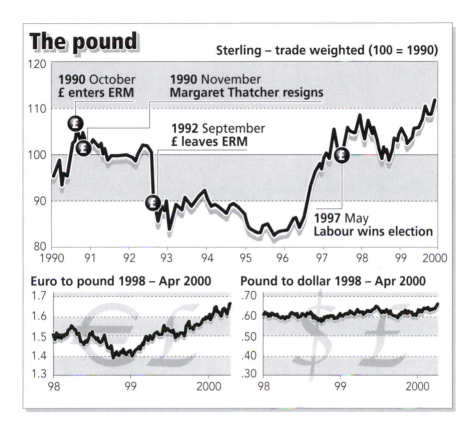

FIG. 7.2 The pound 1990–2000   Source: Reuters/EcoWin

TOP TIPS ON WHEN TO BUY YOUR HOLIDAY MONEY

Here are a couple of things to look out for to make sure you get the most out of your pound when you go abroad.

- **Interest rates.** Changes in interest rates can have a significant effect on the value of a currency. As a rule, higher rates mean stronger currencies, so if the Bank of England looks likely to tighten policy, the pound may strengthen. Conversely, if you are heading to Florida and the US central bank, the Federal Reserve, looks set to raise rates, the dollar may rise and the pound fall.

- **Sentiment.** This is a hard one to pin down but again can have a substantial impact on the exchange rate. If investors think an economy is in bad shape or that the government is doing a poor job of running the country, they may take a dim view of the currency and sell. Things to look out for include disappointing growth figures, signs that inflation is about to take off, and negative press stories on the government's handling of the economy.

- ■ **Politics.** Any serious sterling watcher will keep a close eye on government policies, particularly in relation to the European single currency. Hints about when Britain may join the euro and at what rate could have an enormous impact on the pound. For example, if Labour signalled its intention to sign up to monetary union, but at a lower, more competitive rate than the prevailing one, sterling could fall.

- ■ **Rumours.** There is very little the man in the street can do to keep track of all the rumours that fly around the foreign exchange market, and often very little point anyway. Currency movements on the back of gossip tend to be short-lived and are unlikely to affect exchange rates offered by high street banks.

If you plan your holiday far enough in advance and follow the suggestions above you could find yourself left with a little more change from your decaff and pretzel than otherwise. However, the very fact you are forced to go to your high street bank or a bureau de change to get your dollars means you will never get a particularly good deal regardless of when you buy.

The average difference between the buy and sell prices for the sterling/dollar exchange rate in the foreign exchange market is just five ticks – 0.05 of a cent. The difference in Barclays is about 10 cents. Admittedly, part of that huge spread is because the average holidaymaker buys considerably fewer dollars than an international investor. Buying spending money for a trip to Disneyland will not yield the economies of scale that a multi-million-dollar deal with an investment bank will. Part of it also reflects the fact that high street banks have no guarantee of selling on a currency as soon as they buy it. If Barclays is saddled with huge amounts of dollars and the price of the US currency plunges, the bank will take a hit.

However, the majority of that 10 cents spread is profit margin. Unfortunately for the hapless holidaymaker, there is not a lot he can do about that. Aw, shucks.

Its reach does not stop there. The value of the pound could affect your job and even, indirectly, the size of your monthly mortgage payments. BMW's controversial decision to sell the Longbridge Rover plant in March 2000, for example, was blamed partly on the strength of the pound, which made exports expensive, and partly on Britain's indecision over the euro. A weak currency, on the other hand, could spark inflation, bringing a multitude of problems in its wake (*see* Chapter 4). Interest rates will rise to dampen consumer demand and prevent expensive imports from flooding the economy, and your monthly mortgage payments will bear the brunt.

A happy medium is clearly called for. The trouble is, the foreign exchange market is not known for delivering convenient compromises. It has a mind of its own and it is not afraid to use it.

EXCHANGE RATE SYSTEMS

Fixed exchange rate. When the value of one currency is held constant against the value of at least one other, no matter what happens to demand etc, those currencies are said to be fixed. The Gold Standard in the 19th and early 20th centuries was a fixed exchange rate system. For example, in 1914, anyone holding a £1 note could walk into the Bank of England and exchange it for 0.257 ounces of gold. Similarly, a Frenchman could exchange francs for a fixed amount of gold in France, and a German could do the same in Germany, etc. In that way, currencies' values were effectively fixed against each other. Fixed exchange rates fell out of fashion in the 1930s and are usually regarded as too inflexible for today's multi-trillion-dollar currency market.

Currency bloc. European Economic and Monetary Union is an example of a currency bloc. Participating currencies are fixed against each other, and the bloc as a whole fluctuates freely against outside currencies such as the dollar and the yen.

Adjustable peg. Currencies may be fixed (pegged) against each other in the short term, but prone to revaluation or devaluation (adjustable) in the long term, in which case they are said to be on an adjustable peg system. Europe's Exchange Rate Mechanism fell broadly into this category. Prior to monetary union in 1999, ERM members were obliged to keep their currencies within a certain range of each other. In extreme circumstances, however, they could agree a step change in one or more currencies, *vis-à-vis* the central rate, known as a realignment. For example, between 1979 and 1987, the French franc was devalued four times and revalued once after currencies got out of kilter.

Conventional peg. This occurs when one country pegs its currency, formally or de facto, at a fixed rate to a different currency. For example, the Barbados dollar is pegged to the US dollar at BD$2 per US$1, while the Belize dollar is pegged to the US currency at BZ$1 per US$0.50.

Managed or dirty float. Not as interesting as it sounds. This is a system where the exchange rate is determined by market forces, but governments intervene from time to time to alter the free market price of a currency. Examples include the Jamaican dollar, the Kenyan shilling and the Norwegian krone.

Free floating exchange rate. By far the most popular in today's globalised, transient world, the floating exchange rate is one where the value of a currency is determined by market forces. The pound was allowed to float in June 1972 after almost 30 years in an adjustable peg arrangement called the Bretton Woods system (where the world's currencies were anchored to the dollar, which was guaranteed against gold). The dollar, the yen and the euro are all examples of floating exchange rates.

WHY DOES THE POUND MOVE?

The exchange rate is the price at which one currency is convertible to another.
Currencies are bought and sold on the foreign exchange market.

A currency has a price, just like everything else, that is governed by demand and supply. Whereas the price of labour is wages and the price of money is interest rates, the price of a currency is the exchange rate, the amount it costs to convert, say, pounds into dollars.

Britain's exchange rate, like that of the dollar, the yen and most other currencies of industrialised countries, is allowed to move freely; it will rise if demand rises and fall if demand falls. In other words, it is a **floating exchange rate**. In this floating world, the value of the pound is determined by four factors:

- the level of international trade;
- long-term investment needs;
- speculation;
- central bank intervention.

Financing international trade

The need to buy imports forms a small but fundamental part of demand for a currency. If Britain has a current account deficit, UK firms will sell pounds and buy foreign currencies to pay for imports. Meanwhile, fewer exports mean overseas firms need fewer pounds to buy their British goods. The demand for sterling falls along with its value against other currencies.

That is all very well, but a £12.8 billion British current account deficit in 1999 did little to sap the strength from the mighty pound. In fact, the UK currency actually rose by 10 per cent against its main trading partners over the course of the year. That suggests there are far more powerful forces at work on the currency.

Financing long-term investment

One of those forces is long-term investment. For example, if directors at Japan's Nissan want to build a car factory in the Midlands, they will have to sell yen and buy pounds to pay for construction workers and architects, etc. Mergers and acquisitions on the stock market will also influence an exchange rate. For example, when British mobile phone company Vodafone-Airtouch announced it was buying Germany's Mannesmann for €180 billion, the pound fell on the expectation of the large currency shift the deal entailed. Again, this forms only a very small part of overall demand for a currency.

Speculation

Speculation is far and away the most important determinant of an exchange rate. About $1.5 trillion worth of currencies changes hands in the world's foreign exchange markets every day. Global exports and imports amount to just over $6.5 trillion each, a year,[5] so clearly it is not the need to finance exports and imports that dominates demand. It is effectively gambling on the direction of currencies.

Any number of factors can drive speculative demand, including:

- **Interest rates.** The higher the rate of return an investor can earn in a country, the more likely she is to put her money there. For example, at the beginning of 2000, the official interest rate in the euro area was 3 per cent, substantially lower than the 5.5 per cent in Britain. One of the reasons the single currency was struggling at the time was that investors could earn more money by changing their cash into sterling and putting it in a British bank account than they could by doing the same in euros.

- **Inflation.** If price rises in a country appear to be heading out of control, two things could happen. Investors may sell the currency for fear that inflation will erode any interest earned on it, or they may buy it if they think interest rates are on the verge of going up to choke off that inflation. That is why the currency market watches RPI figures so closely.

- **Politics.** Politics can be just as important for a currency as hard economic data can. For example, the pound fell slightly in the immediate aftermath of Labour's landslide victory in the 1997 general election because the market was unnerved by the size of the new government's majority. However, sterling soon recovered because underlying fundamentals were still strong. About a week later it dipped again on rumours that Tony Blair was considering taking Britain back into the European Exchange Rate Mechanism at a rate 10 per cent below prevailing levels.

- **Rumours.** Gossip is the life-blood of the foreign exchange market. Such whisperings are impossible to predict and have won and lost currency traders trillions of pounds over the years. A few years ago, a rumour that a nuclear weapon had been fired from Russia sent the dollar sharply higher against the German mark (any anti-Russian gossip has an adverse impact on the German currency simply because of the latter's proximity to the former Soviet Union). The 'nuclear weapon' in question turned out to be a Norwegian weather balloon, but not before investors in the mark had had their fingers and their bank balances badly burned.

The morning before US employment figures are released is another volatile time for foreign exchange markets. These data are extremely important for currencies since it gives the very latest indication of growth and inflation in the US and hence the likely path of interest rates. On one occasion in November 1998 the US Department of Labour mistakenly put the job figures on its website ahead of the scheduled release time. For a long time afterwards, every month around the same time, the dollar started to skip around as someone, somewhere started a rumour that the figures had been pre-released again.

Central bank intervention

Countries can also influence exchange rates by using their reserves of foreign currency to manipulate demand (as discussed in Chapter 3). If the yen is falling, for example, Japan may sell some of the dollars it holds and buy the domestic currency, artificially boosting its demand and price. This so-called intervention is pointless unless the balance between demand and supply is finely poised. The most memorable example of the futility of intervention is the failure by the Bank of England to stop the pound from crashing out of the European Exchange Rate Mechanism in September 1992 (*see* box below).

BRITAIN AND THE ERM: A NATIONAL HUMILIATION

16 September 1992 will be forever remembered in the City as Black Wednesday, the day the pound almost died.

The story begins almost two years earlier on 8 October 1990. Under John Major's chancellorship, Britain joined Europe's exchange rate mechanism, a grid system designed to keep member countries' exchange rates within specified bands against each other. After the 8–9 per cent price rises of the late 1980s, the government was desperate to regain its anti-inflation credentials. The ERM was a relatively painless way of achieving that, and one which would also manoeuvre the country back into the inner circle of Europe. At least, that was the plan.

The pound signed up at a central rate of 2.95 marks and was allowed to fluctuate up to 6 per cent either side of that level. In other words, the government had to make sure sterling was worth no less than 2.7780 marks and no more than 3.1320. Instead of being allowed to float freely, it was now partially fixed.

Initially, the policy was roundly applauded. A strong pound would rule out imported inflation and pave the way for interest rate cuts as prices fell, went the logic. But the Herculean nature of the task ahead soon became clear.

The burden of reunification forced the Bundesbank, the German central bank, to raise its interest rate to a record 8.75 per cent in July 1992. Investors immediately poured money into the mark, weakening the other currencies in the ERM in the process. The pound was particularly precarious since many believed it had entered the system at an artificially high level in the first place. Recession and rising unemployment in Britain had only diminished sterling's popularity further and before long massive selling meant it was bumping dangerously along the bottom of its lower limit against the German currency. Drastic action was called for.

The beginning of the end of the pound's love-hate relationship with the ERM came on a bright, sunny day in August. The chancellor at the time, Norman Lamont, made a statement, telling sceptical markets he wanted to remove any 'scintilla of doubt' about the government's commitment to keep sterling in the currency grid. They did not believe him.

The avalanche of selling gathered pace and the Bank of England was forced to intervene, spending more than $1 billion of its foreign reserves in what turned out to be a futile attempt to prop up the pound. Meanwhile, the government refused to surrender to the speculators. There were a few weapons left in its arsenal and each would be used before Britain capitulated.

Plan A involved Lamont 'breaking all the rules', as one EC minister put it, by putting pressure on Germany to cut its interest rates. He only made matters worse. Incandescent at being told what to do about its own monetary policy, Germany dug in its heels and refused to budge.

An increasingly desperate John Major, by now prime minister, turned to Plan B. In a speech at the beginning of September he staked his reputation on keeping the pound in the ERM, ruling out devaluation as 'a betrayal of our future'. He was determined not to suffer the humiliation that befell Harold Wilson when the Labour government was forced to devalue in 1967. Major let pride get in the way of politics.

Then the pound was dealt another body blow. On Monday 14 September the Italian lire, which was also struggling to maintain parity in the system, devalued by 7 per cent, in return for a quarter-point cut in Germany's main interest rate. With nothing left to distract them, speculators trained their sights firmly on sterling.

The dying days of Britain's foray into the ERM had an almost farcical ring to them. Major was ensconced in 18th century Admiralty Arch in London while Downing Street was being reinforced against terrorist attack. Since it was only a temporary arrangement, there was no switchboard, no Reuters screens and no computer network. Anxious civil servants were sent scurrying back and forth to Number 10 to check on the latest developments in the foreign exchange markets while others were despatched to search for a radio.

In a last-ditch attempt to stem the flow of speculation against the pound, the government raised interest rates from 10 per cent to 12 per cent. The pound did not move. The Bank of England was buying sterling at the rate of tens of millions every few minutes and it was still only just clinging to its bottom rate of 2.7780 marks. Investors knew it was all but over and were like vultures circling their victim.

Not even the announcement of a further rate rise to 15 per cent made at 2.15 pm on 16 September could stop the haemorrhaging. Britain suspended membership of the ERM after close of trade that day, effectively devaluing the pound.

Exactly how much money the government spent in its abortive attempt to stay in the ERM has never been confirmed. We know that at the start of September the Bank had $44.4 billion in its coffers, $6.5 billion of which was held in gold and IMF special drawing rights. It is probably fair to say that most of that was spent. But a lot of those reserves had been accumulated over a number of years at different exchange rates and would be paid back at varying rates, too. So the net cost to the taxpayer is probably a substantially lower – though nevertheless painful – £3 billion to £4 billion.

Hungarian-born financier George Soros took a large chunk of that. Convinced the government's ERM resolve would weaken, he converted £10 billion into German marks and then sat back and waited for sterling to plummet. When it did, he converted his relatively strong marks back into weak pounds, paid back what he had borrowed, and pocketed a reputed $1 billion profit. He later called it 'an obvious bet, a one-way bet'. It was a pity the government didn't see it that way, too.

IF YOU REMEMBER SIX THINGS FROM THIS CHAPTER …

- It is still worthwhile for countries to trade with each other, even if one can produce everything more cheaply than the other. This is because of comparative advantage.

- Free trade helps to lower prices and give consumers more choice. There is also evidence that it boosts economic growth.

- A country's balance of payments records everything that comes into the nation – all the goods, services, investments and loans – and everything that goes out. It is split into a current account and a capital and financial account.

- Current account deficits do not matter if the underlying economy is robust and the currency is strong. However, they may be a source of concern if left to build up indefinitely.

- The pound is an example of a floating exchange rate, in that its value is determined by demand and supply. Currencies may also be fixed or a hybrid of the two extremes.

- Factors to look out for when buying your holiday money include relative interest rates, the general state of the economy, political events, particularly those relating to monetary union, and rumours.

ENDNOTES

1 Global Trade Protection Report, 1999, Rowe & Maw.

2 The WTO website can be found at www.wto.org

3 The OECD website can be found at www.oecd.org

4 Social Policy and Governance in the East Asia and Pacific Region, World Bank, November 1999.

5 Based on 1998 WTO figures.

CHAPTER 8

"You'd be upset too —
the tooth fairy left a euro
under her pillow"

REDRAWING THE EUROPEAN ECONOMIC MAP

A guide to monetary union

"I fear that in 50 years' time,

the UK's decision not to join the euro

from the start

may be the

European tragedy

of the present generation of

British leaders."

Yves-Thibault de Silguy, outgoing European Commissioner for monetary affairs, 1999

"God separated Britain from

mainland Europe

and it was for

a purpose."

Margaret Thatcher, December 1999

INTRODUCTION

European economic and monetary union (EMU) is shaping up to be the defining issue of our time. A country's currency and the way it interacts with the rest of the world is like an umbrella covering the whole economy. If it does its job well, employment, growth and trade will all thrive in a low-inflation environment. But spring a leak or two and all those good intentions could get washed away in a flood of market speculation and ill-conceived patch-up policies.

On a more personal level, the question in Britain of whether to swap pounds for euros could have repercussions for everything from the size of people's mortgage payments to the amount they pay in tax. It could affect the flow of foreign investment into the country and therefore the number of jobs, the success of the City of London and the volume of British exports. It is easy to get side-tracked by the emotive issues that monetary union entails, but it is about so much more than that. Once the sound bites have faded and the pithy newspaper editorials are wrapping up fish and chips, it boils down to just one question: will Britons be better off inside or outside the single currency? This chapter addresses that question.

Monetary union began on 1 January 1999 when the currencies of 11 countries on the Continent were irrevocably fixed. Until 2002, Germans will still use marks and Italians still spend lire, but the values of those currencies no longer fluctuate against one another on foreign exchange markets. Instead, they move in union against the rest of the world. They act as a single unit of money called the euro.

True to form, Britain played the role of the reluctant European and stayed out of the first wave of EMU. It took 15 years to join the Common Market, and 11 to enlist in the Exchange Rate Mechanism. So on past performance, we should be earning and spending euros anytime from about 2010 onwards (although it could happen as soon as 2005). Certainly, some European neighbours think it is only a matter of time before the UK joins the single currency club. Former Dutch Prime Minister Ruud Lubbers commented during the 1991 euro negotiations in Maastricht: 'History teaches us that, if one or two lag behind, they always follow.'

Will history repeat itself? Will Britain make a half-hearted bid to join EMU in a few years' time, loath to miss out on any euro spoils but unable to shake nagging doubts about relinquishing national sovereignty?

That depends on the British voter. Any decision to scrap the pound – one of the most controversial and complicated issues of our time – will almost certainly be subject to a referendum. No doubt that means months of jingoistic headlines and frantic flag-waving from one side and accusations of xenophobia from the other. Sifting fact from fiction, rhetoric from reality, will be difficult, not least because objective analyses of the subject are scarce.

This chapter gives a simple, unbiased account of all the issues surrounding European Economic and Monetary Union. By the end of it, with a bit of luck you will not only know where you stand on the single currency, you will also be able to hold your own in any debate on the subject. Among other things, the chapter discusses the following.

- **It explains exactly what EMU is and how it works.**
- **It discusses how the single currency has divided Britain's politicians, businesses and the public.** This chapter looks at where the political parties stand on the single currency, and at how the newspapers have stirred up the EMU debate, often treading a fine line between patriotism and nationalism.

▪ **It gives a short history of currency unions.** The euro is not quite as groundbreaking as it seems. Currency unions were first initiated by the Ancient Greeks in 400BC, and were a regular feature right up to a Latin Union between Belgium, France, Italy and Switzerland in 1865.

▪ **It examines the theory behind the single currency.** In 1961, Canadian-born economist and Nobel prize winner Robert Mundell published a seminal article on optimum currency areas. This research posed the question of when it was advantageous for different regions to relinquish monetary sovereignty in favour of a common currency. This chapter looks at that theory and applies it to the euro area.

▪ **It outlines the arguments for and against British membership of the European single currency.** Using Mundell's theory as a starting point, the chapter goes on to give an unbiased account of the issues surrounding British membership of EMU.

▪ **It explains the government's five economic tests.** In October 1997, the newly elected Labour government outlined five tests it said must be met before it would lead Britain into the euro.

▪ **It traces the history of the euro.** The single currency is the climax of 50 years of closer European integration, intended to banish the threat of war and enhance the Continent's standing in global politics. Unearthing the euro's roots, from the six-nation Coal and Steel Community in 1952 through to the creation of the single currency in 1999, helps to understand how the project got this far.

▪ **It gives a snapshot of who is in the euro, who is part of the EU and who wants to join Europe's elite economic club.**

▪ **It identifies a number of issues ahead for the EU, including the possibility of greater political integration.**

EMU is a huge leap of faith. It could be more than 100 years before a definitive statement of its consequences can be safely ventured. In the meantime, the best we can do is use economics to decide whether we are europhiles or europhobes – and then cross our fingers.

€CONOMICS AND THE €URO

WHAT IS THE SINGLE CURRENCY?

The euro is just like any other currency, except that it operates across 11 countries instead of one (at the time of writing). Those countries are Austria, Belgium, Finland, France, Germany, Ireland, Italy, Luxembourg, the Netherlands, Portugal and Spain. Up until 2002, everyone in those nations will continue to use francs, guilders, etc. – established national currencies – when they go shopping, as euros are available only in cheque or electronic form (so when you go on holiday to Portugal, you will still need to buy escudos from your bank for the time being). But from 2002, national currencies will disappear and will be replaced by euros at exchange rates that have already been set.

Just like a single country's currency, the 11 euro nations are subject to the same interest rate. This is decided by the **European Central Bank,** which is composed of representatives from each member nation (as long as Britain stays out of the single currency, it will not have a seat on the ECB's main governing council). The area operates like one country in other ways, too. People are largely free to move and work anywhere in the **euro-zone** (and indeed anywhere in the EU) and money and goods can typically cross borders without having tariffs slapped on. At the moment, that is as far as the co-ordination goes. Each country can still decide its own tax rates and government spending levels (although strict rules on how much debt they can build up mean those choices are limited).

The United States is an example of a highly successful currency union. All states use dollars and all are subject to the same interest rate, set by the country's central bank, the **Federal Reserve.** There is a strong sense of national identity, and workers are free to move around in search of jobs. However, the US differs from the eurozone because it is a political as well as a currency union. There is one federal government that decides income tax (although individual states may set their own taxes to a degree) and passes laws (although again, states can set laws themselves).

Value of pound sterling to euro

FIG. 8.1 The fall of the euro   Source: Reuters/EcoWin

Britain is also a political and currency union, although on a much smaller scale. England, Wales, Scotland and Northern Ireland all use pounds and all are subject to the same interest rate, set by the Bank of England. Westminster is in charge of setting tax rates, although post devolution the Scottish parliament may vary income tax by up to three pence in the pound. Government spending helps to smooth out regional imbalances, although as Chapter 5 showed, vast differences persist, particularly between the north and the south of the country. To see how the euro has fared against the pound, *see* Fig. 8.1.

PATRIOTISM OR NATIONALISM?

BRITONS DRAW BATTLE LINES OVER EUROPE

The single currency has an extraordinary ability to stoke patriotism (or is it nationalism? Author and poet Richard Aldington wrote in 1931: 'Patriotism is a lively sense of collective responsibility. Nationalism is a silly cock crowing on its own dunghill.'). The pound is no longer just a unit of account in some eyes – like shells, metal and even cigarettes before it – but a symbol of self-determination and national identity.

It is an issue that has split the country in two.

> **❝It (EMU) cannot, they tell us, possibly fail. It will be the veritable *Titanic* of the economic world.❞**
>
> Lord Tebbit

The political view

Leading the confusion are the politicians. Incessant euro squabbling, both within and between parties, has left the electorate drowning in rhetoric. The Labour Party, broadly in favour of the single currency, has taken a 'wait and see' stance. They have set five economic tests for euro entry (see box on p. 244) and have pledged to hold a referendum on the issue before signing up. That referendum could come as early as 2002 if Labour were to win a second term in office, meaning Britons could be using euros as soon as 2005.

The Conservatives have claimed the anti-euro ground, although deep divisions remain within the party. Leader William Hague has pledged to keep the pound for the lifetime of the next parliament (which must be chosen by May 2002 at the latest), vowing to 'rally the British people in defence of our democracy'. He has accused Tony Blair of riding roughshod over the public's euro concerns and of planning to bounce the nation into the single currency with a 'rigged referendum'.

Not all his fellow Conservatives agree. A vocal pro-euro lobby within the Tory party, which includes former Chancellor Kenneth Clarke and Michael Heseltine, has branded Hague's stance as 'barking mad ... single-minded anti-Europeanism'. Others believe the leader has not gone far enough in protecting Britain's monetary heritage and have founded a Conservatives Against a Federal Europe group which is campaigning to renegotiate UK membership of the entire EU, an issue well beyond the single currency.

Meanwhile, the Liberal Democrats have emerged as the most pro-euro of the lot, although their limited political clout means they are likely to remain on the fringes of the debate.

The business view

It is not just the politicians who cannot make up their minds about the euro. British businesses are also at loggerheads. On the one side is the Confederation of British Industry (CBI), a lobby group for medium-sized firms, which broadly supports the single currency, but has felt increasingly let down by the government's softly, softly approach. On the other side is the Institute of Directors, which represents 43,000 UK businessmen, and the Federation of Small Businesses. Both want to keep the pound and use every opportunity to say so.

WHAT THE PAPERS SAY

British tabloid newspapers, with their jingoistic headlines and xenophobic editorials, are notorious for stirring up anti-European sentiment. *The Sun* famously ridiculed the French architect of the euro, Jacques Delors, in 1990 with the headline 'Up yours, Delors', urging its readers to 'tell the French fool where to stuff his Ecu', and entreating them to 'kick the French in the Gauls'. Nine years later it told German Finance Minister Oskar Lafontaine to 'Foxtrot Oskar' when he called for harmonisation of European tax rates.

Such blatant euro-bashing has drawn angry criticism from the European Commission, which has accused the British press of peddling 'jingoistic rubbish' with the express aim of distorting the news and damaging Brussels. Geoffrey Martin, the head of the EC office in Britain, complained: 'We are faced with an avalanche of misrepresentation. It is wilful. It is conscious. It is propagandist.'

It is not just European politics that gets newspaper editors reaching for their Union Jacks. Just about anything is used as an excuse for a spot of euro-phobia. *The Mirror* drew a torrent of criticism for its June 1996 headline, 'Achtung! Surrender', printed after Germany got knocked out of Euro '96. Another football tournament, the ▶

1998 World Cup, and another headline. 'Frogs need a good kicking', said the *Daily Star* after the French were accused of keeping too many tickets for home fans and not distributing enough to away supporters.

Rows over British beef, British chocolate (which was close to being called vegelate in Europe at one stage because of it vegetable oil content) and even imperial weights and measures have all served to fan the xenophobic flames. The nature of the debate means the pro-euro lobby do not have an equivalent weapon with which to fight the anti-Europe onslaught. The best Blair and other europhiles can do is hope to get the tabloids on side before D-day.

The public view

With politicians and businesses so divided, it is hardly surprising the British public is having trouble fathoming the debate. They are constantly bombarded with sound bites from bickering businessmen, triumphant insults from feuding politicians and provocative headlines in tabloid newspapers.

Finding the 'right' answer among all the hyperbole is incredibly hard. There is no black and white, it is all a muddy grey. Economists can argue a convincing case either way, leaving only one thing for certain. The eventual decision on whether to join monetary union will impact on the lives of every person in the country. It will affect prices, jobs, bond and share markets, taxes and interest rates.

In the following pages the theoretical case for a single currency is first outlined then applied to the euro. Its chances of survival are debated, and the arguments for and against British membership discussed.

BEEN THERE, DONE THAT: THE HISTORY OF CURRENCY UNIONS

Monetary union is often portrayed as an historic, groundbreaking venture, whereas in fact Europe has been there before, many times.

Currency unions are almost as old as money itself. One of the earliest recorded examples dates from around 400 BC, not long after the Ancient Greeks introduced coins. Seven states stretching from what is now Turkey to Lesbos in Greece shared a single currency. Just like the proposed euro, the coins had a common design on one side (the baby Heracles wrestling with a snake), leaving the reverse free for the national designs of union members.

Although that alliance was short-lived, its collapse did little to deter future generations. Archaeologists have unearthed evidence of currency unions in at least three other areas of Greece between the fifth and second centuries BC, including silver coins inscribed with goats, dolphins and thunderbolts.

In the late first century BC, the spread of the Roman Empire ushered in the first monetary union to encompass almost the whole of western Europe, including Britain. The need to pay conquering soldiers meant Rome's silver denarius and gold aureus came to dominate from Spain in the west to the Balkans in the east; from Britain in the north to Sicily in the south. It was an informal arrangement that helped to smooth trade between Rome and the rest of the world.

Numerous alliances followed, including Napoleon Bonaparte's 'Empire Français' which saw the franc become official tender in parts of Spain, Italy, Switzerland, The Netherlands, Belgium and Luxembourg.

Whereas that union was imposed by force, a **Latin Monetary Union**, founded on the Continent in 1865, was entirely consensual. Fluctuating gold and silver prices had led to instability in the French monetary system, which, by this time, was used as an informal benchmark for neighbouring currencies. To counter that instability, and formalise monetary union, Belgium, France, Italy and Switzerland introduced silver and gold coins of equal weight and quality. Hence a 20-franc gold coin was worth the same as a 20-lira gold coin, which, upon the inclusion of Greece in the system in 1876, was worth the same as a 20-drachma gold coin.

Meanwhile, across the Channel there was a fearsome debate about whether Britain should join the alliance. The Master of the Royal Mint was all for it and argued for combining the move to European monetary union with decimalisation. The possibility was taken seriously enough in 1867 for the Mint to design a silver coin worth both 10 pence and one French franc. However, it was a case of Empire versus Europe, and in the end Empire won and Britain stayed out.

Many countries on the Continent took a more positive view. Although there were no official new members of the alliance, a number of countries including Serbia, Romania, Liechtenstein and Finland adopted an identical monetary standard. Even the Papal state began issuing gold coins worth 20 lire. However, the First World War brought an end to such widespread co-operation and the system collapsed shortly before the outbreak of hostilities.

If there are any lessons to be drawn from these monetary unions they are twofold. Firstly, currency union will work only if the market accepts it. When coins were made of gold or silver – in other words, they had an intrinsic value – that was relatively straightforward. Maintaining confidence in paper money that costs just a few pence to print is much harder. Secondly, monetary unions that have political origins will work only as long as those politicians are talking to each other. As soon as the First World War put a stop to European esprit de corps, the Latin alliance collapsed.

THE THEORY BEHIND EMU

In 1961, Canadian economist Robert Mundell led a body of research examining the economics behind currency unions. He concluded that there were a number of gains to be had by sharing currencies across borders, provided certain conditions were in place. Those gains, which formed part of his theory known as **optimum currency areas**, were as follows.

- **Transparent prices.** A single currency allows direct comparison of cross-border prices, encouraging greater competition between companies and hence lower prices in shops. A single currency in the UK, for example, discourages HMV from charging more for CDs in Cardiff than it does in London.

- **Lower transaction costs.** Swapping one currency for another can be costly for both firms and holidaymakers. The former face potential foreign exchange losses (or gains) when they conduct business overseas and the latter pay commission when exchanging money. A single currency eliminates both costs, thus encouraging trade, which should act as a catalyst to growth.

- **Greater certainty for investors.** An overseas investor will be happier to pour money into a country if he knows his capital will not be eroded by a fall in the local currency. One cross-border unit of money takes care of that concern. More investment generally means more growth.

- **Price stability.** If a single currency area has one monetary policy, enforced by an independent central bank, inflation in previously unstable countries will fall. This will again encourage investment and growth.

Fans of the euro believe it will generate savings worth billions of pounds thanks to these benefits. However, few are blind to the inherent risks of the project. Having sketched out the advantages to a single, cross-border currency, the theory went on to recognise two main dangers.

- **Loss of independent monetary policy.** All countries in a single currency union are subject to the same interest rates. If the currency covers a wide, economically diverse area, that may cause problems. For example, within Britain alone, struggling manufacturers may need low borrowing costs, but buoyant service sector firms may be more tolerant of higher ones. Finding the right balance in a single country is hard. Achieving a sound compromise over a number of countries could be impossible.

- **Loss of exchange rate flexibility.** One country may be hit by an asymmetric shock, in other words, an event that affects it differently from the surrounding region. For example, a country reliant on oil imports will suffer if the price suddenly rises, while one that exports oil will benefit. If those countries have separate currencies, the exchange rate can change to mitigate the effects of the shock. However, if they are tied into a currency union, exchange rates are effectively fixed, leaving jobs and growth to take the strain.

Optimum currency theory recognised the problem of asymmetric shocks and proposed three ways of dealing with them. Firstly, via a *mobile workforce*. If people are willing and able to move between union countries, they can go where the jobs are, softening the impact of an adverse event. For example, imagine that demand for executive cars like BMWs plunges, putting thousands of Germans out of a job, but that for more affordable Renault Clios is booming. If those Germans are willing to move to France to find work, the adverse effects of the initial shock will be reduced. There will be fewer people out of work in the union as a whole. America is often held up as a shining example of labour mobility, with people willing to move interstate in search of work.

Secondly, if *wages and prices can move up and down easily*, they can take the strain of an unexpected, adverse event instead of the exchange rate. Take the example of an oil price rise again. If workers in an oil-importing country were willing to accept lower wages (which, in practice, is highly unlikely), they could offset the impact of the oil price rise on final prices. That would leave demand, hence growth and jobs in the region, intact.

Thirdly, given the lack of independent monetary policy, there needs to be plenty of *government spending* available for regions that are struggling. Interest rates are set for the whole currency union, hence won't change if one country is in trouble but the rest are fine. The only way of helping that country is via increased government spending. Again, if a country's industry suffers because of an oil price rise, it may need government help in the form of grants, retraining allowances or benefits to redundant workers to stop the whole area from going under.

Given these caveats, optimum currency theory concludes that to have the best chance of success, a single currency area must have the following five characteristics.

- **Asymmetric shocks should be rare.** Countries should have a similar make-up and be at similar stages of their business cycle to reduce the chances of being hit harder than their neighbours in times of trouble (hence Labour's oft repeated five economic tests).

■ **A single monetary policy should affect members in similar ways.** The one-interest-rate-fits-all policy that comes with monetary union means member countries must ideally respond to rate changes in similar ways.

■ **No barriers to labour mobility.** That means no cultural, linguistic or legal impediments to the free movement of labour. In the case of the euro, Italians must be willing and able to work in Finland, for example, or Portuguese in Austria.

■ **Wage flexibility.** Wages should change easily to allow workers to take the strain of shocks, since the exchange rate and the interest rate cannot. France, a core EMU member, has notoriously rigid wages backed up by a strongly unionised workforce.

■ **Should be a system of stabilising transfers.** To cushion the blow of bad news, in the absence of interest rate changes there should be a pool of government money available to spend on struggling regions. The European Stability and Growth Pact, which penalises EMU countries for running excessive deficits, means the scope for fiscal tinkering is limited. The pan-European Union budget amounts to around 1.5 per cent of GDP (and this also covers the four EU members not in the eurozone). Some economists suggest a level closer to 7 per cent is needed to provide adequate funds for adjustment.

MEMBERS OF THE EUROPEAN CLUB

Following is a list of member countries of the European Union. Those marked with a * joined monetary union in the first wave in January 1999.

Austria*	Germany*	Netherlands*
Belgium*	Greece	Portugal*
Denmark	Ireland*	Spain*
Finland*	Italy*	Sweden
France*	Luxembourg*	United Kingdom

Of those four EU countries that stayed out of the first wave of currency union, Greece is the most enthusiastic euro supporter. It is due to join the euro zone in 2001. But integration for the remaining three countries outside EMU may take longer than previously anticipated after Denmark rejected a proposal to ditch the krone in favour of the euro in September 2000. That decision raised the prospect of a two-tier Europe, split between the 'ins' and the 'outs'. It was also expected to reduce the chances of early entry for Britain and Sweden.

ASPIRING MEMBERS

There are several countries eager to join Europe's elite in the EU. An initial wave of enlargement could include the Czech Republic, Estonia, Hungary, Poland, Slovenia and Cyprus. Six other countries are hot on their heels – Latvia, Lithuania, Slovakia, Bulgaria, Romania and Malta. *See* Fig. 8.2. Any decision on even the first wave of enlargement is unlikely before 2005.

FIG. 8.2 European Union membership   Source: Reuters/EcoWin

PUTTING THEORY INTO PRACTICE

Economic theory casts doubt on the chances of EMU success. People are reluctant to accept lower wages, particularly in heavily unionised countries like France, language and cultural differences make moving jobs across borders hard, and the scope for government spending to redress economic imbalance is curtailed. Yet the author of the research, Robert Mundell, is a fan of the single currency (in fact, he is popularly known as the godfather of the euro), which suggests the benefits of EMU might outweigh the costs. In other words, greater trade, enhanced competition, price transparency, low inflation and lower transaction costs could deliver substantial savings that make the euro risk worthwhile.

Take the lack of labour mobility. Many workers were reluctant to move within their own country before monetary union, yet their economies survived perfectly well. In addition, the problem of rigid wages on the Continent is well known and is being confronted, if reluctantly. As for the remaining hurdles, maybe they are best tackled from within a currency union. Many economists believe that the longer the single currency is in operation, the more confidence it will inspire, hence the benefits will rise and the costs diminish. The trouble is, that is very hard to prove.

BRITAIN'S FIVE ECONOMIC TESTS

In October 1997, the Labour government devised five economic tests it said had to be met before it would lead Britain into economic and monetary union:

1 **Business cycles and economic structures must be compatible, so the UK could live comfortably with euro interest rates on a permanent basis.** In other words, the European and British economies must have converged. They must have similar levels of unemployment, debt and inflation, and be growing at a similar pace, under the same interest rates. Only then will a single monetary policy be workable. For example, it would be disastrous if Britain were to join EMU just as it was about to slide into recession if the rest of the euro economies were in mid boom.

2 **If problems emerge, there must be sufficient flexibility to deal with them.** This criterion takes a dig at Europe's strict labour laws, which make hiring and firing workers particularly hard, thus limiting the ability of firms to cut jobs in a downturn. Britain has spent the past 20 years nurturing labour flexibility and would be reluctant to give it up.

3 **Joining EMU must create better conditions for firms making long-term decisions to invest in Britain.** Thousands of British jobs depend on overseas investment. These must be protected in any decision on the future of the pound.

4 **What impact would entry into EMU have on the competitive position of Britain's financial services industry, particularly the City?** The Square Mile earns a lot of money for Britain. Again, that money must be safeguarded when debating the future of the currency.

5 **In summary, will joining EMU promote higher growth, stability and a lasting increase in jobs?** This sounds like a tall order. However, if EMU is not going to bring more jobs and greater wealth, what would be the point in joining?

These criteria have been lambasted for being too woolly. Without any hard figures to aim for, say critics, Labour could pronounce the tests met at any point it chose, making them practically worthless.

❝The purpose of studying economics is
not to acquire a set of ready-made
answers to economic questions, but to learn
how to avoid being deceived
by economists.❞

Joan Robinson, economist, 1955

MARKET FORCES OR FORCING MARKETS?

THE PROS AND CONS OF BRITISH EMU MEMBERSHIP

Mundell's theory provides a useful benchmark for assessing Britain's chances of success within the European single currency area. In the following two sections the *economic* arguments both for and against UK membership are reviewed (the emotional ones are harder to pin down and are probably best left to the newspapers).

Arguments in favour of British membership of EMU

- **Reduces exchange rate uncertainty.** A single, cross-border currency eliminates the exchange rate risk associated with trade. If companies know their profits cannot be wiped out by an unexpected move in trading partners' currencies, they are more likely to do business there. Economics predicts that more trade allows more specialisation, economies of scale and greater growth. Around half of British trade is with European Union countries (*see* Fig. 8.3). That could be threatened if the country stays outside the single currency.

- **Stable exchange rates encourage investment.** This is one of the most persuasive arguments for British membership of EMU and could be the clincher in the debate. Britain attracts more inward investment than any other country in the EU. Relatively cheap, flexible labour means many overseas companies looking for a foothold in Europe head for the UK, bringing jobs and growth with them. However, if Britain stays outside EMU, there is a danger that investment will dry up. For example, a Japanese car factory in the UK, such as Nissan, will have to pay costs in sterling, but will receive most of its revenue in euros, by selling cars on the Continent. If the pound remains strong versus the single currency, a lot of its profit will be wiped out. German

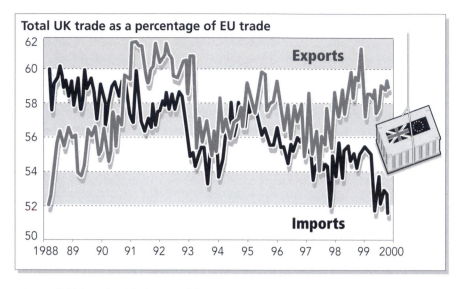

FIG. 8.3 British trade with the rest of Europe

Source: Reuters/EcoWin

carmaker BMW said the strong pound was one reason behind the sale of the troubled Rover group in early 2000, while Mitsubishi has urged Britain to join the euro as soon as possible, saying it could find it 'difficult' to keep its European base in the UK otherwise.

- **Reduced transaction costs.** As Mundell pointed out, a single, cross-border currency greatly reduces transaction costs for both firms and holidaymakers, saving money and encouraging more trade.

- **Protection for the City of London.** A permanent place outside the euro may jeopardise London's status as a leading financial centre, although hard evidence on this is difficult to find. Given the substantial amount of money earned by the financial sector for Britain, any knock to the city would be extremely damaging for the whole economy.

- **Britain has a poor inflation and exchange rate record.** This argument is starting to look a little dated. In the past, a poor inflation performance meant the UK would have had much to gain in entrusting interest rates to an independent bank like the ECB. Advantages would have included a fall in long bond yields and lower inflation, which would have brought with it greater investment and hence GDP growth. However, given Britain's impressive inflation performance in the latter part of the 1990s, it arguably does not need to borrow credibility from other central banks any more.

- **Greater price transparency.** Direct price comparisons under a single, cross-border currency will encourage competition between retailers, hence lower prices in shops. However, easy access to

Europe with the single market and the Internet is already highlighting price discrepancies between countries. For example, a recent Competition Commission report found that private consumers in Britain were being overcharged by up to £1 billion a year for cars. Britons have been paying around 30 per cent more for Volvo S70s than their French, German or Italian counterparts, and 20 per cent more for Volkswagen Golfs.

- **Globalisation.** As cultural and economic barriers fall, only a few world currencies will come to dominate on the global stage. The dollar will be one of them, and the euro could be another, simply because of the 300 million people using it. The pound, with its 57 million customers, could slip into obscurity.

- **Greater fiscal discipline.** The rules of monetary union prevent governments from racking up unsustainable debts (thanks to the Stability and Growth Pact). That means less money spent on interest, but it also means that if people want more public services, they will have to pay for them in taxes rather than relying on borrowing. However, Britain already has fiscal rules intended to discourage government profligacy.

So there you have it. Eight reasons for Britain to join European economic and monetary union. Convinced? Before you decide, here is a word from the detractors.

Arguments against British membership of EMU

- **Relinquishing monetary sovereignty.** The loss of interest rate control is the biggest argument against Britain joining a single currency. Rates are a powerful tool in manipulating the economy, and if set at an inappropriate level can cause runaway inflation or deep recession. At the beginning of 2000, a year after the euro was launched, borrowing costs in the single currency area were 3.0 per cent, while those in Britain were 5.5 per cent. Bringing the latter down to the former's level would have been disastrous. Inflation would have taken off, forcing the government to raise taxes or cut spending to try to syphon off some of the excess demand.

  Anti-euro campaigners also argue that Britain now has a perfectly good inflation framework of its own in the form of the Bank of England's Monetary Policy Committee. The Bank's symmetrical 2.5 per cent target is arguably better than the ECB's 2 per cent or less, which carries with it risks of deflation. The MPC is also far more transparent than the ECB – the minutes from its monthly rate meetings, for example, are released two weeks after the event, compared with 17 years in the case of the ECB.

- **British economy is more sensitive to rate changes.** One criterion for a successful monetary union is that each country has a similar response to interest rate changes. Heavy reliance on overdrafts and variable-rate mortgages in Britain could mean the UK is more sensitive to changes in short-term borrowing costs than its Continental neighbours (around 75 per cent of UK mortgages are variable while they make up only 5 per cent of home loans in France and Germany). Thus a rate rise could squeeze spending and growth harder in Britain and a rate fall may trigger inflation more readily. Many pro-euro economists dispute this argument, saying there is no evidence that Britons are any more susceptible to rate changes than their Continental counterparts.

- **Lack of exchange rate adjustment.** Another danger is the absence of exchange rate adjustment in the face of an adverse, asymmetric shock. For example, a rise in the cost of raw materials in Britain would put the country at a competitive disadvantage. Its products would be more expensive to make than those overseas. Under a flexible exchange rate system, the pound could fall to compensate, making exports cheaper and thus maintaining demand. Under a fixed system, however, unemployment could rise, possibly to politically unacceptable levels, as demand for British goods falls.

- **European labour markets are more rigid.** Copious rules and regulations in euro countries make labour markets less flexible than their British counterparts. Workers are harder to fire, which discourages firms from expanding for fear of being saddled with unwanted employees if growth slows. This could impede enterprise. If the UK were to join the single currency, it may have to fall in line with these social policies, risking its prized labour flexibility and the investment that comes with it. (However, some counter with the argument that Britain could keep its flexibility, thus giving it a competitive advantage over its neighbours.)

- **Government spending is constrained by the Stability and Growth Pact.** With interest rates set by the ECB, governments must rely more on spending and taxation to steer their economies. However, the Stability and Growth Pact among euro members puts strict restrictions on the amount of debt each country can accumulate, curtailing the main area of control left open to domestic authorities. Some in the anti-euro camp also warn that monetary union could end in a form of fiscal union, with tax levels across the zone set by politicians in Brussels.

- **Lack of flexibility.** This encompasses the last two arguments. A lack of labour mobility and fiscal leeway – two essential criteria for an ideal optimum currency area – make dealing with asymmetric shocks incredibly difficult. A single currency may be tested to the limit in a downturn.

Those are the main arguments for and against British membership of the European single currency. I have deliberately left out the emotional views – giving up the pound, being run by bureaucrats in Brussels, etc. – because this is supposed to be an unbiased, *economic* look at the issue. If you are still undecided, you may find those aspects clinch it for you. Either way, you won't have to rely on politicians and newspapers for an opinion.

THE SINGLE CURRENCY: GOING BACK TO ITS ROOTS

The single currency is the culmination of a 50-year journey towards greater European integration intended to banish the threat of war, stamp out economic nationalism and give the Continent more clout in foreign policy. Back in 1952, six countries – Belgium, France, Germany, Italy, Luxembourg and the Netherlands – established the **European Coal and Steel Community**. The idea was to put the raw materials of war into the hands of a supranational authority, thereby controlling old Franco-German rivalries. To some extent, that remains the European Union's binding legacy.

Five years later, those same nations signed the **Treaty of Rome**, founding the **European Economic Community (EEC)**. The treaty, which came into effect on 1 January 1958, called for the abolition of internal tariffs, which was completed by the original six members ten years later. At this stage, there was no mention of monetary union. That only came to light in 1970 when a group of European experts devised the **Werner plan** (named after Luxembourg's Prime Minister Pierre Werner), which envisaged a single European currency by 1980. Extreme currency volatility and the oil crisis meant the plan was thwarted.

In 1979, the **European Monetary System** was founded which established a grid of stable but adjustable exchange rates, known as the **Exchange Rate Mechanism**. By this time, Denmark, Ireland and the United Kingdom had joined the EEC. The UK remained outside the currency grid, where it stayed until October 1990.

Over the years, the EEC, which was renamed the European Union (EU), acquired more members. By 2000, the original six, plus the three latecomers, had been joined by Greece, Spain, Portugal, Austria, Finland and Sweden.

Momentum towards monetary union really started to gather pace in the 1980s. In 1986, the **Single European Act** officially recognised the objective of a single currency and a European single market (signed on behalf of Britain by Margaret Thatcher in the days when she was notorious for 'hand-bagging' European colleagues when their federalist tendencies came to the fore). Architects of the treaty believed that by pooling all

▶

the resources in the EU, and then creating a single currency, Europe's twin ambitions of global power and lasting peace would be assured.

In 1989, the blueprint for monetary union was approved and in December 1991, in the Dutch city of Maastricht, EU ministers drew up a route map on how to reach a single currency by 1999.

Over the remainder of the decade, the building blocks for the euro were put in place. The **European Monetary Institute (EMI)** was set up in 1994 as the forerunner to the **European Central Bank (ECB)**. It was charged with assessing each country's suitability for euro membership. Aspiring nations had to have low inflation and low long-term interest rates, sensible levels of government debt and stable exchange rates.

Eleven countries were approved for EMU membership in May 1998 (Austria, Belgium, Finland, France, Germany, Ireland, Italy, Luxembourg, the Netherlands, Portugal and Spain). On 1 January 1999, their exchange rates were irrevocably fixed and the euro was born. The ECB took control of setting interest rates on the same day.

Participating countries will continue to spend their national currencies until 2002. They will then have six months to exchange their francs, marks, lire, etc. for euros, and will be able to use either when they go shopping during that transition period. In July 2002, national currencies will be abolished for ever.

THERE MAY BE TROUBLE AHEAD ...

Even if the euro is a success and matures into a strong currency capable of delivering low inflation, more trade and greater competition, it could still encounter problems. Some economists predict it will exacerbate the trend to globalisation, freeing companies even more from their national roots and rendering governments increasingly impotent.

It could distract policymakers from wider issues such as EU enlargement. Many countries in Eastern Europe are knocking on the door of the European Union, eager for a taste of western prosperity, low inflation and the strength that comes in numbers. What they gain in economic credibility, the EU gains in greater security by injecting stability into volatile, conflict-prone areas. And if enlargement plans do progress, the tricky issue of how far and when to integrate them into EMU arises.

There is also a debate as to whether the structural reforms necessary to promote flexible labour markets within Europe will be helped or hindered by the single currency. Britain is one of the loudest advocates of flexibility, but holds limited sway from its position on the sidelines. If the commitment to flexible labour markets were to founder, it would significantly increase the chances of problems within the euro area in the future.

Finally there is the highly sensitive, emotive issue of greater political integration within Europe. History suggests that currency unions crumble more readily in the absence of political commitment. And even though words such as irrevocable and permanent are used about the single currency, it is not impossible for a country to leave, or even for it to break up. However, just the idea of a European superstate, where decisions are centralised in Brussels, is enough to make many people quake. (I met someone a few years ago who had taught his three-year-old daughter to recite the words: 'No to a Federal Europe, no to a single currency.' It was a bizarre and slightly disturbing performance.)

IF YOU REMEMBER SIX THINGS FROM THIS CHAPTER …

- European economic and monetary union (EMU) began on 1 January 1999, when the national currencies of 11 countries on the Continent were irrevocably fixed against each other. Those countries were Austria, Belgium, Finland, France, Germany, Ireland, Italy, Luxembourg, the Netherlands, Portugal and Spain. Each currency has been replaced on foreign exchange markets by one single currency, the euro. This still fluctuates against currencies like the dollar and the pound.

- Economic theory highlights four advantages to a single, cross-border currency: transparent prices, lower transaction costs, greater certainty for investors and price stability.

- The two downsides are the loss of independent monetary policy and the loss of exchange rate flexibility. Both could be sorely missed if one country within the single currency area was knocked sideways by a negative event, but all the other countries remained unaffected (an asymmetric shock).

- Economics is only part of the argument, however. Politics and patriotism play an equally important role and could prove decisive in Britain's decision about whether to join EMU.

- EMU is the culmination of almost 50 years of greater integration in Europe, initially intended to prevent the outbreak of another war, halt rampant economic nationalism and create a global economic power. The process continues with the introduction of euro notes and coins in January 2002, which will run alongside national currencies for six months.

- Interest rates in the EMU area are set by the independent European Central Bank, which comprises representatives from each euro member country.

CHAPTER 9

ALTOGETHER NOW

Institutions for a globalised world

66 Bureaucracy is not an obstacle to democracy but an inevitable complement to it. 99

Joseph A. Schumpeter

There is a saying in financial circles that when the US stock market sneezes, the rest of the world catches a cold. Such is the integration between countries today that you cannot afford to consider any nation in isolation. Money, people, goods and ideas can all flow virtually unimpeded across borders, tying each country's prosperity to that of its neighbours'. One economy's recession soon becomes the rest of the world's downturn, as shown to clear effect in the summer of 1997 when a number of Asian countries saw growth plummet. Global growth took a severe knock in the months that followed, falling to 1.7 per cent in 1998 from an expected 4 per cent.

It is because of that integration that the world's independent central banks and supranational organisations like the International Monetary Fund (IMF) have come increasingly under the spotlight in recent years. British markets often follow the interest rate decisions of the US central bank, the Federal Reserve, for example, more avidly than they do those of the Bank of England. US figures on inflation and employment garner far more attention than their British equivalents. As soon as US stock and bond markets open for business, in early afternoon UK time, British gilts and London shares slavishly follow the US lead for the rest of the day.

One reason the US has the rest of the world in its thrall is that if its economy were to veer off the rails, it could take out a sizeable chunk of global growth in the process. Statesiders import more than $1.0 trillion worth of goods (1999 figures), bankrolling millions of jobs in the process.

So it is not just the Bank of England that Britons need to watch to get an idea of what the future holds for the UK. It is useful to have an idea of what the Federal Reserve is up to as well.

This chapter considers the role of the Fed and other institutions that affect global jobs and growth. It looks behind the scenes of the world economy at the following issues.

- **It charts the origins and aims of the Bank of England.** It is not just politicians who have a say in how the economy is run, independent central banks also play a significant role. Chapter 4 discussed how the Bank decides interest rates, leaving this section to focus on its other responsibilities, such as lender of last resort and caretaker of the country's multi-billion-pound financial sector. It also gives a brief history of the Old Lady of Threadneedle Street, as it's known, from its creation more than 300 years ago to its new-found independence in 1997.

- **It explains what the US Federal Reserve does.** The Fed is quite simply the most powerful central bank in the world. Its interest rate decisions affect global bond and share prices and wield more influence over British jobs and growth than anything else beyond its shores. That makes the Fed's pragmatic chairman, Alan Greenspan, who is profiled in this chapter, the most influential banker on the planet.

- **It looks at the workings of the European Central Bank.** The ECB will end up deciding the cost of borrowing in Britain if the country joins monetary union. This chapter looks at its structure and at how it allows 11 countries to collectively decide a single rate of interest.

- **It explains the function of the International Monetary Fund.** The IMF is best known for lending billions of dollars to crisis-hit countries like Russia and Indonesia. It may seem far removed from life in Britain and other developed countries, but in fact its influence can be keenly felt. The UK buys and sells millions of pounds of goods and services to countries in Asia, trade that would have been jeopardised in recent years if it was not for IMF help in the region. If you invest in emerging market stocks or bonds you have also arguably benefited from the Fund's financial rescue operations in the latter part of the 1990s.

- **It delves into the workings of the World Bank.** In theory, the World Bank has a more philanthropic agenda. Its aim is to eradicate global poverty by lending money to poor countries for sustainable economic development. This chapter explains how it gets that money, exactly where it spends it, and why it has come in for some harsh criticism in its 50-year lifetime.

■ **It examines the origins and aims of the World Trade Organisation.** The WTO has been the focus for angry protests against globalisation recently because of its trade liberalising agenda. Again, although it may seem a remote, bureaucratic institution that has little relevance to everyday life, its influence can be felt on British jobs and prices.

THE WORLD'S MAJOR CENTRAL BANKS

THE BANK OF ENGLAND

Behind every great man there's a great woman, and in the case of the British economy it is the Old Lady of Threadneedle Street, otherwise known as the Bank of England.

THE OLD LADY OF THREADNEEDLE STREET

The Bank of England earned its nickname in the early 19th century when, in theory, all bank notes were readily exchangeable for gold. A series of runs on its bullion, caused by the uncertainty of the Napoleonic wars, drained the Bank's reserves to the point where it was forced to suspend that guarantee. This Restriction Period, as it was known, prompted the Irish playwright and MP Richard Brinsley Sheridan to refer angrily to the Bank as '… an elderly lady in the City'.

This was swiftly changed by cartoonist James Gillray to the Old Lady of Threadneedle Street, a name that has stuck.

Origins

Founded in 1694 to finance King William III's war against France, the Bank is one of the oldest central banks in the world. It has outlived 13 monarchs, almost 100 prime ministers and numerous wars. It has even survived a potential raid on its gold vaults.

In 1836, the directors of the Bank are said to have received an anonymous letter stating that the writer had access to their bullion and would meet them in the gold vaults at any hour they chose. Despite their scepticism, they eventually agreed and assembled one night in the vast cellar under the Bank's Threadneedle Street offices. At the appointed hour, the mystery man appeared beneath them, displacing a few floorboards. The story has it that he was a sewerman and had discovered the old drain underneath the vaults during routine repair work. Despite the obvious temptations, he had taken nothing and was awarded £800 for his honesty – a princely sum in those days.

During the Bank's early years, from 1715 onwards, its main task was to raise money for the government by selling bonds. It moved to its present-day premises at Threadneedle Street, in the heart of London's financial district, in 1734, gradually expanding to fill the three-acre site. During the 1800s, its powers grew. In 1827 it opened its provincial branches, and in 1844 it was given a formal monopoly on issuing notes in England and Wales.

Throughout this period, the Bank was privately owned, although for many years it had acted in the public interest. It bailed out Baring Brothers in 1890, for example, after a series of injudicious loans in South America left the ill-fated bank sitting on a pile of worthless Argentine bonds. This established the concept of the Bank of England as lender of last resort, which meant it stood ready to loan money to banks in financial difficulty, whose collapse could threaten the stability of the whole financial system.

The Nationalisation Act in 1946 transferred ownership of the Bank to the government. The Banking Act 33 years later confirmed its powers in law and gave it formal responsibility for the supervision of commercial banks, a role it was subsequently relieved of in 1998. But what the government took away with one hand, it had already given with the other. In May 1997, a few days after its sweeping election victory, Labour's Gordon Brown stunned financial markets by handing the Bank power to set interest rates. Since then, in a move which must reflect the MPC's anti-inflation credentials, the opposition Conservative Party has pledged to maintain the status quo.

Aims

The Bank of England has three purposes: to maintain the integrity and value of the pound, to ensure the stability of the financial system and to promote the efficiency and competitiveness of that system. Its customers are the commercial banks in Britain such as Barclays and Lloyds (plus any foreign banks that have branches here), overseas central banks and the government. It also has around 8,000 private account holders, most of whom are staff or pensioners of the Bank.

Protecting the value of the pound

The most important function of any central bank is to safeguard the value of the currency, in terms of what it will buy both at home and abroad. To that end, the Bank must keep prices as stable as possible. As explained in Chapter 4, its nine-member Monetary Policy Committee is charged with keeping underlying RPIX inflation at 2.5 per cent. If it moves more than one percentage point either side of that mark, the governor must write an open letter to the Chancellor of the Exchequer explaining why.

As to the pound's value overseas, the government is responsible for determining the country's exchange rate policy while the Bank merely advises and implements that policy by buying or selling the nation's foreign exchange reserves. At the time of writing, the pound was free to float against other currencies, but that would change if Britain were to join European Economic and Monetary Union. The Bank does, however, have separate foreign exchange reserves of its own, which the MPC may decide to use for monetary policy purposes.

Prior to April 1998, one of the Bank's functions was to manage the sale and redemption of government bonds. However, that responsibility has now been passed to an agency of the Treasury, the Debt Management Office (DMO).

Ensuring a stable financial system

Without a stable financial system, the Bank of England's ability to impose its interest rate policy would be curtailed. It is therefore up to the Bank to make sure everything in the City runs smoothly. Up until June 1998, that involved supervising all banks that had offices in Britain. That task now falls to the Financial Services Authority (FSA), but it is still the Bank's duty to intervene if there is a threat to the stability of the financial system as a whole.

It could do that by acting as the *lender of last resort*. In the rare situation where the failure of one institution could bring down other, otherwise viable, institutions, the Bank can step in and bail out the bank concerned. For that reason, in September 1984 it rescued Johnson Matthey, buying it for £1 and putting in its own managers to run it.

More recently, when Barings collapsed in February 1995 under the weight of $1.4 billion of losses on unauthorised derivatives trades in Singapore, the Bank kept its distance. Rather than lend it money again, as it had done more than 100 years previously, it waited for the private sector to come up with a solution. It duly did, and Dutch bank ING took over the troubled institution instead.

Keeping the City competitive

The City of London, a square mile of densely packed offices between St Paul's Cathedral and the East End, earns vast amounts of money for Britain. The bankers, brokers, insurance salesmen and traders who pack into the district by day (and leave it deserted by around 9.30 at night when many of the bars close) make up one of the most lucrative sectors in the country. It is one of the Bank's jobs to make sure it stays that way.

London is the world's leading international financial centre thanks to its openness, flexible regulations, skilled personnel and willingness to innovate and adapt. The Bank plays a key role in that success by implementing slick back-office systems for the payment of shares and bonds and, more recently, by making sure information technology could handle both the change to the year 2000 and the switch to the euro on the Continent.

The Bank of England's website is at www.bankofengland.co.uk

THE LIFE AND TIMES OF THE POUND NOTE

The Bank of England first issued bank notes more than 300 years ago. Today, it is easy to accept that something that costs less than three pence to make is worth £5 or £10 or £100, but back in 1694 the public took a bit more convincing.

Therefore, when they were first issued, Bank of England notes were backed up entirely by gold. Handwritten on Bank paper was a promise to pay the bearer the sum of the note on demand, meaning that anyone presenting it at the Bank could immediately exchange it for bullion or coinage.

That link ended with the First World War, however, because the government needed to preserve its stock of gold. It was partially restored in 1925 and finally scrapped in 1931. Ever since then, note issue has become *fiduciary*, that is, wholly backed by securities instead of bullion.

Unlike today, notes were rarely used by the general population when they were first introduced because their denominations were so high. From 1696, the minimum tender was £50 – more than double the average annual income of £20. By 1745 notes ranged from £20 to £1,000, the latter being equivalent to more than £68,000 today.

With such staggering sums at stake, counterfeiting was rife. The first recorded case was in 1695, when Daniel Perrismore was fined and pilloried for manufacturing 60 £100 notes. He had a lucky escape. Two years later, new laws meant his crime would have been punishable by death.

▶

During the Second World War, the problem of counterfeiting grew. By 1943, the German government was producing around 500,000 fake 'British' notes a month in an attempt to undermine the country's financial system. Most were captured by advancing allied forces, although some did find their way into circulation, so to counter the problem the Bank introduced a metal thread into the currency.

These days, the Bank of England prints its notes at a factory in Loughton in Essex. Around 1.3 billion are made each year, enough, if put end to end, to stretch halfway to the moon. The paper used, produced specially for the bank by a company called Portals, is made from cotton which gives it its distinctive feel and increases its toughness and durability. The average lifespan of a note varies – £5 notes last only around a year, while £50 notes last up to three or four years. Old notes are shredded and used as landfill.

THE US FEDERAL RESERVE

The US Federal Reserve is a giant among central banks. Not only does it control the fate of its own, $9 trillion economy, it also has the rest of the world hanging on its every word. US interest rate meetings are the most eagerly awaited, hyped event on the economic calendar. For days beforehand there is talk of nothing else in currency, bond and share markets, simply because if the US economy was allowed to stumble, it could drag the rest of the world down with it. Such is the power of its 270 million consumers that if they decided to stop spending money, countries from Australia to Zimbabwe would feel the pinch. (If it had not been for a voracious US appetite for imports in the latter half of the 1990s, the global economy could well have sunk into recession thanks to the economic collapse in Asia.)

Origins

For one so powerful, the Fed, as it is known in markets, is surprisingly young. Less than a third of the age of the Bank of England, it was founded in 1913 under President Woodrow Wilson's administration. A network of 12 regional banks was established a year later, charged with executing Fed business across the country. Branches from Boston to San Francisco meant 'no (commercial) bank should be more than one night's train ride from its Federal Reserve Bank', as one senator put it at the time. The geographic spread also meant interest rate policy could not be hijacked by overbearing bankers on the east coast and skewed towards their economic needs.

The Fed had a troublesome adolescence. By the time it was 21 it had been through two world wars and a Great Depression which had seen half of the nation's banks fail. The rest of the century passed relatively peacefully in comparison. The US economy had highs and lows, just like Britain, but the 25 per cent unemployment and plunging share prices of the 1930s never recurred. Inevitably for an institution so powerful, the Fed has attracted its fair share of criticism over the years. Some say its rate policies exacerbated the 1930s depression and contributed to the stock market crash more than 50 years later in October 1987. But on the whole it has acquitted itself well and is worthy of its august reputation.

Aims

The Federal Reserve's duties are fourfold. It must decide interest rates, regulate the country's banks, make sure the US financial system is stable, and provide certain services to the government, the public and foreign official institutions.

Its most public role is undoubtedly the first of those – setting interest rates. Eight times a year, its MPC equivalent, the Federal Open Market Committee (FOMC), meets in Washington DC to decide whether to change the cost of borrowing. The 12 members who comprise the committee at any one time (consisting of seven from the board of governors and five regional reserve bank presidents) discuss factors such as prices, wages, employment, consumer spending and business investment. They reach a decision by consensus, typically led by the board's highly respected chairman, Alan Greenspan (*see* box below).

The Fed's mandate is fuzzier than the MPC's. There is no specific target for inflation, simply a responsibility to promote stable prices, sustainable economic growth and full employment.

The Federal Reserve website can be found at www.federalreserve.gov

GREENSPAN SAYS …

Alan Greenspan, the Fed's judicious, highly respected chairman since 1987, is the most powerful central banker in the world. He speaks, markets move. When he declared in December 1996 that stock market investors were showing signs of 'irrational exuberance', equity prices in the US plunged 10 per cent. When he cautiously accepted that the US economy might be able to grow faster and longer than ever before without igniting inflation, the public took him at his word and the stock market soared.

A keen tennis player and accomplished musician, Greenspan likes to cultivate an unworldly image that belies his impressive career. He ran a highly successful economic consulting firm before becoming Fed chairman, and advised both Presidents Ford and Reagan in the 1970s and 1980s. His respect for free markets is renowned. Having studied at New York University in the 1940s under the libertarian thinker Ayn Rand, the young scholar developed an enduring admiration for *laissez faire* economics that was to hold him in good stead in later years.

The word most often associated with Greenspan is pragmatic. He is said to have a keen eye for detail and a voracious appetite for fact and figures. This 'watch everything' attitude served him well during the Asian crisis in 1997 and 1998. Many believe that it was his deft handling of the world's largest economy during that time that saved the rest of the globe from recession.

It also compounded his growing popularity among both the public and the markets. Unlike his predecessors, Greenspan has garnered widespread admiration, verging on cult status in the US. Central bankers are not supposed to be liked – as former Fed chairman William McChesney Martin put it, their job is to take away the punchbowl just as the party gets started. But Greenspan seems to be an exception. He even has an unofficial fan club (at www.getexuberant.com).

However, he is not without his critics. The one-time saxophonist from New York has been blamed for precipitating the stock market crash in October 1987 and for overstimulating the economy in the aftermath. Some also worry about his handling of the dot.com sensation in the US. While his supporters believe that it is his matter-of-fact approach to inflation control that has allowed the US to chalk up its longest non-inflationary expansion in history, detractors warn he is playing with fire. They worry that the rule book has not changed, and that the US stock market is riding towards a fall. A central banker is only as good as his country's economic credentials and Greenspan could yet go down in history as the perpetrator of the biggest stock market crash in history.

THE EUROPEAN CENTRAL BANK

The European Central Bank is by far the youngest of the institutions profiled here. Established in June 1998, six months before the advent of the single European currency, its main role is to keep inflation down within the 11-nation eurozone. It has had a rocky induction thanks largely to the skittish behaviour of its young charge, the euro, which fell almost 30 per cent against the dollar in its first 20 months. Not only did that add to inflationary pressures on the Continent, it also posed a diplomatic conundrum. The ECB faced two choices: try to bolster the flailing currency via intervention or let the currency find its own level and in the meantime (gratefully) reap the benefits of greater competitiveness and therefore stronger export growth. The ECB initially chose the latter, but resorted to intervention when things looked to be getting out of control in September 2000. A major concern at the time was that the weak currency would stoke eurozone inflation.

Origins

The ECB has evolved into what it is today over a number of years. Its earliest incarnation was as the European Monetary Institute, founded in January 1994 to help guide aspiring single-currency members towards successful EMU entry. The EMI was different from the ECB in one important sense – it lacked any autonomous power, being bound instead by member national authorities. That meant it had no right to make interest rate decisions, it simply helped to strengthen the co-ordination of monetary policy among eurozone countries.

The EMI gave way to the ECB in 1998, at which point the latter took responsibility for deciding interest rates in the eurozone. All 11-member nations have a say in that decision via their individual central bank governors, making the ECB's twice-monthly meetings an enormous exercise in compromise.

At the helm is Wim Duisenberg, a white-haired, chain-smoking former Dutch central bank chief. He has yet to establish a reputation among markets as solid as Alan Greenspan's and probably only has until 2002 to do so. At that point French central bank governor Jean-Claude Trichet is tipped to take over as ECB president.

Aims

Just like the Bank of England, the ECB has a specific target for inflation. However, unlike the Old Lady, that target is asymmetric. The ECB must keep HICP inflation (the harmonised measure) at 2 per cent or less. That means it could drive it down to 1 per cent or even 0.5 per cent if it saw fit, whereas the MPC must not let RPIX deviate from the 2.5 per cent target. Some say the ECB's open-ended target is dangerous since it increases the possibility of deflation. You will recall from Chapter 4 that this may trigger a downward spiral of job losses and economic contraction.

Criticisms

The ECB also comes in for criticism over its decision not to publish the transcript of its rate meetings. Some say this lack of transparency is damaging and encourages unhealthy speculation in currency, share and bond markets. The ECB counters that its post-meeting news conferences give ample opportunity to scrutinise its thinking.

The trouble is, ECB members often make comments about interest rates outside of those meetings. Trying to get 11 central bank chiefs to speak with one voice is proving extremely difficult and on more than one occasion small contradictions about likely policy have emerged.

The jury is still out on the ECB. It has had a rocky initiation but appears to be holding up well, albeit with a few teething problems. By the time Britain joins EMU – if indeed it does – those difficulties will hopefully have been ironed out. Assuming, of course, it survives its bumpy initiation.

The ECB website, which contains links to other EU central banks, is at www.ecb.int

THE INTERNATIONAL MONETARY FUND

SAVING COUNTRIES FROM BANKRUPTCY

The **International Monetary Fund** offers financial help to indebted nations in return for economic reform, ensures currencies can be easily exchanged, thus oiling the wheels of trade, and offers training to officials in less developed economies.

If you continually borrow money without any apparent means of being able to pay it back, there will come a point when no one will lend you any more. You will be blacklisted by banks and credit companies, and you could face bankruptcy.

The same can happen to countries, but on a much larger scale. Those that wrack up bigger and bigger debts, either for investment purposes or simply to buy more goods, face the risk of defaulting on their loans (particularly if those investments have been unwise). The chain reaction in such a scenario could be devastating. If banks do not get repaid, they could collapse, which means thousands of depositors from all over the world could lose their money.

The International Monetary Fund exists to make sure that does not happen. The IMF is like a huge credit union funded by more than 180 countries that provides emergency finance to nations which cannot pay their bills. In theory, each country that contributes to the fund can borrow from the kitty when they need to, but in practice, it is the rich nations that put money in, and the poor ones that take it out.

The IMF has a fund of almost $300 billion thanks to contributions from its 182 members. When each country signs up, it pays a subscription, known as a quota. The richer the country, the bigger the quota, and the larger the voting power. The world's leading economy, the United States, contributes 18 per cent of quotas, or $35 billion, and wields the greatest influence. Britain is the fourth largest contributor along with France, with each providing around $10 billion. Quotas are reviewed every five years and can be raised or lowered according to IMF needs and the prosperity of members.

Origins

The IMF was founded in 1947 with 29 member countries after lengthy talks in the New Hampshire town of Bretton Woods. Its original aim, devised in part by Keynes, was to supervise the system of fixed global exchange rates negotiated after the breakdown of world trade in the 1930s. The fund stood ready to bail out countries that could not pay their import bills under the new regime (under fixed exchange rates, countries have to borrow money or devalue their currencies to cover a balance of payments shortfall).

Aims

In today's world of floating exchange rates, the IMF's original *raison d'être* no longer exists. In theory, countries no longer have to borrow large sums of money to see them through mounting current account deficits. They can simply sit back, wait for their currency to weaken, and then watch demand for their exports rise as prices fall. In practice, however, things are often very different.

The Fund has had to carve out a new role for itself, one that fits into today's increasingly globalised, market-oriented world. It has done so in three ways. It lends money to countries struggling to pay their debts, makes sure currencies can be easily exchanged, therefore facilitating trade, and offers technical assistance and training to officials in less developed economies.

The first of those roles, to effectively bail out indebted countries on the verge of collapse, is its most controversial. It is best explained by way of example.

THE IMF AND ASIA

In the summer of 1997, a tidal wave of panic washed over the economies of south-east Asia that sent international investors sprinting for the exits. After years of unparalleled economic growth, it seemed that countries such as Thailand, Korea and Indonesia could no longer afford to pay back their mounting international debts. Poor-quality investments, a lack of adequate governance by the authorities and the sheer amount of unhedged, short-term money that had been pumped into the region sparked a speculative attack on the Thai baht that saw it lose almost 30 per cent of its value in three months.

The rout soon spread to neighbouring countries. Something needed to be done. South Korea alone was the world's 11th largest economy. If it was allowed to go bankrupt it would undoubtedly take other countries down with it and cause untold damage to the global economy.

It fell to the IMF to take action. In 1997, the Fund approved around £35 billion of IMF financial support for reform programmes in Indonesia, Korea and Thailand. It also led to the mobilisation of around $77 billion of additional financing from multilateral and bilateral sources.

But there were strings attached. Whenever financial support is extended to member countries, the IMF demands that certain policies, aimed at economic revival, be implemented in return. In the case of Asia, the Fund insisted that recipient countries raise interest rates in order to halt the run on their currencies and demanded that sound fiscal policies be imposed. In addition, it called for penetrating structural reforms such as the break-up of monopolies and the dismantling of trade barriers, factors it believed had exacerbated the crash in the first place. Unviable financial institutions were closed and domestic financial systems were opened up to foreign participation.

CRITICS ABOUND

However, not everyone believes in this image of the IMF as global saviour charging to the rescue. Critics abound, just as one of its primary architects, Keynes, warned they might. 'There is scarcely any enduringly successful experience of an international body which has fulfilled the hopes of its progenitors,' he told the 1946 inaugural meeting of the Fund in Savannah. 'Either an institution has become diverted to the instrument of a limited group or else it has been a puppet – sawdust through which the breath of life does not flow.'

■ The most common grumble about the IMF is that it encourages **moral hazard**. If countries know that someone else will pick up the bill in the event of a disaster, they will be more gung-ho in their economic decisions. This devil-may-care attitude could encourage the very scenarios the IMF is there to prevent.

- The Fund's *one size fits all* policy prescriptions that come attached to loans also come in for criticism. Detractors want a move away from the traditional calls to devalue the currency and increase taxes (to restore current account surplus) towards a more innovative, tailor-made approach. The Fund's advice to Russia as it moved from communism to capitalism has been a particular target for critics. Almost a decade after reforms began, around 60 million people – half the population – still lived below the poverty line, income inequality had risen, and life expectancy had plummeted.

- Equally unhelpful, they say, is the IMF's *domineering, overbearing style of crisis management*. Instead of swooping in and imposing non-negotiable policies, it should let local economists and government officials decide the best course of action. That way, the country in question will not only learn more from the experience but will also be more inclined to implement the necessary reforms.

- Some Fund members complain that IMF loans are used as *political levers* by the west, particularly the US. When Russian commitment to free-market economics looked like floundering in the 1990s, the promise of billions of dollars in IMF help was enough to keep it on the straight and narrow path to capitalism.

- Finally, what is the point of the IMF if it fails to spot crises? There was little warning of the Asian turmoil that engulfed the world in 1997, for which some blame the Fund. If it wants to keep its $300 billion budget, it may have to be a little more vigilant in future.

More information on the IMF can be found at its website at www.imf.org

THE WORLD BANK

HELPING THE POOR

The **World Bank** lends money to poor countries for spending on projects that encourage sustainable economic development. It also supports private businesses in needy areas, channels foreign capital into investment-hungry economies, and offers extensive training and technical assistance.

The World Bank is often confused with the IMF. Both were established around the same time, both are based in Washington and both lend money to developing economies. But they have very separate roles.

Whereas the IMF provides loans only in emergencies, so as to ensure the integrity of the global financial system, the World Bank's primary aim is to reduce poverty.

It lends around $30 billion each year to 100 developing economies to finance spending in areas such as transport, agriculture, health and education.

Origins

The Bank was established in 1946 to prepare for the reconstruction of Europe after the devastation of the Second World War. Its mandate was agreed at the same Bretton Woods conference that created the IMF.

Aims

The World Bank has four roles: to provide loans to poor countries, to help local businesses get established, to encourage private money into needy areas, and to offer technical help and policy advice.

Lending to poor nations

Almost three-quarters of World Bank funds are raised in financial markets by the **International Bank for Reconstruction and Development**, one of five institutions that make up the Bank group. The IBRD sells AAA-rated bonds to pension funds and insurance companies worldwide, and then loans the money raised to middle-income countries and creditworthy, poorer nations. It charges interest to its borrowers and demands that loans are repaid in 15–20 years. Less than 5 per cent of IBRD money comes from member subscriptions.

The **International Development Association** oversees the rest of the Bank's lending for large-scale projects such as improving sanitation, building hospitals and constructing roads. Established in 1960, the IDA provides interest-free loans to those countries too poor to borrow at commercial rates. Repayment is required in 35 or 40 years and countries have a ten-year grace period before they have to start paying back the principal.

The IDA is funded by donations from almost 40 countries, including developed economies such as the UK, France, Germany and the US, and developing nations like Argentina and Botswana, some of which were once IDA borrowers themselves.

Helping local firms

Developing countries will never escape from the poverty trap unless private sector companies are allowed to flourish. Entrepreneurs are the catalysts for long-term, sustainable growth, but often struggle to raise money. The Bank's **International Finance Corporation**, in partnership with private investors, provides both loan and equity finance for business ventures in developing countries. It has supported around 2,000 companies in 129 nations since its inception and has provided advice to many more.

Encouraging private money into needy areas

When the World Bank was established more than 50 years ago, it was rare for private companies and banks to invest in poorer nations. But the search for high returns plus an explosion of private investment capital has prompted a flood of money into developing countries, particularly those in Asia. The Bank's **Multilateral Investment Guarantee Agency** encourages that flow of money by providing insurance against loss caused by non-commercial risk.

Training and advice

The World Bank has an enormous skills base of clever, dedicated people ready to offer training and advice to poorer nations. There has been a move in recent years to involve those nations in the development process more by devising plans 'owned' by the country itself.

CRITICISMS

A recent report that criticised the IMF's unwieldy structure and its tendency to promote moral hazard also took aim at the World Bank. Its key criticism was that the IBRD makes loans to countries where commercial funds are available. If countries are to fully integrate into the world economy they should tap private money for development, leaving the Bank to concentrate its resources on those really poor nations that have no hope of access to international capital markets.

The Bank has also been accused of excessive meddling in the domestic policies of client countries. Just as the IMF is being urged to let local officials take more control of economic reform, so the World Bank is facing calls to step back from client-country politics and assume a more detached role in the development process.

More recently, anti-capitalist protestors have accused the World Bank of being no more than a debt collector that preys on poor countries. The legitimacy of that view is open to question, but at the very least it suggests a growing impetus for reform.

More information on the World Bank can be found at its website at www.worldbank.org

THE WORLD TRADE ORGANISATION

FREE TRADE RULES

The WTO encourages free trade among its 135 member nations and provides a forum for settling trade disputes amicably.

The World Trade Organisation has attracted more controversy in recent years than the IMF and the World Bank put together. Many believe its crusade to free international trade from tariffs and other barriers is at best misguided, at worst damaging to jobs, the environment and democracy. They equate its free market ethos with corporate greed and the rising power of multinationals, making it a target for every protestor across the spectrum from human rights campaigners to anti-GM food demonstrators.

Pitted against them are the free marketeers, the fans of Adam Smith and David Ricardo who believe more trade means more growth, more choice, lower prices and better standards of living. As Chapter 7 showed, textbook economics would tend to agree with them.

Origins

The WTO was set up in 1995 as the successor to the temporary General Agreement on Tariffs and Trade (GATT). Like the IMF and the World Bank, the latter was established after the Second World War in a bid to prevent the re-emergence of the rabid protectionism that exacerbated the Great Depression and eventually played a part in the outbreak of hostilities.

By and large GATT was a success. It oversaw eight rounds of trade talks that brought tariffs down to their lowest levels ever. In the first round alone, in 1947, 45,000 tariff concessions were negotiated, which affected $10 billion of trade, around one-fifth of the world's total.

However, GATT was always an *ad hoc* organisation with no solid legal foundation. Hence after the 1986–1994 Uruguay Round extended the scope of trade rules, it was replaced by the more powerful WTO.

Aims

The WTO is the epitome of free market economics. It has two key aims: to promote free trade and to arbitrate in trade disputes. This, according to its supporters, will deliver a number of benefits. Those were discussed in Chapter 7, but in case that seems like a long time ago, here is a quick recap.

- **Better use of global resources.** Free trade allows countries to specialise in those areas in which it excels, therefore making better use of the world's limited resources.

- **Stronger growth.** More trade means more income, both nationally and personally. The WTO estimates that the 1994 Uruguay Round of trade talks added between $109 billion and $510 billion to world income (depending on assumptions).

- **More choice.** More trade means consumers can choose from products from all over the world, not just those made in their backyard.

- **Lower prices.** Pretty self-explanatory. Tariffs are taxes on overseas goods and therefore raise prices.

- **More jobs.** This is a controversial one. If free trade means more growth, that suggests more jobs will follow. However, as production moves from one country to another, some workers will inevitably lose out (witness the decline of Britain's car and textile industries). The WTO argues that job losses are far outweighed by gains.

CRITICISMS

Like all the other supranational institutions, the WTO comes in for heavy criticism. Opponents see it as a vehicle for powerful multinationals to extend their market reach and pump up already inflated profits. Frustrations at this and other grievances boiled over in November 1999 at the WTO's trade talks in Seattle. Thousands of rioters went on the rampage through the city, disrupting the meeting, which ended without an approved statement from delegates for the first time in 57 years of trade liberalisation discussion. Their complaints were as follows.

- **Jobs.** Powerful US unions were among the most vociferous protestors in Seattle. They want the WTO to impose minimum labour standards on all its members, thus outlawing cheap child labour in developing countries. This would not only safeguard against human rights abuses, they argue, but would also prevent poor nations from undercutting richer ones through what they see as unfair competition.

- **Penalises developing countries.** Developing countries, however, already feel marginalised by their richer WTO colleagues. They complain that wealthy western nations dictate proceedings, imposing their own selfish agenda via back-room negotiations that pay scant regard to poor country needs. They want more transparency in the system.

■ **Encourages environmental damage.** Some say the battle to cut prices and compete in a free global marketplace encourages countries to ransack the environment in the name of profit, for which they hold the WTO responsible.

■ **Vetos.** Any one of the WTO's 135 members can stop trade negotiations using a national veto. This means talks are continually delayed, making progress painfully slow (the Uruguay Round lasted eight years).

■ **Credibility.** The battle of Seattle did nothing to rescue the WTO's floundering credibility. A protracted row in 1999 over the appointment of a new chief, plus unresolved disputes like the US/EU banana and beef rows, also detract from its authority.

Just like the IMF and the World Bank, reform of the WTO looks inevitable. More violent episodes like Seattle will hasten the process of change, but getting 135 countries to agree to anything is a tall order. Watch this space.

For more information on the WTO, see its website at www.wto.org

IF YOU REMEMBER SIX THINGS FROM THIS CHAPTER ...

■ The Bank of England was founded in 1694 to finance King William III's war against France. Nicknamed the Old Lady of Threadneedle Street, its three purposes are to safeguard the value of the pound, ensure the health of the financial system and promote that system so that it continues to be profitable.

■ The US central bank, the Federal Reserve, was founded in 1913. Its duties are fourfold. It must decide interest rates, regulate US banks, make sure the US financial system is stable, and provide certain services to the government, the public and foreign official institutions.

■ The European Central Bank, founded in June 1998, is responsible for deciding the cost of borrowing in the 11-nation eurozone. It must keep inflation in the area at 2 per cent or less.

■ The International Monetary Fund offers financial help to indebted nations in return for economic reform, ensures currencies can be easily exchanged, thus oiling the wheels of trade, and offers training to officials in poor economies.

■ The World Bank raises money on behalf of poor countries with the aim of wiping out world poverty.

■ The World Trade Organisation encourages free trade among its 135 member nations and provides a forum for settling trade disputes amicably. It has been the target of violent protests in recent years for its role in fostering globalisation.

CONCLUSION

 Liberty is,

to the lowest rank of every nation,

little more than a choice of

working or starving.

Samuel Johnson

Given the multitude of choices that abound in today's wired-up, fired-up world, you would be forgiven for feeling a bit of a Buridan's ass every now and then. This unfortunate creature, dreamt up by the 14th century moral philosopher Jean Buridan, died of starvation when, placed between two equally attractive piles of hay, it was unable to decide which to turn to.

That was 700 years ago. Since then, the burden of choice has become immeasurably heavier. The paradox of progress means people have more opportunities and more options than ever before – and more complications and more stress as a result. We are asked to make hundreds of decisions every week, from the trifling to the momentous.

The quandaries confront us everywhere, from the supermarket to the workplace to the voting booth. To take an example, there are upwards of 40,000 separate products lining the shelves of your local superstore these days, including nearly 100 different types of toothbrush alone. A relaxing trip to the coffee shop has turned into a brain-achingly complicated exercise with up to 6,000 permutations of coffee, milk, topping and sugar to choose from (if you bought one a day it would take nearly 17 years to try them all).

Then there are the more weighty judgements. Where to work, which job to train for, is now a good time to buy a house? All that before you can even think about the questions that send most people into the arms of the nearest financial adviser – how much should you put into your pension, which mortgage should you take out, is the stock market going to collapse or make you a million?

On the one hand, those choices empower – they represent freedom and growing prosperity. But on the other hand, they come with a price. We want supermarkets that open 24 hours a day, but that means someone has to sit behind a cash register at four o'clock in the morning, probably earning a pittance. We want inexpensive cars but feel cheated when multinationals move production to low-wage, developing countries. We want more equality of income and opportunity but many balk at the idea of voting in a government that promises tax increases.

In short, choices have made our lives a lot more complicated. Which is where I think economics can help. Many of the most impenetrable – and important – decisions we are called upon to make demand some knowledge of the subject. That was the inspiration behind this book.

I found various friends – often far more intelligent than me – struggling to make sense of the choices with which they were confronted regularly. They thought the answers were hopelessly complicated and out of reach. This book is intended to show that they are not (although I can't promise you will be any wiser by this stage on whether to buy a tall, skinny, decaff latte or a no-fun cappuccino with almond syrup).

Take the simple question of whether to splash out on a new car, either by running down your savings or borrowing, or whether to tuck your salary into the bank in case things turn nasty. That decision will depend on a whole range of factors, many of which are rooted in economics. If you suspect that inflation is heading out of control and that interest rates may need to rise sharply, you may feel the risk of recession necessitates caution. Or if your chosen profession is under threat, either from a wave of takeovers and mergers or growing competition from low-wage developing countries, again, you may feel happier with some savings behind you.

On the other hand, if investment in the economy is strong, workers are becoming more productive, and prices are under control, you may feel comfortable enough to at least test-drive a BMW Z3. Add in low borrowing costs and you may even find enough money to take a holiday … and of course get the most from your travellers' cheques now you know when to buy them.

That is just one way that economics can work for you. Knowing a bit about growth and recessions, inflation and interest rates, unemployment and job security can help you to pick a path through the increasingly complicated – and cutthroat – new economy.

It can also help you out when it comes to voting. Finding a way through the political spin that dominates modern politics is tricky. It is not just a matter of whether you will be better or worse off financially under a new government, it is also a question of which party will nurture the economy through sustained growth, fostering improved living standards in the longer term. That may mean paying a bit more in taxes for now, and pumping that money into schools and investments, to allow sound finances and a stronger economy in the future.

That is the rub with economics. There are always hard choices to make. There is no quick fix, no formula for individual or collective wealth and prosperity, no rules to follow. It is often a matter of trial and error for policymakers, and in that sense the subject is evolving all the time. Theories are constantly being teased into working and hypotheses compromised into producing results.

But that does not make it redundant. On the contrary, it makes it accessible to everyone exactly because there are no formulas to learn or complex notions to get your head round. The concepts described in this book are, on the whole, simple ideas that just sound complicated when they are dressed up with jargon and when bits are left out because of some assumed knowledge.

This is far from the definitive guide to the subject – more a package of edited highlights. But with a bit of luck, it will make a few decisions a bit easier, relieve that sense of analysis paralysis that the information age has a knack of inducing – which is, after all, just the modern-day equivalent of Buridan and his ass.

GLOSSARY

Absolute advantage If one country can make a good cheaper than another, it is said to have an absolute advantage in that good. It is therefore in both countries' interests to trade.

Accelerator theory This suggests that the level of net investment is determined by the rate of change of national income. In other words, if the economy is growing at an increasing rate, investment will also grow, but if the economy is contracting, investment will fall.

Appreciation A steady rise in the value of a currency relative to other currencies under free market conditions. For example, if sterling were to appreciate against the dollar, one pound would buy more dollars than previously.

Automatic government spending Public spending that the government has no control over, such as unemployment benefit.

Automatic stabilisers Government taxation and spending measures which reduce the impact of changes in the economy on national income. For example, when growth slows and workers lose their jobs, the government provides them with a minimum income through unemployment benefit, thereby cushioning the impact of the downturn. Equally, when growth surges, people will pay more in income tax and VAT, relieving some of the potential inflationary pressure in the economy.

Balanced budget A government will balance its budget when it receives the same amount of income in tax revenues as it spends. Classical economists argue that this should always be the aim of governments, but Keynesian economists recommend running a deficit to boost the economy when it is slowing, and a surplus to take some heat out of growth when it is rising. In this way, the government could balance the budget in the long run instead.

Balance of payments A record of all the exports and imports that flow into and out of a country. It is split into the current account, which measures the flow of goods and services, and the financial and capital accounts, which measure the flow of money. Total inflows must always equal total outflows, hence the balance of payments always balances.

Bank of England Britain's central bank. The Bank of England has three purposes: to maintain the integrity and value of the pound, to ensure the stability of the financial system, and to promote the efficiency and competitiveness of that system. Its customers are the commercial banks in Britain such as Barclays and Lloyds (plus any foreign banks that have branches here), overseas central banks, and the government. It also has around 8,000 private account holders, most of whom are staff or pensioners of the Bank itself.

The Bank's most important function is to safeguard the value of the currency, in terms of what it will buy both at home and abroad. To that end, the Bank must keep prices as stable as possible. Its nine-member Monetary Policy Committee (MPC) is charged with keeping underlying RPIX inflation at 2.5 per cent. If it moves more than one percentage point either side of that mark, the governor must write an open letter to the Chancellor of the Exchequer explaining why.

Bear market A market in which prices are falling or are expected to fall. Bear markets in shares generally last about a year.

Bond A form of loan that usually carries a fixed amount of interest and must be repaid after a fixed period of time. Bonds may be issued by companies, in which case they are called corporate bonds, or by governments, in which case they are called government bonds. They may be short-dated, in which case they have up to seven years left to run, medium-dated, with between seven and 15 years to run, and long-dated, anything with more than 15 years to go.

Bretton Woods The site in New Hampshire, USA, of an international conference in July 1944 to discuss proposals relating to post-war international payments problems. Agreements resulted in the establishment of the International Monetary Fund and the World Bank.

Budget The annual announcement of the government's fiscal policy changes by the Chancellor of the Exchequer. It usually takes place in March. It includes details of tax and spending plans for the coming year and a forecast for the economy. The Budget is made law by the Finance Act after debate in Parliament.

Bull market A market in which prices are rising or are expected to rise. On average, bull markets in shares last about four years.

Bundesbank Germany's central bank. Before European Monetary Union, the Bundesbank was one of the most powerful central banks in the world. However, since interest rate decisions are now taken by the European Central Bank, it is just a shadow of its former self.

Business (or trade) cycle Regular fluctuations in the rate of economic growth over a number of years. Cycles typically go through four phases: a boom, followed by recession, after which the economy hits a trough, and then recovers.

Call option An option, but not a commitment, to buy a financial instrument such as a share at a future date at a predetermined price.

Canons of taxation Criteria set down by Adam Smith, used to judge whether a tax is 'good'. They are:

- the cost of collection of the tax must be low relative to the revenues it yields;
- the timing and amount to be paid must be certain to the payer;
- the means and timing of payment must be convenient to the payer;
- taxes should be levied according to ability to pay.

Capacity constraints Limits to the amount an economy can produce without igniting inflation. Capacity can be expanded by investment.

Capital account A subdivision of the financial account in the balance of payments. It records transfers of capital for which nothing is received in return, for example the forgiveness of overseas debt. This is also where the buying and selling of things such as copyrights and football players is noted.

Chancellor of the Exchequer The politician in charge of the British Treasury, responsible for handing out public money to other government departments and for the smooth running of the economy. The Chancellor decides on government spending and taxation, in other words, fiscal policy. The title Exchequer comes from the chequered tablecloth which served as a counting board for royal revenue in 12th-century England.

Circular flow of income A model showing how money flows around an economy between households and firms. Households receive income from firms, which may be in the form of wages, interest or profits, and firms receive money from households when the latter buy goods and services.

Claimant count A measure of unemployment in Britain based on the number of people claiming unemployment benefit. Eligibility for this benefit has changed many times over the years, particularly during the 1980s under the Conservative government. The claimant count is therefore largely discredited as a measure of unemployment. The Labour Force Survey is considered more accurate, and has the added advantage of being directly comparable with other countries.

Classical economics One of the main schools of thought in economics. Founded by Adam Smith in the 18th century and developed by David Ricardo, classical economists believe that markets are highly efficient, and that government intervention is counterproductive. They recommend giving the market free rein, a *laissez faire* philosophy. For example, classical economists believe unemployment is caused by wages being too high. They say that by removing impediments to the free market, such as unemployment benefit and trade unions, wages will be bargained lower and unemployment will disappear. Modern-day followers of this philosophy are called neo-classical economists.

Classical unemployment Otherwise known as real wage unemployment, classical economists believe workers lose their jobs because wages are too high. They therefore call this type of unemployment voluntary.

Command economy A country where the state allocates resources, deciding who produces what, through a central planning mechanism. Some goods and services are provided free, some are sold and some are rationed. Command economies are associated with the former communist countries of Eastern Europe and the Soviet Union, although Britain was run along command lines during the Second World War.

Comparative advantage Exists when a country is able to produce a good more cheaply relative to other goods produced domestically than another country. The theory of comparative advantage says that countries will find it mutually advantageous to trade if the opportunity cost of production differs.

Convergence criteria A set of five conditions that countries had to meet in order to join European Economic and Monetary Union. Those conditions were:

- **budget deficits** must be no more than 3 per cent of GDP;
- **national debt** must be no more than 60 per cent of GDP;
- **inflation** must be no more than 1.5 per cent above the average inflation rate of the lowest three inflation countries in the EU;
- **long-term interest rates** must be no more than 2 per cent above the average of the three countries with the lowest inflation rates;
- **exchange rates** must fluctuate within the normal bands of the ERM, with no currency realignments for at least two years.

Corporation tax The tax companies pay on their profits.

Cost-push inflation A sustained rise in prices thanks to an increase in the costs of production. Those costs could be higher wages (maybe due to bargaining by trade unions) or more expensive raw materials, or they may come about because of a rise in taxes. The most dramatic example of cost-push inflation in Britain came in the early 1970s when the price of imported oil rose fourfold. Cost-push inflation can spark a wage/price spiral where high wages trigger higher prices which spark demands for even higher wages, and so on.

Counter-cyclical demand management *See* demand management.

Currency future When a currency can be bought at a fixed price for delivery at some point in the future. Firms use currency futures when they do business abroad, to protect themselves against adverse foreign exchange movements.

Current account A record of everything exported and imported into a country. It is split into a trade balance, which records the movement of goods, and a services, investment income and current transfers balance, which records all services.

Cyclical debt That portion of government debt that arises purely because of a downturn in economic growth. For example, when an economy enters recession and unemployment rises, the amount of tax revenues received by the government falls. Corporation tax falls with lower company profits, VAT falls with lower spending and income tax falls because there are fewer people in jobs. In addition, the amount of government spending increases thanks to a growing number of unemployed drawing benefits.

Cyclical unemployment *See* demand-deficient unemployment.

Deflation A general, sustained fall in the price level.

Deflationary policies Policies that deliberately set out to slow down the economy, usually because inflation is about to rise. Examples include cutting government spending and raising taxes, both of which are known as deflationary fiscal policy, or increasing interest rates, which is called deflationary monetary policy.

Demand-deficient unemployment Unemployment that arises because there is not enough demand in the economy to employ everyone who wants a job. It usually occurs in a downturn and is categorised as involuntary. Keynesian economists argue that this is a major source of unemployment and recommend stimulating demand as a remedy.

Demand management Keynesians recommend controlling inflation and growth by controlling demand. During recessions, the government should stimulate demand and therefore jobs by lowering taxes and increasing spending. Conversely, during booms, it should rein in demand by increasing taxes and lowering spending. In this way, demand management is inherently **counter cyclical**, in that it runs in the opposite direction to the business cycle.

Demand-pull inflation A sustained increase in prices generated by excess demand. Keynesians believe this to be one of the main causes of inflation.

Demerit goods Goods that generate negative externalities. In other words, goods that cause harm or health problems such as drugs or tobacco. One of the government's roles is to restrict the availability of demerit goods, maybe by banning them, or by imposing taxes on them.

Depreciation Has two meanings. It can either refer to a steady reduction in the value of an asset due to wear and tear, or a steady decline in the value of a currency relative to other currencies under free market conditions. For example, if the pound were to depreciate by 10 per cent against the dollar, all other things being equal a British tourist in Florida would be able to buy 10 per cent fewer goods with the same amount of sterling as before.

Deregulation The process of removing government controls from markets. For example, the Conservative government's decision to allow private bus firms to compete in the previously state-controlled sector.

Derivative A financial instrument derived from an underlying stock or asset. Derivatives are used by hedgers and traders.

Devaluation A reduction in the official rate at which one currency can be exchanged for another. Devaluation is the same as depreciation, only it applies to a fixed exchange rate regime.

Direct tax A tax levied on income, for example, income tax.

Discretionary government spending Public expenditure that the government can control and therefore budget for, such as roads.

Dividend A portion of company profits distributed to ordinary shareholders.

Division of labour The idea, first developed by Adam Smith, that workers can produce more when they do specialised tasks. Smith used the example of a pin factory to demonstrate the gains from dividing labour.

Dumping The sale of a good on a foreign market at a loss. Firms may use dumping as a way of establishing a presence in an overseas market and forcing competitors out as a result. Japanese firms have been accused of doing this in the European video market. Alternatively, firms may dump goods overseas because they have failed to sell them. For example, China dumped a surplus of knickers on the world market in the 1980s.

Economies of scale The greater the scale of production, the less it costs to make one extra good. For example, a larger firm may be able to get a discount from suppliers if it buys in bulk, it may be able to organise its production more efficiently, or it may be able to negotiate cheaper loans if it is borrowing a lot of money. All represent economies of scale.

Elasticity A measure of the degree of responsiveness of one variable to another. Price elasticity denotes how much demand for a good changes when its price changes, while income elasticity shows how much demand varies when the income of consumers changes. For example, cigarettes are fairly price inelastic – addicted smokers will continue to buy them even if their price rises. However, a luxury such as eating out is more elastic. If the cost of a meal in a restaurant rises too rapidly, many people will cut down on the number of times they dine out.

Endogenous variable A variable whose value is determined by forces within an economic model. For example, in a model of the market for potatoes, the price of potatoes is an endogenous variable because it will be decided by demand and supply, which are part of the model.

Euro The name given to the single European currency, which began on 1 January 1999. Euros are available only in cheque or electronic form until January 2002, at which point notes and coins will be issued.

European Central Bank (ECB) The central bank for the 11-nation euro area, responsible for keeping eurozone inflation at 2 per cent or less. The ECB sets interest rates for all euro member countries.

European Coal and Steel Community Established in 1952 by six countries – Belgium, France, Germany, Italy, Luxembourg and the Netherlands – the ECSC scrapped all import duties and quota restrictions between treaty countries on coal, iron ore and steel. The idea was to put the raw materials of war into the hands of a supranational authority, thereby controlling old Franco-German rivalries.

European Economic Community (EEC) The EEC was founded in January 1958 after the six members of the ECSC (Belgium, France, Germany, Italy, Luxembourg and the Netherlands) signed the Treaty of Rome the year before, creating a common market. The primary aim of the EEC was to eliminate all obstacles to the free movement of goods, services, money and workers between member countries, and to set up a common external commercial policy, a common agricultural policy and a common transport policy. Ireland, the UK and Denmark joined the EEC in January 1973. Over the years, the EEC was renamed the European Union (EU) and acquired more members. By 2000, the original six, plus the three latecomers, had been joined by Greece, Spain, Portugal, Austria, Finland and Sweden.

European economic and monetary union (EMU) EMU began in January 1999 when 11 countries in Europe irrevocably tied their currencies to each other at predetermined exchange rates to form the euro. Those nations were Austria, Belgium, Finland, France, Germany, Ireland, Italy, Luxembourg, the Netherlands, Portugal and Spain. Member nations' currencies no longer move against each other, they move as one block against other currencies such as the dollar. The ECB sets a single interest rate for the whole of the euro area.

European Exchange Rate Mechanism (ERM) A forerunner to EMU, the ERM is a currency grid that keeps member nations' exchange rates within specified bands in relation to each other. Sterling joined the ERM in October 1990 at a central rate of 2.95 marks and was allowed to fluctuate up to 6 per cent either side of that level. In other words, the government had to make sure the pound was worth no less than 2.7780 marks and no more than 3.1320. A weak British economy and interest rate rises in Germany meant that range was unsustainable, and on 16 September 1992, the pound was ejected from the system after a massive speculative attack.

European Monetary Institute (EMI) Forerunner to the ECB, the EMI was founded in January 1994 in order to pave the way for monetary union.

European Monetary System (EMS) Founded in 1979 among EEC members to establish a grid of stable but adjustable exchange rates known as the Exchange Rate Mechanism. Britain was the only EEC member country to stay outside the currency grid, which it did until October 1990.

European Stability and Growth Pact An agreement among European single currency countries to prevent any one member government from accumulating too much debt. The pact says euro countries should balance their budgets, or run a surplus in the medium term, under normal economic conditions. The idea is to keep deficits below 3 per cent, even during **recessions** when **automatic stabilisers** mean borrowing is likely to increase.

Eurozone The name given to the area covered by the European single currency. In 2000, 11 countries were part of the eurozone, namely Austria, Belgium, Finland, France, Germany, Ireland, Italy, Luxembourg, the Netherlands, Portugal and Spain.

Exchange rate The price at which one currency is convertible to another. Currencies are bought and sold on the foreign exchange market.

Exchange rate policy The name of attempts by governments to manipulate the exchange rate in order to fulfil one or all of their goals of stable inflation, strong growth, low unemployment and a balance in foreign trade.

Exogenous variable A variable whose value is determined by forces from outside an economic model. For example, in a model of the market for potatoes, weather plays an important role in determining the supply of the vegetable and therefore its price, yet the model does not try to predict or explain rainfall patterns.

Exports Goods or services sold abroad.

Externality, negative Externalities occur when the actions of a firm or an individual have an effect on people or places other than themselves. A negative externality is when that action imposes a cost on others. For example, a factory making steel may generate a lot of pollution, which may cause health problems for nearby residents and may damage the environment. The factory does not count those costs as part of the production process, therefore they are an externality.

Externality, positive When the actions of a firm or individual generate a benefit for others that is not taken into account as part of the production process. A firm may set up a training programme for computer engineers which increases the availability of skilled workers for a competitor.

Factors of production Resources that go into making something. There are four factors of production: natural resources, workers, money and technology.

Federal Reserve The central bank of the United States. The Federal Reserve System consists of 12 regional banks across the country. Its duties are fourfold. It must decide interest rates, regulate the country's banks, make sure the US financial system is stable, and provide certain services to the government, the public and foreign official institutions.

Financial account That part of a country's balance of payments accounts that records all the money flowing into and out of the country.

Fine-tuning An attempt by governments to use fiscal policy and Keynesian demand management to move the economy to a very precise level of unemployment and inflation, etc. Fine-tuning was popular in the 1960s and 1970s, but it soon broke down and is now largely discredited.

Fiscal drag Fiscal drag occurs when inflation increases nominal earnings and propels taxpayers into a higher tax bracket, even though *real* earnings may be unchanged.

Fiscal policy That part of government policy concerned with raising revenue through taxation and deciding on the level and pattern of government spending.

Fixed exchange rate A rate of exchange between at least two countries where it is constant over a period of time. The gold standard in place during much of the 19th century and the start of the 20th century was an example of a fixed exchange rate system. Each major trading nation made its domestic currency convertible into gold at a fixed rate. So, for example, in 1914, anyone holding a £1 note could walk into the Bank of England and exchange it for 0.257 ounces of gold. Similarly, a Frenchman could exchange francs for a fixed amount of gold in France, and a German could do the same in Germany, etc. In that way, there was effectively a fixed exchange rate between the major countries in the world.

Floating exchange rate An exchange rate where the value of a currency relative to others is determined by market forces. The pound has been floating since June 1972. Most of the world's currencies are floating.

Foreign exchange reserves Assets such as gold or foreign currencies, held by a country's government or its central bank, for the purpose of intervening in the foreign exchange market. The dollar is a popular reserve currency as it can be easily bought and sold in the market.

Free market economy A country where resources are allocated through the market. The price mechanism determines who produces what, how it is produced and for whom. Government involvement is limited. The state provides public goods, maintains a sound currency and enforces a legal framework, leaving the rest up to the private sector. The United States is an example of a broadly free market economy – public health care is limited to the very poor and old and there are strict rules on benefits. Advantages to the system include the fact that it provides choice, incentives to innovate and room for economies to grow. Disadvantages include the emergence of inequalities. Friedman is a free market enthusiast, as was Adam Smith.

Free rider A person who receives benefits that others have paid for without making any contribution themselves. For example, certain goods, called public goods, are available to everyone, regardless of who pays for them – streetlights illuminate roads for everyone and traffic lights control traffic for all road users. In that case, it is up to governments to provide the services involved.

Free trade The free exchange of goods and services between countries, unencumbered by artificial obstacles such as tariffs and quotas.

Frictional unemployment If someone loses their job, or maybe leaves it voluntarily, it may take them some time to find a new one. While they are out of work and searching, they are said to be frictionally unemployed. The better a country's system of matching vacant jobs to unemployed, the lower frictional unemployment will be.

Friedman, Milton A Nobel prize winner and modern-day champion of free markets, Friedman is typically associated with the theory that inflation is a direct consequence of changes in the money supply. Margaret Thatcher was an enthusiastic convert of this so-called monetarism, and for years British interest rate decisions were based on the size of the money supply.

Full employment When everyone who wants to work is able to get a job. Classical economists think the economy will automatically tend towards full employment whereas Keynesians believe it is the government's responsibility to steer the economy in the right direction through taxation and spending.

Gilt-edged security The name given to bonds issued by the British government, usually shortened to gilts. A staple investment of many pension funds.

Globalisation The removal of barriers between countries, either culturally, technologically or economically. Globalisation allows the free trade of goods, services, information and money both within and between nations.

Golden rule One of the Labour government's fiscal policy rules, intended to prevent the country from accumulating too much debt, thereby reassuring the markets and the voters that there will be no return to the tax and spend days of 1970s Labour. The golden rule says that over the economic cycle, the government will borrow only to invest. In other words, it can issue bonds and add to its debt if it is going to spend the proceeds on building more schools or hospitals. But spending on things like unemployment benefits must come out of tax revenues. In this way it can run a *total* budget deficit over the cycle, but not a *current* one.

Government capital expenditure Government spending on investment, such as roads, schools and hospitals.

Government current expenditure The government's day-to-day spending, including items such as bandages for the NHS and books for schools.

Gross domestic product A measure of the size of an economy, the total amount of goods and services produced in a country over a specific period. GDP is calculated in three ways: by adding up total spending in the country, total income and total output.

Gross national product Similar to GDP, but it includes any income that has been earned abroad, such as dividends received on shares, minus any income that the country has had to pay abroad.

Harmonised Index of Consumer Prices (HICP) A measure of inflation used in both Britain and the rest of Europe, allowing EU countries to directly compare price rises. The HICP is calculated differently from the Retail Price Index and uses a different basket of goods, but the principle is similar. Should Britain decide to enter European Monetary Union, HICP would take over from RPIX as the target inflation rate.

Headline inflation A measure of price rises based on the Retail Price Index. The RPI tracks the prices of more than 600 goods and services every month, from postage stamps to petrol. Unlike the underlying inflation rate, which strips out the effects of volatile mortgage interest payments, there is no official target for headline inflation in Britain.

Hedging Action taken by a buyer or seller to protect his business or assets against a change in prices. For example, take a British furniture manufacturer who wins an order to supply sofas to a US firm, and who will get paid in dollars in six months' time. If the dollar weakens in that time, his profit margin may be wiped out when he converts the US currency back into pounds. To protect against that – to hedge against that – he could take out a contract in the futures market when he wins the order, to buy pounds for dollars at a set exchange rate, at a set point in the future. Of course, if the dollar has strengthened in the meantime, he could lose out, but he is in the business to make money from sofas, not from betting on the foreign exchange market.

Hire purchase A form of consumer credit, where a purchaser pays a deposit on an item, then pays off the rest, plus interest, in instalments over the following six months to two years. Popular in Britain before credit cards. Controlling the volume of hire purchase business was a key way of controlling inflation in the 1960s, as it reigned in the amount of credit consumers could take out.

Hysteresis The term for when an economic variable changes but does not bounce back to its original position when economic circumstances change. For example, unemployment will rise in a recession. Hysteresis occurs if it then stays high once the economy has recovered.

Imports Goods and services bought from overseas. Britain tends to be a net importer of food, drinks and tobacco, of precious stones, cars, and consumer goods.

Indirect tax Tax that is levied on spending, for example VAT and excise duties on cigarettes and alcohol. Indirect taxes account for around a quarter of British tax receipts.

Infant industry argument This may be used as justification for imposing trade barriers. A new industry in a developing country will find it very hard to compete with established industries in advanced nations because the latter have the advantage of experience and economies of scale. It may be necessary for the developing country to impose tariffs on imports in order to protect its industry until it has had time and room to grow.

Inflation A general, sustained rise in the price level. Inflation is caused by too much demand in the economy or by an increase in the factors of production that go into making something, such as wages or raw materials. Monetarists believe inflation is caused by an increase in the money supply. It can damage an economy in a number of ways. It distorts decisions, redistributes income from lenders to borrowers and discourages investment. A weak currency can lead to an increase in inflation by making imports more expensive.

Inflation target The Bank of England must keep underlying, RPIX inflation at 2.5 per cent. If it deviates more than one percentage point either side of this, the governor of the Bank must write a public letter to the Chancellor of the Exchequer explaining why.

International Bank for Reconstruction and Development The main body of the World Bank, the IBRD sells AAA-rated bonds to pension funds and insurance companies worldwide, and then loans the money raised to middle-income countries and creditworthy, poorer nations. It charges interest to its borrowers and demands that loans are repaid in 15–20 years. Less than 5 per cent of IBRD money comes from member subscriptions.

International Development Association The IDA oversees that part of World Bank lending for large-scale projects in poorer nations, such as improving sanitation and building hospitals, that is not run by the IBRD. Established in 1960, the IDA provides interest-free loans to those countries too poor to borrow at commercial rates. Repayment is required in 35 or 40 years and countries have a ten-year grace period before they have to start paying back the principal. The IDA is funded by donations from almost 40 countries, including the UK, France, Germany and the US.

International Finance Corporation Part of the World Bank. The IFC, in partnership with private investors, provides both loan and equity finance for business ventures in developing countries. It has supported around 2,000 companies in 129 nations since its inception and has provided advice to many more.

International Labour Organisation (ILO) Established in 1919 under the Treaty of Versailles, the ILO is now affiliated to the United Nations. Its aims are to improve working conditions throughout the world, spread social security and maintain standards of social justice. It also provides a standard for measuring unemployment across the world, which allows countries to compare jobless levels. Britain uses the ILO measure of unemployment and the claimant count measure, which is based on the number of workers claiming Jobseekers allowance.

International Monetary Fund The IMF offers financial help to indebted nations in return for economic reform, ensures currencies can be easily exchanged, thus oiling the wheels of trade, and offers training to officials in less developed economies. Based in Washington DC, it was set up by the Bretton Woods agreement of 1944, partly on the advice of Keynes, and came into operation in 1947. It is best known for its high-profile rescue operations in Asia in 1997, and for lending to Russia in its transition to capitalism. It has come in for much criticism lately.

Intervention The term given to attempts by central banks to influence the value of an exchange rate by buying and selling foreign currency reserves. Intervention is often futile, particularly if it is going against the force of the market. The most famous example of intervention in Britain was the government's 1992 attempt to keep the pound in the European Exchange Rate Mechanism, by selling foreign currency reserves and buying sterling. It ended in spectacular and costly failure.

Investment trusts Formed in 1868, investment trusts are limited companies that issue their own shares and use the proceeds to invest in other companies. Anyone who buys a share in an investment trust automatically buys a diversified investment. These shares are listed on the stock exchange and can be bought and sold just like any other equity. There are more than 350 investment trusts operating in Britain with combined assets of more than £60 billion.

Invisible hand An expression derived by the 18th-century economist Adam Smith to describe the action of markets. Smith believed that if left to its own devices, the market would ensure the best outcome for all concerned, despite everyone being motivated by self-interest.

Keynes, John Maynard Renowned 20th-century economist who challenged the classical belief that markets worked best. In his 1936 book the *General Theory of Employment, Interest and Money*, Keynes recommended that governments should interfere in the economy to either increase or decrease demand and therefore control unemployment and inflation.

Laissez faire A term used to describe an economic system where government intervention is limited, and the private sector organises the bulk of activity through markets. Classical economists were great fans of *laissez faire*.

Latin Monetary Union A European currency union established in 1865 between Belgium, France, Italy and Switzerland. It was based on gold and silver coins in each country of equal worth. Hence a 20-franc gold coin was worth the same as a 20-lira gold coin, which, upon the inclusion of Greece in the system in 1876, was worth the same as a 20-drachma gold coin. There was great debate in Britain about whether to sign up to the union, but it eventually decided to remain outside. The Latin union collapsed shortly before the outbreak of the First World War.

Lending ceilings Restrictions imposed by the Bank of England in the 1960s on the amount of money banks could lend. Lending ceilings were far tighter for personal customers than for businesses and were seen as a useful way of controlling inflation.

Life assurance companies Firms that sell a variety of long-term investment products such as personal pension plans and endowment policies. The insured pays regular contributions to a fund over a number of years, typically ten or more, then receives a guaranteed lump sum at the end.

London Stock Exchange Founded in 1801, the LSE is the main market in Britain where shares are bought and sold. Its functions are to channel savings into productive investments, allow investors to dispose of shares quickly if they wish, and to facilitate **takeovers** and **mergers**, which encourage firms to be efficient. In April 2000, the LSE demutualised.

Maastricht Treaty An agreement negotiated in the Dutch town of Maastricht in December 1991 between the leaders of what were then the 12 European Community countries. The treaty, which set out a detailed timetable for Economic and Monetary Union (EMU), was signed in February 1992. It also set out the convergence criteria for countries wishing to join EMU.

Marginal rate of tax That rate of tax paid on the next pound earned. In the case of income tax, the marginal tax rate will increase as workers move from one tax band to the next.

Marx, Karl Author of the *Communist Party Manifesto*, Marx believed that capitalism was simply a stage in the process of evolution from the primitive agricultural economy towards the elimination of private property and the class structure. Far from imposing a kind of discipline over people, he argued that market forces allowed a few people to make more and more money at the expense of exploited workers. He believed that those workers would become increasingly alienated and would end up rebelling against the system and bringing about the downfall of capitalism.

Medium Term Financial Strategy First published by Chancellor of the Exchequer Geoffrey Howe in the 1980 Budget, the MTFS set out targets for Britain's money supply with the aim of keeping inflation under control. It was believed that if the amount of money in the economy could be kept within a certain range, price rises would remain low, too. This monetarism formed a central plank of Margaret Thatcher's early years as prime minister.

Menu costs Periods of high inflation mean firms will constantly have to update their prices, an expensive and inconvenient exercise which gives rise to so-called menu costs.

Merger The fusion of two or more separate companies into one, as distinct from a takeover which occurs against the wishes of one company. Mergers will be horizontal if they involve two firms in the same industry at the same stage of production, for example, two carmakers. They will be vertical if they involve two firms at different stages of production in the same industry, such as a clothes factory and a department store, and they will be conglomerate if they involve two firms with no common interest At all, for example, a drinks company and an insurance firm.

Merit goods Goods which are underprovided by the market mechanism, for example, education and health. The government often spends tax revenues on increasing the supply of merit goods.

Minimum wage Imposed in Britain in April 1999, the minimum wage sets a floor under earnings, ensuring every worker gets paid a minimum amount per hour. Classical economists argue that a minimum wage may lead to unemployment, as it prices some workers out of a job. This fear has so far proved unfounded in Britain, but its real test will come with an economic downturn.

Mixed economy A hybrid of the **command economy** and the **free market economy**. Many resources are allocated by both the government and the private sector, for example healthcare and education. Britain is a mixed economy. The degree of mixing is open to debate – more government provision means higher taxes but a generous welfare state, less government provision means a lower tax burden but less help with medical costs and stricter rules about benefits.

Monetarists People who believe that inflation is caused by an increase in the amount of money in an economy. Margaret Thatcher was Britain's most famous monetarist in the 1980s.

Monetary policy The deliberate control of interest rates (or the money supply) in order to control inflation. In Britain, if inflation looks like rising above the government's 2.5 per cent target, the Bank of England's Monetary Policy Committee may increase interest rates, thereby imposing a contractionary or deflationary monetary policy. If it looks likes falling significantly below target, maybe thanks to an approaching recession, the MPC may reflate the economy by lowering interest rates.

Monetary Policy Committee (MPC) A nine-member committee that meets once a month to determine interest rates in Britain. The MPC comprises five high-level Bank of England employees, including the governor and the two deputy governors, and four 'outside' members, outside in the sense that they can come from academia, industry or the City, thus providing a different perspective on monetary policy. The MPC meeting typically starts on the afternoon of the first Wednesday of the month, and continues on Thursday morning. The rate decision is announced just after noon.

Monetary transmission mechanism The way in which a change in the money supply translates into a change in GDP and other real variables such as unemployment.

Moral hazard Someone who is fully insured against crashing his car may drive less carefully than someone covered only for third-party fire and theft. Likewise, if a country knows the IMF will bail it out if it gets into debt, it may be less stringent in its economic polices than otherwise. Both are said to be experiencing moral hazard.

Multilateral Investment Guarantee Agency Part of the World Bank, based in Washington DC. The MIGA encourages a flow of private money into developing countries by providing insurance against loss caused by non-commercial risk.

Multiplier effect Keynes argued that an increase in investment would lead to an even greater increase in income. For example, imagine Japanese car company Nissan spent £100 million building a factory in Britain. Part of that investment would go on paying construction workers, architects, electricians and plumbers, etc. They would spend their wages on anything from clothes to food to a holiday, so now demand for, say, trousers would have risen too. Textile manufacturers would hire more workers to make more jeans, increasing their income, which would also be spent. And so on. The £100 million invested by Nissan would have triggered a chain reaction and increased overall GDP by much more than the original amount. There has been a multiplier effect.

National debt The amount of money the government owes. It represents a stock of borrowing, the total debt outstanding, rather than an annual increase in borrowing, which is the deficit.

National Statistics Britain's government-funded statistics office responsible for compiling and publishing all sorts of UK data, from inflation to unemployment to trade.

Natural rate of unemployment That rate of unemployment that persists even when the economy is in full swing. Any unemployment at the natural rate is said to be voluntary in that everyone who wants a job has one. It comprises classical, seasonal, frictional and structural unemployment. Many economists believe the only way to reduce the natural rate is to use supply-side policies to improve the quality and quantity of available workers.

New Deal A £5 billion employment scheme devised by the 1997 Labour government to wean Britons off welfare and into work. Funded by a windfall tax levied on privatised utilities, the programme was initially aimed at the long-term youth unemployed but has since been extended to cover the older unemployed, lone parents, the disabled and those over 50.

The young unemployed – still the flagship part of the programme on which its success or failure rests – go through a four-month 'gateway' period during which they have interviews with personal advisers and receive help with job chasing. If they still have not found work at the end of this period they face four choices: full-time education and training, a job subsidised by the government, work on an environmental taskforce, or a voluntary job. Returning to benefit is *not* an option.

Nominal GDP The total amount of goods and services produced in an economy, measured in money terms. In other words, it does not strip out the effects of price rises, it just adds everything up at face value. If you are trying to get a realistic gauge of how much an economy has grown, it is much better to use **real GDP**, which takes out inflation and leaves you with the actual, physical increase in output.

Non-accelerating inflation rate of unemployment Otherwise known as Nairu, this is the rate of unemployment at which inflation is stable. Most economists believe there is a trade-off between inflation and unemployment in the short-run – if inflation is allowed to rise, unemployment will fall and vice versa. But in the long run, it is argued that unemployment always returns to its Nairu rate, regardless of inflation. The Nairu is broadly comparable to the natural rate of unemployment, and is best reduced through supply-side policies.

Non-excludability A characteristic of a public good, non-excludability means that once a good is provided, no person can be excluded from benefiting from it (or suffering, in the case of pollution). A country's defence service is non-excludable – you will be protected by the army whether you like it or not, you cannot opt out.

Non-rivalry When consumption of a good by one person does not diminish the amount available for anyone else. For example, the birth of one more baby will not reduce the amount of defence protection afforded to everyone else in the country.

Normative Concerned with values and ethics and opinions of what *ought* to be, rather than things that can be proved. Examples of normative statements include: taxes should be imposed on polluters, unemployment should be reduced, and every country should have a minimum wage.

Occupational immobility When people are trained for a specific job, such as shipbuilding, they find it hard to get new employment elsewhere if demand for their skills dries up. They are said to be occupationally immobile. They will need to retrain to stand any chance of getting new work.

Optimum currency areas That area that is best suited to having just one, single currency. In 1961, Canadian-born economist Robert Mundell argued that a successful currency area must be able to cope with asymmetric shocks, in other words, events that affect one part of the potential currency area differently from the others. In order to smooth out the effects of those shocks, he said workers must be mobile (willing to move across the whole area in search of jobs), wages and prices must be able to move up and down easily and there must be plenty of government spending. Optimum currency area theory has taken on new resonance recently with the advent of European Economic and Monetary Union. Many argue that the euro area is far from being an optimum currency area, but Mundell disagrees.

Ordinary share An ordinary share signifies ownership of a part of a company. It is the most common type of share, and it gives the holder the right to vote on a company's future (usually on a one-share, one-vote basis) and receive a **dividend** (a proportion of the company's profits). Ordinary shareholders are the very last people to get their money back if a firm goes bust. So if the price of a share falls and you hold it until the bitter end, you will probably end up with nothing.

Organisation for Economic Co-operation and Development Founded in 1961, the OECD provides its 29 member countries with a forum for discussion and development of economic and social policies. These discussions may result in governments adopting formal legislation, for example codes on the free flow of money and services, or simply sharing best practice. More information can be found on the OECD's website at www.oecd.org.

Pegged exchange rate When the value of a currency is linked, at a fixed, predetermined rate, to that of another or a basket of currencies. For example, the Barbados dollar is pegged to the US dollar at the rate of BDS$2 per US$1.

Pension funds Sums of money laid aside and invested to provide a regular income on retirement. There are two types of schemes: the *defined benefit* pension and the *defined contribution*. As their names imply, the former provides a guaranteed, specific pension related to the number of years of service and salary reached, the latter provides an income dependent on the level of contributions made and the fund's investment performance. Falling gilt yields and less favourable tax laws have sparked a move by British firms to defined contribution funds in recent years.

Pension funds tend to like bonds with longer maturities to match their long liabilities, and are fond of lower risk investments, hence their penchant for gilts. In 1999, there was about £800 billion under management in pension funds in Britain, about 20 per cent of which was invested in bonds. Some 70 per cent was invested in equities, with the remainder split evenly between cash and property.

P/E ratio Price to earnings ratio. It is a measure of the price that has to be paid for a given income from an equity share. A company's earnings determine the amount of dividend it is able to pay. If its earnings are growing, dividends are likely to rise in future, which means investors may be willing to pay more for the share (hence the high p/e ratios of many Internet companies). The p/e ratio is calculated by dividing the quoted price of an ordinary share by the most recent year's earnings per share. P/e ratios vary according to the market's assessment of risk. Thus a reasonably large company with a good earnings record might have a p/e of 20/1, in other words, the shares sell at 20 times earnings. But a company with a poor record might have a p/e ratio of much less than that. Generally, a high p/e ratio suggests a growth company and a low p/e ratio suggests one with a more static profit outlook.

Perfect competition A theoretical, ideal environment where there are many buyers and sellers, each extremely well informed. Among such cut-throat competition, there will be no excess profits as each is a price-taker, rather than a price-maker. Perfect competition rarely exists in the real world – even the ubiquitous Internet falls short. Economists therefore use it mainly as a benchmark against which to compare more realistic environments. The opposite to perfect competition is the monopoly, where there is only one seller capable of making an enormous amount of money.

Phillips curve A curve devised by A.W. Phillips, a professor at the London School of Economics, which showed an inverse relationship between inflation and unemployment. Phillips found that as unemployment fell, workers could command higher wages and vice versa. Economists still hold that relationship to be true in the short run, but now believe that in the long term, unemployment will eventually revert to its natural, non-accelerating inflation rate, no matter what happens to inflation. In effect, it means the long-run Phillips curve is vertical.

Positive models Simplified representations of the real world, models that show how processes work. They are concerned with what actually happens and therefore rely on a lot of statistical information. Different from **normative** models which show what ought to happen. An example of a positive model is the **price determination model**.

Pound The UK currency, also called sterling. The name is used for the currency units of several other countries, including Cyprus, Egypt, Lebanon and Syria.

Poverty An inability to afford an adequate standard of consumption. A subjective concept. In developing countries, poverty is taken to mean starvation, but in industrialised countries such as Britain and the United States, it is usually defined as a relative concept, in other words, an inability to afford what average people have. In this sense, it will always be with us. In Britain, poverty is often defined as having less than half, or less than 40 per cent of average income.

Poverty trap A taxation and benefits system that discourages people from working or getting a better paid job and therefore keeps them in a cycle of unemployment and poverty. By definition, means-tested benefits fall as income rises. Therefore, by getting a job, some may actually be worse off.

Preference share A share that signifies part ownership of a company. Preference shares entitle the investor to a fixed dividend, decided at the time of issue. Preference shareholders are ahead of their ordinary neighbours when it comes to both dividends and creditors, but they do not have voting rights.

Price determination (model of) This model says that prices are determined by supply and demand. If supply of a product outweighs demand, prices will fall until enough people are persuaded to buy the excess. If there is more demand than supply, prices will rise.

Price elasticity of demand Measures the responsiveness of demand to a change in price. See also **elasticity**.

Prices and incomes policies In the 1960s, the British government tried to control inflation by putting strict, legal limits on price rises and pay increases. These were known as prices and incomes policies.

Price-maker A firm that sets the price of a good or security by offering to buy and sell at announced prices.

Price-taker Where an individual or a firm takes the prevailing market price, since its own transactions will not influence things. That may be because there are a large number of traders on each side, in a **perfectly competitive** environment.

Privatisation When government-owned entities are sold to the private sector by issuing shares. Examples of privatised firms include British Telecommunications and British Gas.

Producer prices Prices charged by the producers of goods or services. In Britain, producer prices are split into input prices – the cost of raw materials into the production process – and output prices – the price of goods leaving the factory gate.

Production possibility frontier A theoretical line that represents the maximum amount of goods and services a country can produce, given its natural resources, workers, money and technology. A production possibility frontier may be pushed out by improvements in productivity.

Productivity Usually refers to the amount of output produced by each worker, although it could also apply to other factors of production such as output per unit of land, or per piece of capital equipment. In the case of workers, productivity can be increased by a number of factors: longer hours, more effort, better skills, more up-to-date machinery or better management. Britain's productivity lags that in Germany, France and the US. It is an issue that the 1997 Labour government pledged to address. For example, more money for education and tax breaks to encourage modern technology could both help.

Progressive tax A tax where the revenue collected rises more than proportionally to income. Britain's income tax system is progressive because high earners pay higher tax rates than low earners.

Propensity to consume Consumers' tendency to spend money. If someone spends most of their earnings, they have a high propensity to consume; if they save most of them, they have a low propensity to consume (but a high propensity to save); an economy's propensity to consume determines the size of its **multiplier** – how much growth results from an original increase in spending.

Proportional tax A tax where everyone pays the same percentage of tax, no matter what the income of the taxpayer. It is halfway between a **progressive** and a **regressive** tax. Value added tax in Britain is an example of a broadly proportional tax. Barring a few exceptions, it is levied at a flat rate of 17.5 per cent on all goods and services (some items such as books and food are zero-rated, while domestic fuel carries a levy of just 5 per cent).

Protectionism The imposition of tariffs, quotas and other devices to restrict the flow of imports into a country. Arguments in favour of protectionism include:

■ some industries, like food production, must be allowed to flourish away from the ravages of international competition in order to ensure a continuous supply in the event of war;

■ likewise, reliance on foreign suppliers for defence goods could be dangerous in times of conflict;

■ many young firms face higher costs than their long-established competitors because they cannot reap the rewards of economies of scale, or they have to climb a steep learning curve. The infant industry argument says tariffs can be imposed to deter foreign competitors and give domestic producers room to grow to their optimum size;

■ a country may impose tariffs to protect itself against **dumping**. For example, a firm may deliberately sell its goods overseas at a loss either to rid itself of excess stock or to drive firms in its key export markets out of business.

Methods of protection include:

■ **tariffs:** taxes imposed on imports;

■ **quotas:** physical limits on the quantity of a good imported or exported;

■ **voluntary export agreements:** as their name suggests, voluntary agreements with other countries to restrict exports;

■ **non-competitive purchasing by governments**: governments can award public sector contracts like road building projects to domestic firms, even if there are more competitive, overseas alternatives;

■ **safety standards:** countries sometimes use rules on safety as a reason for not importing overseas goods. For example, the EU has banned hormone-treated beef imports from the US for the past decade on the grounds that it poses a potential cancer risk;

■ **customs delays:** a simple but effective way of deterring imports is for customs officers to delay their entry into a country.

Public goods Goods or services provided by the government which are open to use by all members of a society. Public goods are **non-excludable** and **non-rival**. In the case of the former, it means if one person consumes them, it is impossible to prevent others from doing so as well. In the case of the latter, it means that consumption by one more person will not reduce the amount available to everyone else. Defence is a classic example, as is street lighting.

Public sector The whole of government, including any nationalised industries and public corporations.

Public sector net cash repayment The excess money the government may be left with at the end of the month, once spending has been taken out of tax receipts. If the economy is buoyant and lots of people have jobs, tax receipts will be plentiful. Conversely, government spending on things such as unemployment benefit will be lower, hence there may be a surplus of cash at the end of the month.

Public sector net cash requirement The amount of money the government needs each month to make up any shortfall between taxation and spending. If the economy is in the doldrums and unemployment is rife, tax receipts will take a battering. Government spending on things such as unemployment benefit will be high, however, hence the government may run out of cash at the end of the month. PSNCRs can be financed either by printing money (or selling assets to the banking private sector) or by borrowing.

Put option A right, but not an obligation, to sell something – maybe a good or a share or a currency – at a certain price at a certain future date. A put option will be exercised only if the market price is below the agreed option price when the time comes to sell. Put options may be used simply as a gamble, a way to bet on the price of a share and possibly make lots of money, or as a way of protecting against future losses.

Quotas Physical limits put on the quantity of a good imported or exported, with the aim of protecting a home market. For example, if the number of overseas cars allowed to enter Britain was restricted, more domestically built vehicles like Rovers would be bought.

Rate of interest The price of money. The interest rate on a loan is the proportion of money a borrower has to pay a lender for the privilege of using his cash. The Bank of England's Monetary Policy Committee sets Britain's main interest rate, leaving banks and building societies free to set their lending and deposit rates accordingly.

Rating agencies Companies, such as Standard & Poor's and Moody's, that assess how likely borrowers are to default on their debt and then assign them a mark accordingly. Corporate bonds are given ratings so that investors know how risky they are. These vary from AAA, which is top notch, suggesting a company's debt is only slightly more risky than US government bonds, to CCC, which denotes considerable uncertainty about the ability of a firm to repay a loan. These are often called junk bonds. They represent high risk but deliver a high return. The lower a corporate bond's rating, the more expensive it will be for a firm to borrow money.

Real GDP Gross domestic product, divided by a suitable price index, in order to strip out the effects of inflation. An easier way to calculate it is to take **nominal GDP** and subtract inflation. For example, nominal GDP growth of 5.0 per cent sounds very impressive, but if inflation is running at 2.5 per cent, that means real GDP has gone up by only 2.5 per cent – about average. Any expression in economics with *real* in front of it usually means that the impact of price rises has been siphoned off.

Real wage unemployment Classical economists believe that a lot of unemployment is generated by workers asking for too much money. They believe that the cure for this real wage unemployment lies in curbing the power of trade unions and reducing unemployment benefits, both of which will tend to lower wage demands.

Recession Technically, a country is in recession if it has contracted in size for two quarters in a row (in other words, if real GDP growth is negative for two consecutive quarters). Symptoms of recession include a rise in unemployment. Recessions are a feature of the business cycle.

Regressive tax This is where the proportion of income paid in tax falls as the income of the taxpayer rises. The notorious poll tax introduced into England in 1990 by Margaret Thatcher was regressive since someone earning, say, £10,000 paid the same amount as someone earning £100,000. The unfairness of the tax sparked violent riots in central London, forcing the Conservatives to back down and introduce council tax instead. A tax system can be made regressive by imposing indirect taxes at relatively high rates on goods heavily consumed by the poor.

Retail Price Index (RPI) The official British cost of living, or rate of inflation index. The RPI is based on a monthly survey of the prices of more than 600 goods and services, everything from the cost of a cinema ticket to a meal out. The headline RPI includes mortgage payments and indirect taxes, so will be affected by changes in both the cost of borrowing and VAT. The US equivalent to the RPI is the Consumer Price Index, or CPI.

RPIX or underlying inflation An alternative measure of inflation. Based on the same survey as the **Retail Price Index**, but excluding volatile mortgage interest payments. That means it will not be affected by a change in interest rates. The **Band of England's MPC** is responsible for keeping RPIX at 2.5 per cent.

RPIY Another alternative measure of inflation. Based on the same survey as the **RPI** and the **RPIX**, but excluding mortgage interest payments *and* indirect taxes. It is therefore unaffected by changes in either interest rates or VAT.

Schumpeter, Joseph Austrian economist and one-time finance minister born in 1883, famous for his work on business cycles. Schumpeter believed the highs and lows of economic development could be explained by innovation. He argued that entrepreneurs appeared in bursts, which in turn facilitated the appearance of others, triggering an upswing in the business cycle. The downturn sets in thanks to smaller profit margins due to imitation, until the diffusion process is completed. Schumpeter identified the Industrial Revolution in 1750 as the beginning of one expansion, the railroad and construction boom in the mid-19th century as the start of another, and the spread of electricity, cars and chemicals at the start of the 20th century as a third. Some argue that the Internet could be the catalyst for the next long period of growth.

Seasonal unemployment Workers are seasonally unemployed if the demand for their labour varies with the time of the year. For example, a grape picker in the south of France will find employment scarce in winter. Seasonal unemployment is common in the tourist, agricultural and construction sectors.

Services, investment income and current transfers balance The official name given to that part of Britain's trade accounts where all the country's service sector exports and imports are recorded (it used to be called the invisibles balance). For example, if a law firm does work overseas or if a bank sells its expertise abroad, this will show up here. Also included here are things like royalties on music, books and films.

Share Represents ownership in a company. It gives the holder the right to receive a portion of company profits. In the United States, shares are called stocks.

Shoe leather costs The time and money wasted by consumers in looking for reasonably priced goods in a high-inflation environment.

Single European Act A 1986 amendment to the **Treaty of Rome** which committed each member state of the European Union to setting up a single market in the EU by 1992. It involved the abolition of exchange controls, the recognition of qualifications, the abolition of restrictions on internal transport, liberalisation of the market in air services and public procurement tendering, and the abolition of border controls.

Smith, Adam Popularly known as the grandfather of economics, Adam Smith laid the foundations for the subject as we know it today in his 1776 work *An Inquiry into the Nature and Causes of the Wealth of Nations*. He concluded that despite the fact that people act out of a selfish desire to 'better their condition', the **'invisible hand'** of the market ensured that everyone got what they needed. He was the original free-marketeer and forged what became known as the **classical** school of economics.

Stagflation A nasty combination of both *stag*nation and in*flation*. In other words, when an economy is suffering from both high unemployment and high inflation. At one point, economists thought stagflation was impossible

– as unemployment increased, more idle workers would ensure lower wages and a fall in inflation. However, in the 1970s, a fourfold increase in oil prices simultaneously drove prices sky high and plunged much of the developed world into recession. That experience suggested high unemployment and high inflation are incompatible only in the extreme long run, if at all.

Stock Exchange A market in which securities are bought and sold. They used to be buildings where traders would gather and shout out the prices of shares (open outcry system). These days most are institutions with traders linked by computer networks and telephones. There are stock exchanges in most capital cities. The largest in terms of market capitalisation (the quoted price of shares multiplied by the number outstanding) is the New York Stock Exchange, followed by London. Other important markets include the Tokyo Stock Exchange and Nasdaq (which stands for the National Association of Securities Dealers Automated Quotations system). Nasdaq is purely a computerised dealing system that provides price quotes for so-called over-the-counter shares. It specialises in high technology equities.

Structural debt That amount of money owed by the government after the effects of the business cycle have been stripped out. In other words, it is what would be owed if the economy was in neither a boom nor a recession. The OECD produces estimates of its members' structural debt, but it is a fairly imprecise concept.

Structural unemployment Unemployment that arises because of a change in demand or new technology that leads to an oversupply of labour with particular skills or in particular locations. Thousands of British shipbuilders were structurally unemployed after most shipyards in the country closed down. Structural unemployment is not down to an overall lack of demand in an economy and therefore it cannot be cured by reflation. Retraining or relocation is the only answer.

Supply-side policies Government policies that concentrate on improving the supply of workers and technology in an economy. Supply-side policies include reform of the tax and benefits system to encourage more people to work, better education and training to increase the number of skilled workers available and tax breaks to encourage research and development. Supply-side policies contrast with demand management policies, which aim to manipulate jobs and growth through influencing demand in the economy. Most governments plump for a mixture of the two.

Sustainable investment rule The British Labour government elected in 1997 introduced this rule to prevent the government from racking up too much debt in the name of investment. It says that debt will be held at a *stable and prudent level* relative to GDP over the whole economic cycle. That ratio is stated to be around 40 per cent.

Takeover The acquisition of a company by a new owner. Stock exchanges facilitate takeovers by providing a forum for buying and selling company shares. If a firm is being run inefficiently, its share price will suffer. Another firm may then come along and buy the shares either with cash or, more likely in the case of large takeovers, with a combination of cash and the promise of shares in the new company.

Tariffs A tax on imported goods. Used as a way of making overseas goods more expensive than domestically produced goods, thereby diverting demand to the latter.

Trade in goods balance That part of Britain's **balance of payments** that records all exports and imports of goods (as opposed to services).

Treasuries Bonds issued by the US government. Considered more or less risk-free, they therefore carry relatively low yields.

Treaty of Rome Agreement signed in 1957 by Belgium, France, Germany, Italy, Luxembourg and the Netherlands to establish the **European Economic Community (EEC)**. The treaty, which came into effect on 1 January 1958, called for the abolition of internal tariffs.

Underlying inflation *See* RPIX.

Unemployment When people do not have jobs but would like them. Economists classify unemployment in five ways:

- **Cyclical or demand deficient:** occurs when there is not enough demand in the economy to sustain the required number of jobs. This type of unemployment typically occurs during recessions and is termed involuntary. It was how Keynes tended to categorise unemployment.

- **Classical, or real wage:** classical economists believe unemployment is the result of workers asking for too much money. Cures therefore include reducing unemployment benefits and curbing the power of trade unions. Can occur in boom conditions and is therefore considered voluntary. Some economists feared the minimum wage would push the lower paid into classical unemployment.

- **Seasonal:** occurs when demand for labour varies with the time of the year. Fruit pickers, construction workers and Father Christmases are particularly vulnerable.

- **Frictional:** those jobless who are in between work and are likely to find employment soon. Sometimes known as search unemployment, this is also considered voluntary.

- **Structural:** occurs when demand for labour is less than supply in a particular sector of the economy. Structural unemployment has bedevilled British industry as manufacturing has declined in importance. It is largely responsible for a perceived north/south divide in the UK.

Unit trusts Funds of money run by a professional manager who follows guidelines set out in a trust deed. Investors can sell their stakes in a unit trust at any time, in which case the manager would have to sell some investments to repay the unit holder. Each investor is entitled to a pro-rata share of the value of invested funds.

Voluntary export agreements Just as their name suggests, agreements between trading nations, often to restrict sales of foreign goods.

Wealth effect When the prices of assets such as shares and houses rise, people feel wealthier, borrow more money against their new-found wealth (maybe remortgage their home) and spend it. This is called a wealth effect. In other words, rises in asset prices feed through to the real economy. Central banks keep a close eye on potential wealth effects as they are powerful, if indirect, means of fuelling inflation.

Werner plan A report named after Luxembourg's Prime Minister Pierre Werner, drawn up in 1970 by a group of European experts. The Werner plan envisaged a single European currency by 1980, but extreme currency volatility and the oil crisis meant the scheme was thwarted.

World Bank Washington-based institution that lends money to poor countries for spending on projects that encourage sustainable economic development. It also supports private businesses in needy areas, channels foreign capital into investment-hungry economies, and offers extensive training and technical assistance.

World Trade Organisation (WTO) The WTO encourages free trade among its 135 member nations and provides a forum for settling trade disputes amicably.

Yield The amount of interest a bond pays relative to its market price. Yields fall as bond prices rise and vice versa.

INDEX

Bold indicates Glossary entries.

models, economic 37–8, **295**, **297**
monetarism 14, 47, 76–8, 105, 106,
        109–10, 116, 160, 288, 292, **293**
    see also money supply
Monetary Policy Committee (MPC) 76,
        113, 114–15, 116, 117, 119, 129,
        160, 247, 258, 280, **293**, 300
monetary transmission mechanism 104,
        106, **293**
monetary union *see* Economic and
    Monetary Union (EMU)
money supply 28, 104–105, 106, 107,
        109–10, 116, 288, 293
    see also monetarism
moral hazard 266, 269, **294**
mortgages 96, 116–17, 125, 248
Multilateral Investment Guarantee
        Agency 269, **294**
multinationals 206, 207
multiplier effect 23, 46–7, **294**
multi-skilling 139
Mundell, Robert 234, 240, 243

Nairu (non-accelerating inflation rate of
        unemployment) 149, 150,
        152–4, 165, **295**
Nasdaq (National Association of Securities
        Dealers Automated Quotations
        system) 303
National Debt 171–2, **294**
National Statistics 44, 45, 53, 65,
    99–100, 116, 140–41, 154, 157, **294**
Nationalisation Act 257
nationalism 236, 251
natural resources 40, 52
negative equity 124–6
neo-classical economic theory 82–3, 281
new paradigm 153–4
New York Stock Exchange 185, 303
Nikkei 225 Index 195
non-excludability 63, **295**
non-rivalry 63, **295**
normative models 37–8, **295**
north/south divide 134, 157–62, 165

occupational mobility **295**
Okun, Arthur 50, 64
optimum currency theory 240–44, **295–6**

ordinary shares 181, **296**
Organisation for Economic Co-operation
        and Development (OECD) 53,
        68, 74, 127, 209–10, **296**, 303
output 44
overseas sector 42, 47

patriotism 236, 251
peg systems 223
pension funds 96, 176–7, 178, 179–80,
        296
    defined benefit 176
    defined contribution 176
perfect competition 38, 127, 128, **297**,
        298
permanent income hypothesis 28
personal pension plans 177
Phillips curve **297**
poll tax 66
pollution *see* environmental damage
portfolio investment 212
positive models 37–8, **297**
poverty 133, 140, 142–3, 209, 210–11,
        256, 267, 268, **297**
preference shares 181, **297–8**
price determination model 38, 297, **298**
price/earnings (p/e) ratio **296–7**
price elasticity 284, **298**
price mechanisms 15, 16
price transparency 240, 246–7
price-makers **298**
prices and incomes policies 109, **298**
prices, falling 119–21
price-takers **298**
private sector 47
privatisation 70, 83, **298**
producer prices 116, **298**
production possibility frontier 41, 47, 51,
        80, **298**
production, factors of 39, 40, 55, **286**
productivity 41, 53, 134, **298**
profit 16, 18, 19, 101, 137, 182, 193–4
propensity to consume 46, **298–9**
protectionism 204–205, 207–209, 211,
        299
public sector **300**
    net cash repayment 86, **300**
    net cash requirement 86, **300**